Tension in the Tank

Tension in the Tank

Embracing Interfaith Mysticism
Without Leaving the Church

Barbara Lee

Foreword by
Jaco J. Hamman, PhD

RESOURCE *Publications* • Eugene, Oregon

TENSION IN THE TANK
Embracing Interfaith Mysticism Without Leaving the Church

Copyright © 2014 Barbara Lee. All rights reserved. Except for brief quotations in critical publications or reviews, no part of this book may be reproduced in any manner without prior written permission from the publisher. Write: Permissions. Wipf and Stock Publishers, 199 W. 8th Ave., Suite 3, Eugene, OR 97401.

Resource Publications
An Imprint of Wipf and Stock Publishers
199 W. 8th Ave., Suite 3
Eugene, OR 97401

www.wipfandstock.com

ISBN 13: 978-1-62564-595-1

Manufactured in the U.S.A.

Scripture quotations marked (NRSV) are taken from the New Revised Standard Version Bible, copyright 1989, Division of Christian Education of the National Council of the Churches of Christ in the United States of America. Used by permission. All rights reserved.

Scripture quotations marked (NIV) are taken from the Holy Bible, New International Version®, NIV®. Copyright © 1973, 1978, 1984, 2011 by Biblica, Inc.™ Used by permission of Zondervan. All rights reserved worldwide. www.zondervan.com The "NIV" and "New International Version" are trademarks registered in the United States Patent and Trademark Office by Biblica, Inc.™

Scripture quotations marked (NASB) are taken from the New American Standard Bible®, Copyright © 1960, 1962, 1963, 1968, 1971, 1972, 1973, 1975, 1977, 1995 by The Lockman Foundation. Used by permission.

To everyone who lives on the edge

Contents

Foreword by Jaco J. Hamman • ix
Preface: Fish Food • xi
Acknowledgments • xv
Introduction: Extended Grace • xix

1 An Interfaith Adventure: Celebrating Christmas • 1
2 An Integral Perspective • 18
3 Faith in the Midst of Pain: A Lenten Journey • 46
4 A Compassionate Response • 61
5 Whining as a Spiritual Discipline • 72
6 Who's to Blame? Revisiting the Book of Job • 91
7 Don Miguel Ruiz' *The Four Agreements* • 99
8 Real Relationships • 116
9 Embracing Mysticism • 136
10 Advent: The Terrible Journey to Christmas • 167

Epilogue: Creating a New Groove • 179
   Appendix A: EG Worship Template • 183
   Appendix B: Integral Practice • 186
   Appendix C: Chat Ground Rules* • 188

Bibliography • 191

Foreword

THE JOURNEY OF SPIRITUAL growth is fraught with challenges and opportunities. It is best undertaken with good conversation partners, caring folk who will nurture and challenge as your life calls forth. We need trustworthy, wise individuals who can be guides on the journey. We need a community supporting us as we stumble, fall, get up again, and continue the journey. Barbara Lee is such a sage and pastor and in Extended Grace we know that such communities exist. *Tension in the Tank* will stimulate your curiosity and compassion, empower your love to flourish, and deepen all your relationships. Moreover, Barbara will invite you to experience God anew.

Tension in the Tank reminds us that life is messy. So too are our physical lives, our relationships, our emotional lives, our professional lives, and our relationship with God. Still, we want to love deeply, feel passionately, belong strongly, trust unconditionally, experience vital intimacy, work with integrity, and believe with clarity. Like Eve in the Garden of Eden—who wanted to gain knowledge to be like God—we too search for transformational experiences that will inform our sense of self and change our relationship with the Divine. Contemplation and meditation introduce us to the Divine, God fully known while remaining an utter mystery. This paradox, as Barbara persuasively argues, holds the promise of calm and peace amidst tension and anxiety. Furthermore, when we engage the great spiritual and religious narratives and practices of humanity, we can move beyond fear, anxiety, and isolation. We no longer need to wear masks that hide and protect.

I had the privilege of being a witness as Barbara made her way through theological education and Lutheran rules and regulations and gave shape to Extended Grace. What impressed me then, and what is apparent in this book, is that she sees things differently. Her intellectual curiosity, creative imagination, vulnerable transparency, and her compassionate leadership took her into conversations, relationships, and settings few of her colleagues could follow. Inevitably, such a way of approaching ministry and leadership will induce tension. Her multi-vocal lens, especially the aspects of embracing mysticism and interfaith dialogue, enriches the way she reads Scripture and reflects on the experience of church. It is thus no surprise that Barbara and Extended Grace found life, love, and community in unexpected places and ways. She was and remains courageous. When most would walk away from interpersonal and emotional pain, she walked towards it, knowing that healing and wholeness does not come if we follow our natural instincts to avoid our hurts. She moved personal and vocational boundaries, while staying close to the narratives of Scripture and the life and teachings of Jesus. Maybe she ventured too close, for those who are uncritically loyal to tradition and doctrine struggle to follow her. As a modern mystic, however, Barbara finds meaning in the disappointments of life and creates space where others can grow.

To discover a life filled with simplicity, gratitude, friendship, community, compassion, contemplation, and hopeful anticipation is a gift, not a given. It is grace that every person can grow into being a mystic. *Tension in the Tank* shows that an awakened life in union with the Divine, enriched through conversations with wise men and women from all faith traditions, is possible.

The Hebrew prophet Joel witnessed the destruction of locusts. Most persons know the locusts of life. Barbara is a witness to the searching and suffering that many persons know intimately. *Tension in the Tank* is not afraid to name pain and suffering, whether in divorce, interpersonal violence, self-harm, early pregnancy loss or even significant spiritual doubt. Spiritual practices such as mindfulness, friendship, lament, and prayer, to name just a few of the practices Barbara highlights, lead to a life where anxiety and worry no longer rule one's life. Imagine a river that flows from the Divine, nourishing you, those you love, and the community you keep. The prophet Joel saw that river. The prophet Ezekiel, the psalmist, and the Book of Revelation describe nurturing and healing qualities of this river. This river drips from the pages of *Tension in the Tank*. Do not fear getting wet!

Jaco J. Hamman
Vanderbilt University

Preface

Fish Food

THIS BOOK WILL ADD tension to your life. Now, I know you woke up and said to yourself, " I can't wait to sit down with a good book because then I will feel more tension!" Am I right? Well, not if your images of tension are all negative—and so often they are. My initial challenge, then, is to convince you of the need for positive tension in your life.

When this country was still relatively new, fishermen out east tried transporting cod across land by freezing it first. However, by the time it reached its destination, it had lost its flavor. So they tried shipping the cod live in salt water. Now not only did it lose its flavor, but it was soft and mushy upon arrival. Next they started to ship the cod with its natural predator—the catfish. The catfish chased the cod all over the tank. When it arrived, not only was the flesh of the fish firm, but it also tasted better than ever. This is the phenomenon of "Tension in the Tank" and it serves as a metaphor for many aspects of our life.

When there is no tension, there is the opportunity for complacency. There is no need to act. The result is soggy fish or a soggy life. When there is no tension, the stage is set for a no-consequences approach to life. In a no-consequences culture, people feel secure no matter how poorly they perform or how little they work. People feel that something or someone owes them something for nothing. People concentrate on the activity of the moment rather than on long-term results. We all know individuals, families, businesses, and organizations that operate that way.

Not everyone contributes to this mindset. Some people adopt an attitude of fear. These people act in stress or out of panic, fearful for their livelihood, their relationships, their possessions, and their physical needs. They struggle in their insecurity to please others, to try to be good enough, to attempt to measure up. They know whatever they do will never be quite good enough. They anticipate loss. Often, they despair.

Finally, there are individuals who operate with a mindset of accountability. It is here that people are challenged to perform at their best. They don't take what they receive for granted. The goals they set are high, maybe even risky, but they believe they can be met. It is as if they swim with catfish, but with the confidence that they will arrive whole at their destination.

The metaphor applies equally well to our spiritual lives. We have known the temptation of adopting a no-consequence approach to our spiritual lives. After all, in every faith tradition there is a path to God that is promised for all who seek. No matter how poorly we behave, we know we can return to this path and eventually find our way to Salvation, Rebirth, Enlightenment, or Supreme Liberation. We even find our human nature trying to convince us that we "deserve" the blessings we receive, as well as those that haven't materialized yet but must be coming. However, if we stop there, with the promise alone, we miss our call to discipleship and ignore our call to put our faith into action. We become as tasteless fish.

Of course there is the other extreme. Those are the people who have not heard the promise or can't quite accept that the experience of God is a gift that can never be earned. They find themselves living in fear of God's wrath, punishing themselves for their weaknesses and failings, living out the words of the law, and missing the promise of grace entirely. Alternatively, they may choose to avoid God completely in order to avoid God's harsh judgment. They do not realize that even in the confines of the tank, the catfish did not consume its prey.

We have another option. We have been challenged to be disciples, bringing the saving word of grace to the spiritually homeless, caring for our brothers and sisters in need, demonstrating a living faith that shows itself in action. The scriptures of all major religions are clear—the fate of impoverished people is God's litmus test of faithfulness. Because of the promise, we do not need to worry about our own needs because God will provide for us. But we do have a responsibility to care for each other, to meet each other's needs.

We need sources of tension in our spiritual life to keep our faith alive. Tension comes first of all from the presence of the Divine within us. It comes out of our faith and calls us to more and more action as our faith matures. It is the feeling that stirs us to act when we hear about disaster relief efforts, world hunger appeals, or abuse prevention programs. It is the feeling that moves us to help out in a soup kitchen, deliver food to a shelter, hammer a nail for Habitat for Humanity. It is the feeling that makes us restless when we fail to take time to pray, to meditate on God's word, to seek the Spirit's call in our lives.

Tension also comes from living a life that is not always easy, not always comfortable. We are not spared from trials and tribulations. Indeed, God calls us to pick up the cross, an image in sharp contrast to sitting on the EZ-Boy recliner of passive existence. We have known and will know difficulties and hardships, pain, and suffering. But they will never overtake us with God at our side. Our faith will be tested and will grow from such adversity. The trials and tribulations, the catfish we encounter, add seasoning, flavor, and texture to our lives. They prepare us in ways we cannot imagine to serve our world, to serve each other.

Other outside forces can also create tension in our spiritual lives. They include the movies we watch, the music we listen to, and the books we choose to read. Although the image isn't particularly flattering, I suppose as you read this book, you could consider me to be a visiting catfish. You will find many tales of tension from my life experiences and the experiences of those around me on these pages.

The call to be about God's work is one that leads down narrow alleys and tumultuous terrain. It is not easy and it is not fast. But it is never too great a burden to bear. And it is infinitely rewarding. Just as our mandate to serve is clear, so is the promise of joy. In the Christian scriptures, we're told by Isaiah that, "If you offer your food to the hungry and satisfy the needs of the afflicted, then your light shall rise in the darkness and your gloom be like the noonday."[1] "Cast your bread on the water and after many days you will find it again.[2]" That wet, soggy bread just might make good fish food!

---

1. Isaiah 58:10 (NRSV).
2. Ecclesiastes 11:1 (NRSV).

Acknowledgments

I WAS WORKING AS the Executive Director at Muskegon County Habitat for Humanity when I was tapped by my church body, the Evangelical Lutheran Church in American (ELCA), to begin work as a lay Assistant to the Bishop. I fell in love with the work and over time discerned that I was being called to ordained ministry. When I met with Bishop Gary Hansen to ask for his blessing on this endeavor, he surprised me by asking me to be the Mission Developer for a ministry in Grand Haven. So began the remarkable journey that has lead to the publication of this book and the excited realization that where this journey will ultimately culminate is still unknown.

As I pursued my Master's of Divinity Degree and continued to work as an Assistant to the Bishop, I had the amazing opportunity to come into contact and learn from a diverse group of renowned religious thinkers and teachers. This gave me the unique opportunity of attending a variety of seminaries that also informed my work. They included Western Theological Seminary in Holland, Pacific Lutheran Seminary in Berkeley, Luther Seminary in St. Paul, and Lutheran Theological Seminary in Gettysburg. While I am incredibly grateful for all of the instruction I received, I especially need to acknowledge my pastoral care professor Dr. Jaco J. Hamman for providing me with the underpinnings for serving hurting people with grace and love. At the same time I was pursuing my Christian instruction, I became involved in interfaith education through the Interfaith Institute/Mother's Trust in Ganges, Michigan. Meaningful relations with respected leaders brought me to deeper understanding of a variety of faith traditions. I am especially indebted to Fred Stella for his grounding in the Hindu faith and Steve Sampson for his embrace of the Buddhist tradition.

As I reflect on this journey, I recognize that it began far before I realized. For planting the seeds of my early faith, I need to thank my childhood pastor Rev. Jack J. Horner and my family at Edgewood Lutheran Church.

Pastor Jack was more than a religious teacher to me. He was like another father. Pastor Jack passed away before I recognized my call to ministry, but I know he would have been very proud of me and would have done everything he could to support me in my work. He left us far too soon, but his loving spirit and joyous laughter lives on in the hearts of all of us that he touched so deeply.

As Extended Grace took shape, it became clear to me that the last thing the area needed was another "church." So we set out to be the faith community for those who did not feel welcome or comfortable in a traditional house of worship. We embraced everyone from every faith and sought to learn from everyone we engaged. We didn't try to get people to come to us so much as we tried to figure out where people needed us to be. On the surface we appeared unorthodox and we raised a lot of eyebrows. There were detractors and people within the institution that considered us controversial. But we came to appreciate our unique position that allowed us to push the envelope and challenge traditional thought. In truth, we were becoming ever more deeply rooted in our Christian core even as that opened us up to finding God in the most unlikely places and forms. Rev. Ruben Duran, more than anyone else in the ELCA, understood what Extended Grace was about and the difference we were making in people's lives. I am grateful for his support of this ministry and his attempts to find our niche within the ELCA. I also need to heap gratitude and praise upon my mentor and dear friend, Pastor Reed Schroer. For convincing me that irreverence is not a reason to stay out of ministry and for providing a place of safety and refuge when the winds were assailing me, I thank you for your amazingly kind and gracious heart.

Of course, no one has taught me more than the people who gathered and made up the Extended Grace community. This book is my thank you to each one of you for sharing your lives, your wisdom, and your journey with me. I can never express the depth of my gratitude or adequately thank you for the gift of being invited into your lives. There are far too many people to name and I hope they will forgive me for that shortcoming. At the same time there are a few people who I would be truly remiss if I did not publicly acknowledge the importance of their support and their witness over the course of this ministry. Thank you Larry Sehy for your support as a mission partner. Thank you Pastor John Grostic for being a mentor, a friend, and a partner in this ministry. Your presence will be forever missed. For being there at the very beginning, I thank Werner Absenger and Thom Jorgensen. For taking on a variety of leadership responsibilities, I thank (in no particular order) Meredith Hammond, Jon Lathers, Rosie DeVries, Ryan Dibble, Nate Sterling, Dawn Brown, Neil Freeman, Bill Klemp, Tim Burgess, Val

Porenta, Dale Freye and Chrysteen Moelter-Gray. For the entire Extended Grace community, please know that I love each one of you more than I can ever express.

In any writing endeavor, there are experts in the field who offer encouragement and wisdom. In my case, these people were also my friends. Thank you to my copyeditor who gently reviewed and corrected me when I was in error and who makes me look good in print and to Tricia McDonald who has mentored me and encouraged me to share my writing with others. I am also grateful to Christian Amondson and the team at Wipf & Stock for seeing value in my premise and bringing this book into publication. At the same time, I was gifted with dear friends and family members who took the time to read early versions of this book, to offer their critique, and to encouraged me to continue on this path. They include Chrysteen, Mike and Kris O'Conner, David Rowell, and Bobbi Sabine. There are other friends who have generously shared with me their support, their hugs and a few glasses of wine, while helping me grow professionally into the next stage of my life. My thanks to the Wonderful Women.

Of course, nothing gets accomplished without the support of family. My mother Linda Rowell needs to be mentioned and thanked for selfless love and nurturing through the good and the bad. For loving me even when my work overflowed from my workspace and cluttered the house, I thank Leif Van Horssen who believes in me with his whole being and who has brought Brigid into my life and into my heart. Leif is my stable foundation, my best friend, and my devil's advocate. I know that wherever my path leads, I will always have his wholehearted love and support.

Finally, for being there through it all, I thank my boys Jackson and Alex Selb. When they were young and I was preaching in a variety of churches around Michigan, their antics provided endless sermon illustrations. I used to pay them $1 each time I mentioned them in a sermon or message. I owe them much more than that. I will forever be indebted to Jackson for caring so deeply about everything he does, for his generous nature, and for how hard he has always tried to meet the needs of those around him. And I will be forever indebted to Alex for his sense of humor, pragmatic insights, and genuine empathy for others. It is my deepest desire that you both should know your own value and recognize the Divine that lives in you and that shines out on this world. Please know boys how very special you are and how much I love you.

Introduction

Extended Grace

> *This capacity for mystical sensitivity is a fact intrinsic*
> *to what it means to be human:*
> *we are made in the divine image;*
> *we are interdependent with all beings;*
> *we are bonded together in love.*[1]
>
> —BEVERLY LANZETTA

So with courage and strength, let us speak boldly, pray unceasingly, and act with purpose and direction as our faith calls us to respond to heal the hurts and fill the needs of this worldly life. That means standing up for what is right. It means challenging the status quo. It means choosing to believe in a different reality: one that believes in miracles and promises and the need to embrace and care for our neighbors. To give up all, risking our wealth, our reputation, and our relationships. Beware. Following the call of Spirit means being led into the most unlikely of places.

Extended Grace began as a traditional church start in a traditional Christian denomination but always with a different objective in mind. Extended Grace existed to call into community those who had not felt welcome in the traditional church. It aimed at tearing down all of the barriers we erect between human beings and between world religions.

For the first two years of ministry, we gathered in a bar connected to Wicked Ways Tattoo and Body Piercing. How significant is it that you literally had to walk through Wicked Ways to get to Extended Grace?

---

1. Lanzetta, *Radical Wisdom*, 197.

I thought it was perfect. But not everyone shared my point of view. One day a man ran out of gas while traveling on the highway and came in to use the phone. He looked pretty nervous about the whole encounter. I let him use my cell phone and while he waited for his ride he commented on the surroundings. I told him it was a great place for ministry. I thought he heard me, but when his ride came he literally turned on me. "You call yourself a church and your office is in a place like this? You better rethink what you're doing. I'm a *good* Christian and I don't think you're sending the right message." Then he turned and marched right out the door before I could say a word.

His reaction wasn't the first of its kind and it certainly wouldn't be the last. Our mission was to meet the spiritually adrift where they live in order that they might experience the way in which God is at work in their lives. It didn't look much like you would expect a church to look. And yet its mission was bold enough to take Jesus' words seriously when he tells us, "This is my commandment, that you love one another as I have loved you."[2] Jesus never qualifies that statement. He never instructs us to love some and not to love others. We simply are told in no uncertain terms that we are to love each other . . .

We are to love the Christian, the Taoist, the Muslim, the Jew, the Buddhist, the Hindu, and the Ba'hai. To love the skeptical and the doubtful and the faithless. To love those with body piercings and tattoos, those who are gay or lesbian or transgender, those who struggle with addictions. To love those who are poor and dirty, the mentally and physically challenged, the voiceless and the powerless. We have been told to love them all—just as we have been loved.

While working with Extended Grace, I had the rich opportunity to meet so many of God's wonderful children: a young woman whose faith community will no longer let her in the door because of her facial piercings, a gay couple who had never before found a place they could worship together, an ex-felon and recovering alcoholic who found only barriers when he tried to return to his former church home, a woman who was invited to eat the turkey at a Thanksgiving Community Meal, but who was never invited to come back on Sunday.

Now I'm convinced that someone in each of those settings wanted to reach out to the outcast at the door. But to have done so would have been to risk too much. I'm also fairly convinced that each one of us in our own lives, and I know for sure in mine, have had the opportunity to reach out to

---

2. John 15:12 (NASB).

someone in need—and we chose to look away because the cost was simply too high.

Can you feel it? Can you feel the tension of being torn between two different worlds? Two different value systems? Can you feel the conflict between caring for self and truly caring for others? Then you are hearing Spirit's call. Because Spirit does not call us into a place of relief. Spirit calls us very directly, clearly, and undeniably into a place of tension. What are the sources of tension in your life that keep your faith fresh and vital?

When we try to keep the teachings of Christ safely under wraps, we end up with a faith of infancy, a faith that never grows up. But when we say we are the body of Christ and we mean it, we open ourselves to God abiding in us, walking with us in ways we cannot yet imagine. God becomes part of us and we become part of God. We live in a state of transformation and change and renewal, even as we long for things to stay the same. And let's admit it, much of the time we human beings do want things to stay the same.

There is a major rift in our churches today. Debates and division have arisen regarding "truth." They include ordination of women, whether or not Christianity is the only true religion, the definition of marriage, and views on sexuality. But the real conflict isn't over these few matters of theology or behavior. It is between two comprehensive ways of seeing Christianity as a whole.

In my first year of seminary I had a disturbing experience. No. I had many disturbing experiences. This was among the worst . . .

The professor asked what we would want someone to know who walked into our church. "We are friendly," came one answer, "this is a place or worship" came another. "God is here" was followed by "the location of the bathroom"—that might have been tongue in cheek. Then someone said, "God loves you." Ooh. Hey. Wow. "How does that sound?" asked the professor. "Do we want people to know God loves them?" "Yes, yes," we all affirmed. Whew, one question I could get right.

Then that young guy with dark hair who always sat on the far right side of the room stood up and said—this actually happened—"Wait a minute. Can we really say that God loves everyone who comes to our churches? I mean I've read my Bible and it seems pretty clear to me that God loves some people and he's really upset with others. I've heard you talking about welcoming drug addicts and prostitutes and homosexuals in church and I think God must hate that. I just don't think we can say God loves 'those' people."

I was dumbstruck. After all, I was the minister at Extended Grace. Our whole reason for being was to go out of our way to embrace "those" people. People who had been told they had no place in God's house of worship.

People who had come to church seeking God's grace and then found that the gatekeepers would not let them in.

Jesus warns us in a roundabout way that it is not up to us to close any door. He only ever calls us to follow, to continue in his way. He says if we do, we will be free. And what will happen if we don't? Logic says we will be bound. That makes a lot of sense. When we shut those doors, what are we really doing? Are we keeping someone out? Or are we merely locking ourselves in, and stopping our own journey forward? We can imprison ourselves in the values of the culture and our own desires for black and white answers. We can imprison ourselves by judging others instead of working toward reconciliation. We can imprison ourselves behind a door believing we hold the key that determines which people may or may not be able to access God's grace. And into our imprisoned state Jesus comes, bidding us to open the door and step out of our self-made bonds. "If you continue in my word, you are truly my disciples; and you will know the truth and the truth will make you free."[3] What then is the truth?

Before trying to answer that question, we have to check our inner space. Each of us has inside of us an inner space. That space becomes the container that holds our ability to believe in God. Before we can believe "in" God or anything else, we first must have the capacity "to" believe. Belief suggests trust, to put trust in something or to hold something dear. We are not born with this space, just with the potential for it. It is something that must be nurtured over time in an environment that allows trust to develop.

If this inner space of mine becomes warped, it will impact how I believe in God. And that will impact how I talk about God and relate God to others. The wonderful thing is that we can put ourselves in places with people who can help us to expand that space ever larger. As our inner space expands, we become less anxious in this world.

Unfortunately, the downside of religion is that it has often sought to stuff that inner space so full that there is no room for anything else but a long litany of beliefs "in"—in doctrine, in dogma, and in creeds. A contemporary of Freud, D.W. Winnicott believed it was the scientists who had the greater capacity for belief. "Religion," he said, "replaces doubt with certainty. Science holds an infinity of doubt, and implies a faith."[4] If we can keep from stuffing ourselves with certainty, we can actually expand our capacity to believe. Then we can enter into the kind of freedom that Christ calls us to.

Our belief in God doesn't rest in the work of theologians. Instead it evolves out of our own lived experiences of love and transformation, as

---

3. John 8:31–32 (NRSV).
4. Winnicott, *Home is Where We Start*, 14.

we move beyond beliefs "in" to an understanding of our relationship with the Spirit of God. This relationship calls us into a journey and continually pushes upon us to expand our inner space.

"If you continue in my word, you are truly my disciples; and you will know the truth and the truth will make you free."[5] We pursue truth by opening ourselves up in order to experience a deeper level of reality. We seek to connect the body, the mind, and the spirit with the Divine. What truth can be found comes not just from knowledge, but also from feelings and intuition. The truth is not "out there" but right *here*: in you, in community, in our relationships to each other and to the Divine.

We find freedom when we let go of the fear that drives us to totally pin down God so that we know exactly what to expect. And that is a hard burden to lie down. We have all too often known promises that were broken, plans that went astray. We have experienced our routines shaken because life got in the way. So we fear that if things aren't completely set, if we can't figure out exactly what we can hold God accountable to, then things may not go the way they should.

Interesting that in Hebrew the name for God "I AM WHO I AM" can just as faithfully be translated "I WILL BE WHO I WILL BE." God is still capable of surprising us. Despite all our human efforts, mystery remains and questions are left unanswered. Faith is required because we cannot verify religious truth in the same way that we can verify physical things. We do not know, but we believe.

There are a lot of people selling a religion that says once you find God everything is wonderful. It's the theology of glory. It's the theology that if you only pray hard enough, give enough money, and believe the right things, God will reward you with untold blessings. It's a theology about "me" instead of "the other." And it's a theology that ignores the cross and the pain that comes in following the way. Such a theology leaves people abandoned and hurting when things go wrong. Often it drives people away from churches and, in its worst form, it drives people away from God.

If you are reading this book, there's a good chance you have become disillusioned with that message. You may be among us who have lost faith in human institutions that claim to have God all wrapped up in a tight little box they call "truth." We long for a deep relationship with a God that is beyond human description. We celebrate those faith communities that offer authentic love and acceptance, honest relationship, and an openness to seeking God in a way that does not restrict God to human dogma, or to the boundaries of gender, race, background, ability, and orientation.

---

5. John 8:31–32 (NRSV).

Over and over again I find myself talking to people who think they know what Christianity is all about—and they don't want any part of it. But the Christianity they reject—the God they reject—is not the Christianity I follow or the God I know. There is damage to be repaired. And sound bite answers, no matter how theologically sound, will not suffice.

A few years ago I saw an advertisement in a popular Christian magazine for a book. This book claimed to have *the* definitive answers to the top twenty questions people have. Never again will you have to struggle to find an answer. Here are *the* answers to the big questions of life. Period. Everything you need to know was right here in this book for just $24.99. Wow. There you go. Jesus could have made things a lot simpler for us if he had just written this book.

No wonder people are so often confused by Christian rhetoric. For this is a spiritual quest, one that embraces ambiguity, celebrates community, and recognizes doubt as an important part of any faith journey. We ultimately discover truth by experiencing and practicing it, not by intellectual assent. Faith doesn't revolve around believing questionable things to be true, believing contrary to the evidence, contrary to what reasonable people know. Faith is about a radical trust in God.

If our faith is to remain alive and relevant, we cannot let if become stagnant. The promise of tension, as much as we long for it to go away, is often exactly what it takes to stir us to do the spiritual work we are called to do.

How wonderful it is that God can overcome our human prejudice and our human assumptions. How glorious it is that Spirit is available to everyone. How astounding it is that Spirit changes us so that we are able to love. In fact, not only does Spirit change us, Spirit chooses us and appoints us, not just to bask in the tranquil waters of grace, but to swim with all our might in an effort to love others even when it requires us to experience sacrifice.

The challenges, trials, and tribulations we face as we answer the call, the catfish we encounter in doing God's work add seasoning, flavor, and texture to our lives. Prepares us in ways we cannot imagine to serve our world and each other. Hmmm . . . sounds a little fishy to me.

Namaste

1

An Interfaith Adventure

Celebrating Christmas

*Christmas is not a time nor a season,
but a state of mind.
To cherish peace and goodwill,
to be plenteous in mercy,
is to have the real spirit of Christmas.*[1]

—CALVIN COOLIDGE

Anticipation and Expectation:
How Would Moses Celebrate Christmas?

No matter what time of year it is, we all know Christmas is coming. What are your expectations of Christmas this year? Will it be a time of stress and tension, or will it be a time of celebration and delight? Are you looking forward to time with family or wondering how you'll survive yet another encounter with parents and siblings? Did you start shopping at the after-Christmas sales last year, or will you wait until Christmas Eve to make your purchases? Are you looking forward to trays of holiday cookies, or already beginning to count the calories?

---

1. Coolidge, "Brainy Quote," line 1–4.

Do you expect this will be the best Christmas ever, or hope it won't be worse than what has come before? What are your expectations of Christmas this year? And how will they influence your preparations?

Once Thanksgiving comes and goes, it seems preparation for Christmas begins in earnest. One year my brother-in-law actually stood in line at Toys R Us at 4:30 in the morning on Black Friday just so he could get a deal on a PS2 for my six-year-old nephew! Even when we don't sacrifice our sleep for a great deal and the chance of hitting the consumerism jackpot, the Advent season still can be a time of "busyness," panic, exhaustion, and frenzy as we imagine Christmas morning and want to pounce on its arrival like a cat finally eating up the mouse that has teased it for so long.

In fact, it's so easy to get caught up in the marketing campaign of Christmas that we can forget all about the joy, delight, and celebration of the season. We forget that the journey toward Christmas is a reward all in itself. We lose the splendid sensation of hope and anticipation.

If Moses were among us now, I think he'd remind us of that. The recorded witness of the ancient Jewish people was that they knew how to look forward to a promise. In fact, it didn't even matter if that promise seemed remote and distant and impossible to believe. They trusted that God was with them. They lived in the expectation of deliverance, of freedom, of peace, and of joy.

There is a Veggie Tales Christmas video in which a commercial proclaims: "Kids, if you get everything you asked for this Christmas, then you aren't asking for enough!"[2] You just have to love that sentiment, don't you? An honest reflection of the greed and materialism reaching out to hold us all in its grip. But we could look at it in another way—as a way of taking stock of our expectations. What if we hear these words not as an advertising plea or a marketing slogan, but as the invitation of a God of unbounded generosity?

In the Christian scripture it says, "Ask and it will be given to you."[3] What if we believed God would answer our prayers? What if we began to expect to receive the promises God has already made to us—of grace and joy and abundance? What if we entered into a time of expectation?

The Jewish people got really good at expectation, but not because everything they asked for suddenly appeared before them. It wasn't instant answers or spontaneous results that fostered their faith. In fact, for much of their history they have been waiting. Waiting for God to keep God's word.

---

2. "The Toy That Saved Christmas."
3. Matthew 7:7 (NIV).

Waiting for the fulfillment of the promises God has made to them as chosen people. Waiting for a Messiah.

The Hebrew word for Messiah means anointed one. Originally, the Jewish people believed that the Messiah was any person who was anointed with oil upon rising to the position of High Priest or King or prophet. In a general sense, Messiah means a savior or a liberator of the world.

There is a common rabbinical interpretation of Messiah, that there is a *potential* Messiah in every generation. The ancient Jewish text known as the Talmud tells the story of a highly respected rabbi who found the Messiah at the gates of Rome. He asked him, "When will you finally come?" He was quite surprised when he was told, "Today." Overjoyed and full of anticipation, the man waited all day. The next day he returned, disappointed and puzzled, and asked, "You said Messiah would come 'today' but he didn't come! What happened?" The Messiah replied, "Scripture says, 'Today, *if you will but hearken to His voice.*'"Moses hearkened to the voice. Moses was his generation's Messiah.

Moses was the leader who brought the Israelites out of Egypt in what is commonly known as the Exodus. It happened around 1250 BCE. The people were living as slaves in Egypt longing for their freedom. You may have seen this story in the movie *The Prince of Egypt*.[4] Before Disney took their turn, Charlton Heston immortalized the part of Moses in the movie *The Ten Commandments*.[5] Remember the story?

Moses confronts Pharaoh with demands to let his people go, all the while announcing the plagues that will follow Pharaoh's refusal. Eventually, after the stunning death of all first-born children, Pharaoh relents (before changing his mind again). During that brief window of opportunity, Moses leads the Israelites through parted water and, after securing their liberation, continues to lead the people in the wilderness for forty years in anticipation of reaching the land God has promised him and his people.

Moses was a man of expectation. He believed in God's promises and he acted in anticipation that they were true. Which is not to say that he never had his doubts. In fact, Moses spent quite a bit of time doubting himself. Lots of times Moses tried to talk God out of using him for the tasks ahead. He didn't seem to think a lot of his own abilities and probably figured he would be a liability to the cause. Have you ever felt that way? I know I have.

I especially felt that way the day my boss the Bishop asked me to work in Ionia, Michigan where he was thinking about starting a church. That would mean doing something incredibly difficult: knocking on strangers'

---

4. *The Prince of Egypt*.
5. *The Ten Commandments*.

doors. And something absolutely impossible: (gulp) praying out loud with other people around to hear! Being forced into that impossible situation by people who thought I could do it would ultimately lead me to pastoring a ministry and praying out loud on a regular basis with other people around to hear. It is a good thing other people expected something of me or I might never have accomplished a thing. Fortunately, Moses too puts his self-doubt aside in order to do what he is being asked to do. He does it because he expects God to carry out God's end of the deal.

How would Moses celebrate Christmas? Well, I'm not so sure he would ever get the chance. You might not know it, but after all those years of leading, Moses himself never got to enter the Holy Land. He saw it, but he died before reaching it. So I think Moses would celebrate Christmas by anticipating it to be true. He would expect God to keep God's word. He would anticipate God making God's self known to a world in bondage, in slavery to greed and consumerism, defeated by self-doubt and anxiety. And he would, because of his own experience, have no trouble believing that God's revelation would come in the form of a baby, the least likely of messiahs—just as Moses believed himself to be the least likely of liberators more than 1200 years before.

It is in the Jewish witness to a God that does not abandon God's own that we too can live in anticipation. When they were the most disheartened and the most discouraged, they continued to nurture a vision of God's saving action, of the promise that would transform Israel and bring lasting happiness to God's people. We are reminded in that witness that sinfulness, frailty, sickness, powerlessness, destruction, war, and so many other human problems will always be with us. And we are invited to live in expectation that the coming of God and the manifestation of God's glory will bring promised transformation to us and to our world.

In the midst of the chaos and catastrophe, Moses would move through advent telling us not to give up on the world or on God's presence here. As we struggle with our own dark moments, when we feel our own abandonment, our wandering in the desert, our sense of exile, he would tell us that we are making ourselves victims of our own isolation, neglect, and abuse.

The story of God's people points with confidence to flowing water in the desert and homecoming for the exile. The Jewish people placed their hope and expressed their confidence in the coming intervention of God, and so can we! We know that God is already at work transforming this world and our individual dramas. And we wait with full and open hearts for the unmistakable sign of God's glory, which will be revealed to us in the birth of a child.

Gift Giving: How Would Buddha Celebrate Christmas?

We all know the downside to Christmas. It can be all about overindulgence, greed, materialism, and consumerism. Ever since "Remember the Reason for the Season" bumper stickers began appearing on our neighbors' cars we have received copious reminders of the ways in which we have subverted the meaning of Christmas and replaced it with a decadent display of commercialism run amok.

But really, is that all there is to it? Is Christmas nothing more than a servant to a social reality we should all find repugnant? Should Christmas finally be banned for the good of all? Of course not! Because at its best, beneath the layers of Christmas wrapping paper and piles of newspaper inserts lies the heart of Christmas, and it is a heart full of love. Christmas at its best is about giving. It is about good will and compassion. And each of these virtues is found not just in Christianity but in Buddhism as well. Buddhism helps us to remember the joy and delight we discover in giving of ourselves to others.

While we strive to be generous at all times, Christmas is a time when we get to intentionally engage that practice. Swept up in our day-to-day "busyness" and all the worthwhile activities of living, we can take those we love the most for granted. Blinded by our own needs and worries, we can forget the troubles of others. Stuck in our narrow focus of getting through the day the best we can, we can fail to recognize that doing our best always means doing for others. Christmas is a time that can dislodge us from our preoccupation with our self and expand our vision to include everyone from those closest to us to those we will never lay eyes upon.

Christmas is about gift giving. We simply can't get away from it. A big part of the Christmas tradition *is* exchanging presents. And that really isn't a bad thing. In Buddhism such giving is called "dana" and it is considered a very commendable and praiseworthy activity. Gifts given with thoughtfulness and love become symbols of the affection we hold for others. As we make our shopping lists, we are reminded of the significance other people have had in our lives over the past year and we attempt to show a bit of our gratitude for their presence in our lives.

It is also a time to express our concern for all of God's people. In Buddhism this is similar to the virtue of loving-kindness or "metta." "Metta" expresses itself in selfless concern for others. We give beyond our family and friends to support charities and strangers whom we will never meet. Loving-kindness is often illustrated by the image of a mother loving her child. We are urged to develop this kind of love for all beings without exception. The Christian nativity scene displays this kind of deep devotion and affection— that of a mother for her child. This mother gazes lovingly upon the Jesus child who would grow up to become a teacher of loving-kindness himself.

Finally, Christmas giving moves us beyond tangible gifts to gifts of the heart and soul. Christmas is a time for cultivating compassion itself or "karuna" in the words of the Buddha. "Karuna" moves us beyond considering our own happiness and well-being to acknowledge that there are others who are unhappy and who suffer in all different ways. If nothing else, the heart recognizes that there is suffering and wishes (in the Christian tradition we would say "prays") that it be alleviated in some way.

How would Buddha celebrate Christmas? Perhaps by reminding us that there is more to giving than materialism and that the best presents are not extravagant purchases, but simple gifts that are given not in order to impress or to receive in return. Instead, they are meant to simply express our love, care, and compassion toward family, friends, and all people wherever they gather, whatever they believe.

How can we practice the spiritual act of giving without succumbing to Wal-Mart values? There is something to be said for evaluating our own motivation in giving to see that it comes not out of the stress of meeting holiday expectations, but out of a genuine desire to give of our selves.

One very special way to approach this aspect of Christmas is with alternative giving. I am a huge advocate of buying gifts through the Heifer Project and similar organizations. The idea is that you buy something that will improve the life of a family living in poverty in the name of the friend or family member you want to recognize with a gift. You might buy a goat for a family in Ghana or a chicken for a family in El Salvador. You might buy a well or medicine or any number of other tangible gifts for those in need on behalf of someone you know and care about.

I enjoy making these charitable contributions but admit that I also feel the pull to give something personal to those I love, so a few years ago I began buying fair trade items: baskets, chocolate, toys, and other items that are made in impoverished areas by local craftspeople receiving a fair wage for their work.

Other years when I am mindful of the waste of gifts that aren't really needed, I give the gift of myself, my time. My presence becomes my present. A lot of people regularly get together with family members, but I can easily get caught up in my own life. It is difficult for me to find time with my family arising naturally in our comings and goings. For people like me, giving my time is an act of intentional generosity and sharing. My mother has received certificates from me for a day of antiquing or a trip to Shipshewana. My sister has been invited to share girls' night out with me. My niece has received an invitation for a sleepover with her aunt, while my nephew gets to hang out with my kids. A double gift occurs in the opening of a window for their parents to enjoy a night out, or in, by themselves.

The possibilities are limited only by our imaginations. The more generous, the greater the joy. Generosity, in the end, has nothing to do with how much money we spend. When we sincerely give to others, we have the opportunity to use our creativity and to grow as human beings.

There is a popular saying that the more we give, the more we receive. If Buddha were celebrating Christmas with us, I think he'd be quick to point out the fallacy of such a sentiment, because the gift we receive in giving is not about amounts or keeping score, it is about adopting the heart of a giver. It is about the joy one finds in discovering that in our core, we are givers. Giving is simply an expression of our own True Self. The delight we experience is in the giving and *not* in anticipation of the facial expression of the receiver of our gift. The delight is in the giving and *not* in anticipation of being appreciated. The delight is in the giving; the reaction to that giving is of no consequence at all.

Consider these statements: "I helped him out when he needed it and now when I need a hand he isn't there for me." "I've given my children everything they want and they're still disobedient." "I've given so much to so many, sacrificed my own material wants in order to be generous with my charities, and now I've lost my job. How could God do this to me? Don't I deserve to be treated better?"

Such comments are not uncommon. They speak of the frustration, confusion, and anger we feel when our kindness, generosity, and love for others has gone unappreciated, unreturned, unrewarded. "Why is she so ungrateful?" "Did I help the wrong person?" "Didn't I give enough?"

When my son Jackson finished his three-year discipleship program, I spent a lot of time trying to figure out what to give him as a gift. I had received a ten-speed bike when I was confirmed and it was an important and meaningful gift for me. I had mentioned it to Jackson and he, in the kind of sensitivity toward parents that only a teenager can show, told me whatever I did, he did not want a bike!

Through some kind of mental acrobatics that I have difficulty today even beginning to recall, I decided that for Jackson's confirmation gift, I would give him— what else— a bike! And you know what? He wasn't even a little bit appreciative! I really blew it— and in at least two important ways. First of all, I stubbornly refused to be thoughtful and creative enough to come up with a present that might actually mean something to Jackson. Second, I expected him to appreciate my efforts and my cash investment anyway!

Phra Santikaro Bhikkhu, an outspoken American-born Buddhist monk notes that, "Today, consumerism has shaped the way we give. Our giving has become an act of exchange, or an investment. True giving must be free from expectations of anything in return. If you expect to get even a word of appreciation like "thank you" from receivers, then it is not a free giving, but an exchange."[6] Gratitude must be voluntary; so must an act of giving.

According to Kenneth Leong in *The Zen Teachings of Jesus*, it is in giving that we become more alive, more human, more productive, and more confident in our own abilities. As Zen master Seisetsu puts it, "The giver should be thankful."[7]

How would Buddha celebrate Christmas? By inviting us to consider the free and unconditional way of giving that we find in nature. We all receive breath and sunshine, trees and rocks, animals and other human beings without nature insisting we be grateful in return. Buddha would remind us, as we select gifts and place them under the tree, to give with love that is free and unconditional. Trees give us air without being forced to and without forcing us to repay with our gratitude. Then he would remind us that such giving needs to go beyond our immediate circle of family and friends to embrace all of humanity. He would encourage us to cultivate a heart of universal compassion and be moved by our acts of prayer and contemplation as we offer up our concern for the well-being of all others to God.

Finally, I think Buddha would celebrate Christmas by gazing for hours upon the Nativity. I can see a look of profound love and devotion filling his eyes as he watches the way in which mother and child behold each other. He would urge us to gaze upon the scene as well. Buddha would encourage us to breathe it in so that we might begin to radiate that kind of loving kindness to everyone we meet. And he would remind us that this child, this enlightened one, was born precisely for that—to bring the message of compassion, love, and selfless giving to a world longing to be free of its own trappings. Buddha would remind us that there is indeed a Reason for the Season.

A Child is Born: How Would Jesus Celebrate Christmas?

The preparation for Christmas can be a time of "busyness," delight, panic, joy, exhaustion, and celebration in quick succession or all at once. The first Christmas was likely marked with many of the same emotions, for the

---

6. Bhikkhu, "*The Way of Giving.*"
7. O'Reilly et al., *The Road Within*, 85.

advent of Jesus' arrival came at the conclusion of a normal term of pregnancy by way of a young woman's first delivery of a baby.

Those of you with children can remember the preparations you made as you anticipated an impending birth. Wasn't that activity much the same as what we experience at Christmas? Has a name been selected for a boy and a girl? Is the nursery done? Are suitcases packed and phone numbers handy? Has childcare been determined? How much will it hurt and can I still get out of this if I pray hard enough? The eve of a new birth is a time of nervousness and excitement and of overwhelming thankfulness and joy.

I am especially struck by the humanness of the arrival of this Savior. Jesus the Christ, fully God and yet fully human. Born to a human mother. Raised by a human father, a stepfather if you will, in the company of humans.

Likewise, if there's *anything* my family is, it's human. Not that my own household resembled the model of the Joe Carpenter family any more than it did a Norman Rockwell painting. As my children were growing up, serene reflections on holiday giving were replaced with chants of "gimme, gimme, gimme." My children weren't holding hands while I encircled the tree with lights; they were pummeling each other on the ground, rolling over and crushing ornaments in their way. And they certainly weren't asleep all snug in their beds. These little elves were jumping up and down on beds calling each other new and creative combinations of words usually saved for physician offices and biker bars.

And try as I might, I was not always as patient and understanding as I would have liked to be. I made mistakes, and sadly I still do. When I make a mistake, I start thinking about other mistakes I have made, and mistakes my mother has made, and her mother, and my sister and my friends and my relatives and even the mistakes of complete strangers. They have made lots of mistakes. I'm sure they have.

So given the topic at hand, let's reflect on our most famous mom—Mary. Mary, who although she was blessed beyond any woman, was still human—like you and me. Flawed, imperfect, sinful. That's what the Bible says: "for all have sinned."[8] If the human child Jesus was anything like a normal human child, curious, precocious, determined, and the lot, Mary had to have made mistakes—just like any human mother.

As a virgin, Mary receives the gift of Jesus and he grows within her. This kind of virgin imagery is used by one of the great Christian mystics, Meister Eckhart, to describe the birth of God in each of us. Eckhart was born near Erfurt, Germany, in 1260. He was a Dominican monk, a graduate of the University of Paris where he received his Master's degree, a professor,

---

8. Romans 3:23 (NIV).

priest, and advocate for the poor. He also supported the charismatic lay women's movement of the time. Meister Eckhart is best remembered as a Christian mystic, although he died a heretic of the Church.

Mystics believe in the existence of realities that lie beyond human comprehension. Then they seek to be united with that reality. Philosopher Ken Wilber describes a mystic as "someone who doesn't see God as an object, but who is immersed in God as an atmosphere."[9] If you've ever been in love, then you have had a taste of the mystics' passion for God.

If this all sounds like a lot of nonsense then you can see how problematic mystics have been to the church over the centuries. Despite their contributions to Christian theology, many mystics have been and are charged with heresy. This is what happened to Meister Eckhart who, even despite a movement in the 1980s to exonerate him, is still considered a heretic by the Catholic Church. Other mystics were simply written off as psychotic, delusional fanatics.

Meister Eckhart immersed himself in a God of paradox and then sought to share his experiences through sermons and writings. Through his vivid use of images, he was able to direct his listeners to what lies beyond those images. Eckhart draws us into the mystical indwelling of God through the imagery of the Christmas story. Here is my paraphrase of a portion of Eckhart's Sermon 2:

> Our Lord Jesus went up into a little town, and was received by a virgin who was a wife. Notice carefully what this says. You must be a virgin to receive Jesus. To be a virgin is to be free of all images—as free as you were when you were born. You might ask how it is possible for a person who has lived a full life to be as free of images as when they were born.
>
> But I tell you, if I could have those images and know all of the things I know and at the same time not feel attached to any it, not feel possessive of any of it—if I could simply let all those ideas and pictures and knowledge go as unimportant—then I would be as free and empty as God wants me to be.
>
> Then I would truly be a virgin, as free of any images as I was when I was not. A virgin lives in the present moment, free of possessiveness and empty, because every attachment deprives that person of the freedom to wait upon God in the present and follow. A man or a woman who is this kind of virgin has no obstacles between them and supreme truth.[10]

9. Wilber, *One Taste*, 31.
10. Eckhart, *The Essential Sermons*, 177–182.

an interfaith adventure 11

The mystics, like Meister Eckhart, contend that it is in letting go of the images we carry of God that we are filled with God's spirit. Mystics believe that union with God is the true reality of life and that nothing else is really important. Eckhart's sentiments are echoed in the popular phrase "let it go and let it be." Today brain research is providing us with additional insights. The book *Why God Won't Go Away: Brain Science and the Biology of Belief* argues that genuine mystical experiences are not the products of hallucinations, but the result of normal neurological functioning when a certain part of the brain is deprived of input. Individuals literally experience a lessening of their sense of self and the absorption of their self into some larger sense of reality. Blocking that neural flow can be done on purpose through practices like meditation and contemplation.

Returning to Eckhart's imagery of Mother Mary, allow me to paraphrase Sermons 6 and 22:

> God gives me birth as God's self. God gives birth to me as God's being and nature. In the innermost source, there I spring out in the Holy Spirit, where there is one life and one being and one work. God is not outside one's self, but is one's own and is what is within. Some people think they will see God as if God were standing there and they here. It is not so. God and I, we are one.
>
> The Holy Spirit did not speak to Mary alone, but to every good soul that longs for God. I say this: If Mary had not first given spiritual birth to God, he would never have been born bodily from her. It is more precious to God to be born spiritually from every such virgin or from every good soul than that he was bodily born of Mary.
>
> I accept God into me in knowing; I go into God in loving. Working and becoming are one. God is working and I am becoming. The fire changes anything into itself that is put into it. Whatever is put into the fire takes on fire's own nature. The wood does not change the fire into itself, but the fire changes the wood into itself. So are we changed into God, that we shall know God as God is.[11]

Eckhart believes not only that we are birthed by God, but also that God is birthed in us. If you don't understand all of this, Eckhart says not to worry about it. After all, whatever we do understand isn't God anyway. Instead of chattering about God or trying to understand God who will always remain unknown, it is better to long for nothing, to be empty. For if we are

11. Ibid.,189, 293.

empty God has no choice but to come into us. Eckhart wants us merely to open our eyes and see what has always been the case: that God and the soul are truly one in their deepest ground.

Revisiting Jesus' human family, we come to Joseph. According to traditional Christianity, not only is Joseph a new dad, he also has the challenge of being a stepfather, odd man out. Did he find his own authority questioned and did he question his own authority? He had to have struggled with his place in this family and he had to have made mistakes. Just like any father or stepfather. Mistakes. Lots of them.

But what strikes me most as I ponder this relationship between mother and father today and Mary and Joseph of 2000 years ago is God's faith in weak and flawed human beings. Think about it. God trusted human beings to raise this son, the incarnation of God's own self. How many people do you know that you would trust to raise your own child? Sometimes I'm not all that certain that I should be trusted to raise my own kids. But God is. God trusted me enough to give me two little boys to raise, knowing that I am human, I am flawed, that I will sin. And God also provided a safety net, loving, protecting and nurturing my children all of the time, even when I mess up.

That is the glory of this gift of Christ Jesus. That having become human and lived among us, he knows our needs, our weaknesses, and our hopes. He understands the joy and apprehension of new parents on the eve of the birth of their child. He knows the immeasurable happiness that will follow with the baby's first cry. He calls us to embrace the love and glory that is within that child, just as Mary and Joseph embraced their son, not just on the morning of the birth, but from that moment on.

I have made another mistake. I have felt the coming of the Christ child, warm and wonderful within my soul. Felt the mysterious and awesome gift of birth to a virgin mother. Felt the delight of the baby leaping for joy inside Elizabeth's womb. Sang with Mary, "My soul magnifies the Lord, and my spirit rejoices in God my Savior, for he has looked with favor on the lowliness of his servant."[12] Felt the pull of the star and the joyous arrival of wise men and shepherds. Felt the promise of the saving grace of this infant. And then awakened a few days after Christmas to have lost the glorious feeling of Christ with me, within me, always and forever.

Christmas marks the coming of our Savior. But Jesus doesn't come and then go away again. Each Christmas marks an anniversary of a relationship—a relationship that is meant to continue throughout the year. A new baby stays with his parents and together they grow in love and

---

12. Luke 1:46–48 (NRSV).

understanding over the years. Each Christmas anniversary should be a time to celebrate the deepening of our faith, trust, and love of God and God's Son Jesus Christ, a time for wonder and awe and refection. It should not be a time to be suddenly reminded of this most holy gift, not a time to become reacquainted with a Savior that we will forget again when the lights come off the tree and the carols stop playing on the radio.

Our challenge in each New Year is to hold onto the real presence of Christ in our lives every day of the year. Feel it now and hold onto it as tightly as you would hold your toddler's hand in a busy parking lot. Hold onto it and let it deepen. Nurture that relationship, pray for it, feel it grow. Then go about bringing that love, that blessed relationship, to those that are in need of the same.

Howard Thurman wrote:

> *When the song of the angels is stilled,*
> *When the star in the sky is gone,*
> *When the kings and princes are home,*
> *When the shepherds are back with their flock,*
> *The work of Christmas begins:*
>   *To find the lost,*
>   *To heal the broken,*
>   *To feed the hungry,*
>   *To release the prisoner,*
>   *To rebuild the nations,*
>   *To bring peace among brothers,*
>   *To make music in the heart.*[13]

Eckhart said, "I say yet more, do not be startled, for this joy is near you and is in you. There is no one of you so crude, or so small in understanding or so removed, that you cannot joyfully and intelligently find this joy within you in the truth in which it exists, even before you leave this church today or before I finish the sermon today. You can as truly find it and live it and possess it within you as God is God and I am a man."[14]

It is precisely because we know we fail, even when we try our hardest, that we can find comfort in the humanness of Mary and Joseph. It is in their humanness that we can see evidence of God's faith and trust in people just like us—imperfect, flawed, and sinful. Just like you and me. It is in the reality of that humanness that we can understand how amazing God's gift of forgiveness and life truly is. It is in that humanness that we can hope to grasp the truth that we have all been blessed beyond measure. And it is in

13. Thurman and Smith, *Howard Thurman*, 84.
14. Eckhart, *Meister Eckhart*, 61.

that same humanness that we can know without question that our call and our responsibility is to bring that Good News to all of humankind—to the weak, the flawed, the sinful, the hopeless, the broken, the lost.

Then, with Christ not just lying peacefully in a manger, but traveling with us and within us through all the realities of human frailty, we will begin to see our brothers and sisters differently. We will begin to be able to see in them the same possibilities that God sees in us. We will begin to feel the same faith in ourselves and in all humans that God has in us all. And in this new awareness, we will look into the human face of an infant, a child, a mother or a father, a stranger, a sinner . . . and in them we will behold the face of God.

A Celebration: How Would Shiva Celebrate Christmas?

There are many places where the birth of Jesus is greeted with countless voices raised in praise and in song. *What Child is This? Hark! The Herald Angels Sing! Joy to the World!* All of them powerfully proclaim the Word made Flesh, the Babe, the Son of Mary. In some of the places where those voices join together, there are altars that hold pictures of Jesus, Ramakrishna, and Buddha. These are Hindu temples and the worshippers are there to revere Jesus as a yogi master, a Divine avatar, and an embodiment of the Godhead.

I chose the title "How Would Shiva Celebrate Christmas?" But I could have chosen any of Trimurti—because like Christianity's trinity, Hinduism names three principal deities of the faith: Brahma the Creator, Vishnu the Preserver, and Shiva the Destroyer and Completer.

The easy answer to how would Shiva celebrate Christmas is "by celebrating Christmas." Of all the great religions, Hinduism has the clearest voice of conviction for appreciating the diversity of paths that lead to God. Hindu's widespread embrace of Jesus and Christmas amounts to a particularly dynamic form of multiculturalism in which followers of different religions actually embrace some of each other's beliefs.

According to Hindu teaching, the various religions are simply different languages through which God speaks to the human heart. There is admiration and respect for the variety of textures and tones through which God manifests in creation. Still, beyond the celebration of differences, there is a deep and rich embrace of the reality of the Oneness of all.

There is a story of a man who worshipped Shiva but hated all the other deities. One day Shiva appeared to him and said, "I shall never be pleased with you so long as you hate the other gods." But the man did not change his mind. A few days later Shiva appeared again and said, "I shall never be pleased with you so long as you hate." The man said nothing in reply. After a few more days Shiva appeared again, but this time one side of his body was Shiva and the other side was Vishnu. The man was half pleased and half displeased. He laid his offerings on the side representing Shiva and didn't offer anything to the side representing Vishnu. Then Shiva said, "I tried to convince you that all gods and goddesses are various aspects of the one Absolute Brahman. But your bigotry is unconquerable."

Hindus in general have no trouble believing that our Christian God and their Hindu God are the same. God just comes in different shapes. There may be different paths to God, but God is only ever one. This broad, open-minded faith embraces the gods of many religions, not as separate and competing deities, but as manifestations of the one formless God.

The Hindu tradition includes beautiful iconography. The Icon of Christ the Yogi reminds us that despite our attempts to paint Jesus with blue eyes, he was from the Middle East. If we roughly divide the world into two halves with two worldviews, Jesus falls into the realm of the East while I am in the camp of the Westerners. Although Jesus' stories and parables speak to us in our own context, it is possible to find another dimension of richness and texture by remembering that Jesus' context was that of an Easterner.

To better appreciate this dimension of Jesus' language and to help us understand the Hindu love of Jesus, it might help us to explore for a minute what we mean by the Eastern way of thinking. Swami Vivekananda spoke passionately of the birth, life, death, and resurrection of this Eastern Christ. While we in the West are accustomed to looking around and seeing beauty all around us, the people of the East look for the beautiful from another direction. They tend to look inside, not outside.

The Easterner is a visionary, a born dreamer. The ripples of waterfalls, the songs of birds, the glow of the sun and moon and stars, and the whole of creation are certainly lovely, but they are not enough for the Eastern mind. He or she wants to dream a dream beyond what is seen and felt and heard. He or she wants to go beyond what is immediately obvious.

Perhaps because the history of the area is so old and so full of the quest for kingdoms and power and glory and wealth, those very things in which the country is steeped begin to hold the least attraction. Instead the Eastern mind seeks something that is permanent, that does not change, that does not die. In the midst of this life's hardship and suffering, the desire is for something blissful and eternal. A prophet from the East, and you might notice that all the great religions were founded by prophets from the East, never tires of insisting upon such ideals. Christ was such a prophet.

It was the Hindu sage Ramakrishna who in the 1800s preached about the birth of Jesus as a chance to meditate on the sacred "Christ within." And

Vivekananda who in the 1900s taught Ramakrishna's admirers to celebrate Jesus' birth at Christmas and to follow Jesus' life with the goal of realizing God-consciousness. How would Ramakrishna or Vivekananda celebrate Christmas? By celebrating Christmas, of course!

The Hindu scriptures refer to "great children of light, who manifest the Light themselves, who are Light themselves, they, being worshipped become, as it were, one with us and we become one with them."[15] Our Christian scriptures refer to Jesus as the Light of the World and the promise he makes us is the same, that we can be one with Christ just as he is one with God.

It is the light of Christ that shines from within us as we live in this beautiful paradox. We are each called on a unique and personal journey of the Spirit that leads us ultimately to discover the Oneness we share with all creation, with each other, with God. For this Christ lives within us, pointing us to beauty beyond this world's struggles and hardship.

Can you feel it? Can you feel that light shining out from you? Sometimes I do. I especially noticed it when I worked as a barista at a local coffee house. Too often instead of the light I would feel annoyed at my co-workers or bored as I stared at the clock. Then it would happen. A customer would come in and I would know that while all I was giving them was a smile and a cup of coffee, something much larger was taking place. In their eyes, in my heart, something was registering that was far more potent than anything I alone have ever been capable of. It happens even more often these days, because I no longer find myself so often annoyed and I am almost never bored. In those special moments, the Christ light is almost palpable as it shines out from me.

How about you? Are there times you feel the Christ light shining out from you, lighting up your heart, reaching out to touch others? I hope so. I hope you feel it, because I know it's there, shining out from you.

And as the light of Christ shines out from us, it illuminates our path so that in these days following Christmas we can move with certainty and assurance on our own individual path as the road stretches out before us, leading us all to that one destination, the promise of Christ that in him we do indeed know God.

The Great Religions

The
great religions are the
ships,

---

15. Vivekananda, *Christ*, 17.

> *poets the life*
> *boats.*
> *Every sane person I know has jumped*
> *overboard.*
> *That is good for business*
> *isn't it,*
> *Hafiz?*[16]

—DANIEL LADINSKY

An Invitation for Reflection:

1. How do your expectations affect what ends up happening?
2. When did someone else know you could do something you didn't think you could do? What happened?
3. How do you decide whom to give gifts to during Christmas? How do you decide what to give? How important is it to you that your gifts are received well and appreciated?
4. How does the birth of Jesus make a difference in your life?
5. What images of God do you need to let go of in order for God to be born in you?
6. When do you feel the Christ light shining out from you?

---

16. Ladinsky, "Goodreads," lines 1–10.

2

An Integral Perspective

Everyone of us is shadowed by an illusory person: a false self.
This is the man that I want myself to be
but who cannot exist,
because God does not know
anything about him.
And to be unknown of God
is altogether too much
privacy.[1]

—THOMAS MERTON

Enlightenment: A Cognitive Perspective

WE LIVE AT AN amazing time. For the first time in human history, we have access to virtually every other culture, faith tradition, and social order on this planet. So what if we take everything all of these cultures have to offer us in terms of spiritual, psychological, and social growth and put it all on the table?

Almost 50 years ago Ken Wilber was a medical student practicing Zen Buddhism and engaging in Gestalt therapy. The only thing disconcerting about this combination of practices is that they seemed to be in conflict with

---

1. Merton, *New Seeds of Contemplation*, 34.

each other. Based on the proposition that the human mind is incapable of being wrong 100 percent of the time, he wondered what a model would look like that said everyone is right. From that starting point, he built an Integral Map and created a Theory of Everything.

The Theory of Everything can be used to explore every aspect of human culture, including spirituality. When we look at all the world religions, we find striking differences and remarkable similarities. Integral Spirituality takes all of this into account, seeking what we have in common while also celebrating the particularities of each lineage.

Most of the great wisdom traditions agree that:

1. Spirit, by whatever name, exists.
2. Spirit, although existing "out there," is found "in here," or revealed within to the open heart and mind.
3. Most of us don't realize this Spirit within because we are living in a world of sin, separation, or duality. That is, we are living in a fallen, illusory, or fragmented state.
4. There is a way out of this fallen state; there is a Path to our liberation.
5. If we follow this Path to its conclusion, the result is a Rebirth or Enlightenment, a direct experience of Spirit within and without, a Supreme Liberation, which
6. Marks the end of sin and suffering, and
7. Manifests in the social action of mercy and compassion on behalf of all sentient beings.[2]

All major religions seek rebirth or enlightenment. Now, enlightenment is a curious word. We have a lot of language about the light in the Christian lineage. Jesus himself said, "I am the light" so it seems obvious that to "get" Jesus and to follow his way to its conclusion is to reach a state of enlightenment. But what exactly does that mean? Here the Christian faith of the West seems to get a little squeamish about the teachings of the Western Mystics and of the faith traditions of the East.

Consequently, those of us who seek higher, deeper, and wider paths of spiritual growth can find ourselves in a rather precarious position. On the other hand, not to seek such understanding is counter to the instructions of our own Scripture.

Paul said to the Ephesians: "I pray that God . . . may give you a spirit of wisdom and revelation as you come to know God so that, with the eyes of your heart enlightened, you may know what is the hope to which you have

2. Wilber, et al., *Integral Life Practice*, 200.

been called and what are the riches of this glorious inheritance among the saints."[3] At the same time, the author of Hebrews chides us if we think we have no more to do: "Everyone who lives on milk, being still an infant, is not skilled in the word of righteousness. But solid food is for the mature ... Therefore, let us go on toward perfection, leaving behind the basic teaching about Christ."[4]

Every human being has the potential for spiritual growth, just as we develop and grow physically, cognitively, emotionally, morally, and so on. Hence, we are called to move on toward enlightenment, experiencing the heavenly gift, sharing in the Holy Spirit, and tasting the goodness of the word of God.

Integral is a wave of consciousness that is inclusive, balanced, and comprehensive. It is a map that can help us figure out what is going on in our world and how we can act to make this a better place for everyone to live. In that way, it is a problem-solving device. As we also apply this map to our life, we can accelerate our growth and development into higher, wider, and deeper ways of being.

A tool that can help us with this journey is an Integral Practice. In adopting an Integral Practice, we seek to intentionally grow in awareness as a human being. There are four pillars to any such practice and they are: Cognitive, Psychodynamic, Physical, and Spiritual. In addition, there is a supporting structure we will call Ethics.

In the cognitive realm, we examine our practice, set our intent, and recognize and choose to pursue our vision. We usually begin with the cognitive pillar because in our culture, until we can get our heads around something, it rarely moves below our necks.

In the psychodynamic pillar, we address our emotions and our relationships. Ultimately we seek to move from the need to "get" to the need to "express and give." We learn to welcome in and to reintegrate into our being that which we wanted to leave out.

In the physical realm, we pursue new awareness and friendliness with our body. We notice and welcome all of its energies. We seek health and vitality.

Finally, in the spiritual realm, we seek ultimately to unite with Spirit and relax in the universe. We pursue the realization that love and transcendence are gifts already here that we need only to awaken to.

I was introduced to Ken Wilber's works when a mentor suggested I listen to *Cosmic Consciousness* and read *Grace and Grit*. But my understanding

---

3. Ephesians 1:17–18 (NRSV).
4. Hebrews 5:13—6:1 (NRSV).

was blown wide open and deepened considerably when I had the opportunity to attend the Integral Institute in Boulder, Colorado in the spring of 2005.

I left my Colorado hotel room on a Saturday morning after a total immersion experience in all things Integral, only to arrive late at the airport. I had followed bad advice from the shuttle bus and got to the check in counter minutes after they closed the flight. I wandered slowly through the airport regretting getting up so early, regretting not getting up earlier, upset that I would be home so late, wondering what I would do at an airport with 11 hours before the next flight out, upset by the emotionless automatons making these decisions. Simply stated, I was wallowing in my own self-pity. I was meandering toward my gate, because I didn't have anything better to do, when I heard them call for final boarding.

I approached the attendant behind the desk and asked her if it would have been possible, had I been in the right frame of mind, to have taken this flight and had my luggage follow. "No," she answered, "we can't do that." I figured as much, so I told her I understood and that I would try not to cry. In retrospect that was terribly melodramatic. She replied without any melodrama that she was trying not to cry herself. Her father-in-law had wrecked her truck that morning. She was glad that no one was hurt. Then she told me she was putting me on the last available seat on this plane, but that I would have to go back to the airport to get my luggage as they wouldn't deliver it to me. I couldn't believe it! I was surprised and thrilled. I asked if it was okay for me to hug her and in return I received one of the heartiest hugs of my life.

When I sat down in awe and amazement having found my seat in First Class, I realized I had just met Christ—and then I did start to cry. I realized I have so far to go, so much growing up and out of myself to accomplish. And at the same time I relished the fact that two human beings in that moment were touching, connecting, communicating, serving, and being served. I savored the miracle of an embrace. Because of that experience, one of my spiritual practices since that day is to be more intent on seeing Christ in everyone I encounter.

Psychodynamics: Shadow Boxing

A woman was working in her front yard when a moving van pulled up next door. While the movers unloaded the van, her new neighbors walked over and introduced themselves to her. She was feeling pretty self-conscious, what with the dirt on her hands and face, her hair pulled back, and her figure draped in old worn gardening clothes. A few days later she got an invitation to her new neighbors' Open House. She was so happy to have a chance to make a better impression. She colored her hair, put on a girdle, glossed her lips, put on false eyelashes, got acrylic nails, and popped in colored contact lenses. Stepping back from the mirror admiringly she said to her husband, "There. Now they can see the real me."

For me this whole scenario is more likely to play out on an emotional level. I throw a fit or succumb to a hard sobbing cry and then say something brilliant like, "I don't know what got into me." Because surely that behavior isn't part of *me*. It's an other. An it. That anger thing. That grieving thing. You might be like that. But not *me*. That's not part of who I am.

Or is it?

As soon as my application was accepted, I began to prepare for my trip to the Integral Institute. I thought about whom I would be while I was there. Would I be vulnerable and admit my many growing edges? Or would I be smart and accomplished and play on my strengths? Would I speak up and ask questions? Would I sit silently and listen? What parts of me would I own and which would I ignore? The me that emerged ended up being all of that and more. The psychodynamic pillar and practices involve our emotions and our interpersonal relationships.

I'd like to invite you to do a quick little exercise. First just sit there relaxed and begin breathing deeply into your stomach. Feel the rise and fall of your abdomen. How's it feel? Now tighten your stomach like you are bracing for a punch in the guts. And while your holding your stomach in this tension try to take a few deep, satisfying breaths. Did it work?

The same way a contracted muscle gets in the way of our ability to freely breathe and express ourselves physically, we also contract emotionally, creating barriers to normal, healthy self-expression. If we become aware of that contraction, we can release it, breath by breath, by noticing the deeper Self who is able to see the contraction. David Deida notes that in every moment we have a choice. We can open in love or close in fear. We cannot do both at the same time. We contract when we recoil, rather than extending love, care, and compassion to ourselves and to others.

It's easy for most of us to think about times we have rejected or pushed aside some person in our lives: a relative, an ex-relative, a boss, a neighbor. The truth is we have also rejected and pushed aside parts of our selves. That's part of our being human. Life gives us all kinds of opportunities to diminish our sense of self, and we're usually pretty good at accepting those invitations. Psychodynamic work is about recovering those parts of us that were pushed aside and denied. These are the aspects of ourselves we decided or were told by others were unlovable, so we keep them hidden from others, and even from our own awareness.

I was told often and from an early age that I talk too much. This never comes as a surprise to anyone who knows me well. But the truth is that while I never could quite give up the gab, I also became hypersensitive and acutely aware of my desire to say something. At the same time I developed a parallel compulsion to stay silent because I couldn't imagine having anything to say of any value. Not only that, I became overly critical toward others who seemed to "talk too much" as I projected my own sense of inferiority onto them.

It takes an amazing amount of energy to keep a part of our selves buried. You might think of the parts of yourself as a series of threads or strands that get twisted and knotted together. In psychodynamic work, we seek to tease apart those strands of our self. We practice becoming self-aware in order to release and free up that energy which has been trapped and to reclaim the life force that is always already within us.

I have to tell you, this has become a whole new way for me to look at myself. I have a shadow side. There are parts of my past and my personality that I have longed to be rid of. Moreover, I thought I couldn't be healthy until they were gone. I viewed those parts of myself as festering sores that I not only wanted to heal, but that I wanted to disappear completely. I wanted them to be gone, over, finished. But as many times as I thought I had cast them out, I would find them again, to my deep dismay, buried deep inside.

My thinking modeled the way we often think about illness and was consistent with the familiar way of viewing Jesus' ministry of healing. After all, didn't he cast the demons out of people? As I struggled to reconcile these two seemingly contradictory views of healing, I was drawn to the story of the man from Gerasene.[5] In this healing, Jesus casts out the demons, but first he does something else pretty amazing. He looks at a man possessed and, speaking to his demons, says, "What is your name?" The man replies, "My name is legion for we are many."[6] Do you notice what Jesus did in that instant? He addressed the shadows. He speaks to them and acknowledges their presence. And in doing so he takes away their power to control and contract the human being they have imprisoned.

Jesus doesn't banish the demons by denying them and plunging them into dark denial, but by exposing them to the light. If we are to find our own healing, it also requires us to shine the light on our shadow side. To transcend those things that pull us down, we need first to identify and embrace

5. Mark 5:1–16 (NRSV).
6. Mark 5:9 (NRSV).

them. We need to finally embody what we want to dis-identify with and own our shadow. For it is an important component of what has made us who we are. It has served a purpose in being there. This is the way we become a fully integrated human being, able to bear the love of a gracious God.

Furthermore, unconsciousness operates on at least two dimensions: the lower and the higher. The lower is the part of ourselves that we don't have access to any longer: demons denied, slipped-off parts of our self, difficult emotions and experiences. Higher unconsciousness is that which we don't have access to yet: the god or goddess denied, the not-yet-identified parts of ourselves, the higher potentials we have yet to realize.

Psychodynamic work primarily addresses the lower, but in the hidden basement of our awareness we also recognize that the same defenses that keep us from embracing our demons also keep us from embracing the god/dess within. The energy we use to lock down the gate of lower consciousness is the same energy we use to keep from unlocking the gate of higher realization.

As we become integrated, we ultimately move from fear to freedom. We move from a need to receive to a need to give and to express. We welcome in what we wanted to leave out. And we move from a sense that "this shouldn't be happening" to seeing what really is, while bringing loving intelligence with us. We move from judgment to discriminating wisdom. And in the process we find greater alignment and authenticity between who we are, who we think we are, who we say we are, and who God knows us to be.

As we become more authentic, we strip away unhealthy costumes and masks. When my son Alex was in second grade, he came home from school and told me he was going to the Halloween Party the next day as Captain Underpants. "I don't think so," I said. "I don't think the school would approve." "It's okay, Mom!" he assured me, "Miss Fed said it would be all right as long as I wear the underwear over my clothes."

So the next morning, my 8-year-old put on an old red superman cape around his shirtless back and pulled a pair of underwear over his shorts. Then he proceeded to stuff and shove his shorts into the underwear so they bulged like an inner tube all around him before striking a mighty fine Captain Underpants pose.

I admit I thought he'd back out; that he would get embarrassed and change his mind. But despite my offers to rescue him from this situation, when the bus arrived he jumped out of my car and marched proudly up the steps without a glance back. He *became* Captain Underpants. And I'm not really sure whether *that* Alex materialized because of the mask and costume he put on or because he was finally allowed to take off the mask and costume *I* wanted him to wear.

All of us wear masks. There are the masks we wear because we choose to and there are the masks that are thrust upon us. A mask can be something we hide behind, or something that allows us to be more fully who we really are. There are masks that we wear with great ritual and there are masks we casually put on and take off without much thought at all. Some of our masks harm other people. Some of them harm us. Only when we can put them aside and look at ourselves honestly can we claim the righteousness that Jesus tells us is legitimately ours—not because we pretend to be something we are not—but because we know our inability to do anything without the love of God working within us.

When we can claim that truth, we also find a whole new usefulness for masks—not to disguise our true identity, but to allow us to enter into more caring and authentic relationships with others. These are masks we wear out of respect. Knowing we are flawed creatures, we understand the damage we would inflict if we shared every thought and impulse we have. Have you ever been with someone who is brutally, caustically "honest" all of the time? In the movie *Liar, Liar* the character played by Jim Carey becomes unable to self-censor and discern the right place, the right time, and the right people to share his thoughts with.[7] He hurts the people around him, friends, family, and complete strangers.

Masks help us to be appropriate and to set safe and healthy boundaries. I don't talk to my mother the same way I talk to my life partner. I don't act the same way with my kids that I do with my boss. Different relationships pull something different out of me. And they should.

These masks are not like opaque wooden objects that block us out, but more like colored transparencies that allow our own face, our true self, to shine at different times through a slightly different lens.

No one, we are told, can see God's face and live. None of us can really see into the depth of all God is and survive. And so it is that even God wears a mask in coming into this world. What else is incarnation but God putting on a human mask in order to be able to interact directly with you and with me?

And what are we but the masks God wears? God puts us on and acts through us. We bring God's mercy and grace into this world. We bring God's compassion to those in need. We become the movement of God's hands and God's feet. You and me. Each of us a different colored transparency that the true nature of God shines brilliantly through.

When we introduced ourselves at the Integral Institute one woman said, "My name is Janice. I am fully developed in every one of my lines—except

---

7. *Liar, Liar*. Universal Pictures, 1997.

my spiritual line. I am doing great with everything else. But I'm here because I feel I need to work on my spiritual line."

Right then I didn't like her. I knew that anyone who describes themselves as "fully developed in every one of their lines" was bound to be a royal pain in the butt. This was the only person of the fifty gathered that I made a conscious decision to try to avoid. But try as I might, it seemed like she was always right *there*. Right next to *me*.

And I was right. She *always* had something to say. And she always had the kinds of questions to ask that you would think someone so highly developed would already know.

Even so, that very question or that obvious blunder would inevitably yield good conversation and some really important sharing of ideas and intuitions. Slowly I had to reassess my aversion to Janice. Finally I was able to recognize that what I didn't like about her is exactly what I don't like in myself. I became grateful for the chance to practice loving her and the chance to practice embracing a part of me.

Perhaps, I decided by the time we closed, the Institute should always plant a Janice at its trainings just so she could help someone like me to grow a bit.

I'm worth the effort. Jesus witnessed to that and continues to call me to be my own most authentic self. Never before has love and consciousness combined in such a way that is me. And as marvelous as that is, there is more. Because never again will love and consciousness combine in such a way that is you.

May all of us learn to love and embrace fully the me and the you that we are.

Let's Get Physical

In April 2013, I had the unique opportunity to join colleagues from Rotary in installing water filters in Honduras with my son Alex. We used four-wheel drive trucks and tennis shoes, to climb by vehicle and by foot treacherous terrain that mountain goats would stumble on. We slept in camp, and in the morning found salamanders under our shoes and cockroaches in our beds. We swam in the rivers, ate local food and challenged our bodies to adapt. Unfortunately, not all of our bodies made that adjustment easily. Alex ended up taking Cipro during most of the trip after swallowing a mouthful of river water. And it was weeks before my body returned to any kind of balance in its elimination system. My body had decided not to simply go along but to betray me in some way I couldn't quite understand.

It wasn't the first time my body had been a mystery to me. There was a bout with tendonitis that came out of nowhere. There was the diagnosis of hypoglycemia years ago that really shook me up. There was a series of miscarriages and a stillbirth. There were those bothersome cysts that show up in all the most uncomfortable places. There was the graying of hair and the blurring of vision and the recurrence of PMS that will some day give way to menopause. There are desires and needs over which I seem to have little control—to eat, to sleep, to share sexual intimacy. My body is a mystery to me in so many ways. And yet what am I if not my body? I eat, I drink, I rest, I exercise, I dress, I bathe, I dance, I move, and I stand still. Am I my body or is my body a shell that I simply inhabit?

Are we bodies having a spiritual experience?

Or spirits having a bodily experience?

One of the legacies of most world religions is the idea that the spirit transcends at the expense of the body. The tension between being a body and having a body, between freedom and restraint, sacredness and vulnerability is as old as Plato. In the Hebrew Bible (the Old Testament), a person was never described as being made of separate parts—body and soul. In the Creation story, we read that God "breathed into his nostrils the breath of life and the man became a living being."[8] In the New Testament, early Christians came into conflict with the popular Greek notion that the soul was the highest, finest aspect of being. Instead, Paul asserts that the body is a holy place in which God might come to dwell. The whole human must be understood as body and soul. We are our bodies. We are our souls. One is not better than the other. Both are irreplaceable parts of our human person. And so each are intricately intertwined.

An integral approach recognizes that both body and spirit are essential for our growth and development as human beings and doings. Otherwise we risk going as a mosquito into the light. You've seen that, haven't you? Especially with the advent of bug zappers? The mosquito sees the light: "It's so beautiful. I must go closer. It is all I want, all I need. I must go closer, closer." *Zap.* They're fried. An integral life is a balanced life and one that recognizes the sacred value of the body, even as it desires to reach higher spiritual plains.

Furthermore, an integral approach recognizes that the biological line is the only line that has a terminal impact on virtually all the others. When the body is done, the other lines are pretty much done, too. Extending the biological line allows for greater evolution in all other lines. Lengthening

---

8. Genesis 2:7 (NIV).

the biological line gives us more time to reach stable awakening in the other aspects of our lives.

We hear this recognition in Paul's letter to the Philippians. He longs for a bodiless spiritual unity with Christ, but understands the value of his bodily existence and the life that has been given to him in order to live fully in the present. We also hear this recognition in the bodhisattva vow of the Tibetan Buddhists. This vow is a promise to put off one's own enlightenment and to continue to exist in physical bodily form until all beings are enlightened.

So it is that any Integral Practice must address the Physical pillar. We can attend to our physical bodies in a variety of ways—through nutrition, exercise, massage, Reiki, and sex, to name a few. Strength training can actually turn back the biological clock and reduce osteoporosis. But there is more than one way to approach working with weights. If you approach weight work for the purpose of developing beach muscles, you might get those muscles, but in the process you will actually shut down energy and interfere with subtle energy movement.

A more integral approach includes four steps in doing any isolated exercise. First you bring your awareness to yourself and your surroundings by grounding yourself. Then you take a few short, sharp breaths as a way of charging your energy. Next you channel all of your subtle energy into a single part of your body. Focus on the contraction of the muscle. Instead of disassociating and picturing yourself on the beach, you pour awareness into the pain. Finally, you radically release the contraction, relax, and expand your awareness.

Of course, a formal exercise program is by no means the only way to engage our physical self. Play is severely underrated. If you want to get more exercise, the most important question to ask is "What turns you on? What is rewarding?" I find I can integrate different aspects of my Integral Plan by walking with my life partner or playing tennis with my kids. Play might involve boards and giant balls for balancing, hacky sacks for juggling, rapid-fire card games for hand/eye coordination. And for me, one of these days, it's going to include my first skydiving attempt.

For play to be fun, we need to decide that we will make fearless mistakes. I know I'm going to fail and I don't care. Why do we fail in physical activities? Because of the force of gravity. We fall, we roll, we tumble, we crash. In play we don't attempt to defeat gravity, but to defy it. Gravity is another form of attachment. If we can dance with it and be at peace with it and come to love it, then movement is not something we do but who we are. With balance, patience, and practice, anything is possible!!

Once during a meeting with my doctor, she asked how seminary was going. As we visited, she commented on the amount of pastoral care she does with her patients, though certainly few people would call it by that name. "Of course," I responded, "you must." What happens to our body affects our soul, and what happens to our soul can have profound effects on our body. Both are to be honored and cherished. Every body is worthy of blessing and care.

Not only that, our bodies demand that care. We must eat, we must sleep, we must move and breathe or we cease to be whatever it is that we are. Our bodies are vulnerable and needy. Yet through the needs of the body, we are invited into relationship with God and with each other. Perhaps this is the one thing in the end we all have in common: our bodies are vulnerable. Whether we are rich or poor, male or female, enslaved or free, every body is a fragile temple of God's spirit and worthy of our care. How do we care for our bodies? How do we care for the bodies of others?

The body clearly needs food. In this vulnerability, our need for food, we are sent back to the table, even sometimes in spite of ourselves. Moreover, what has seemed to limit us (our need for food) opens us not just to food, but also to relationship. Through the needs of our bodies, God opens us to one another. Every time we gather for meals with others, God offers us an opportunity to go deeper in our conversations, to plumb our disagreements, to affect one another, to forge new bonds. It is our bodies—hungry, thirsty, needy—that bring us to a place where this is possible.

When we invite others, especially others in need of what our table has to offer, to be seated and served, nourished and listened to, our tables become holy places, a sign of what God desires. At the Christian table we gather and remember Jesus' body broken for us. We remember that on the night he was arrested, Jesus blessed, broke bread, and poured wine for all those sitting at the table. We remember Jesus' life sacrificed. Jesus' suffering does not deliver us from illness. It doesn't make the death of those who die by violence any less tragic or unbearable. But when the community gathers for communion, a space opens up that can hold both suffering and healing, endings and beginnings, life and death and rebirth. A space opens up for hope.

I worked for a few years at a Methadone clinic in Grand Rapids, Michigan. Methadone is the primary treatment for opiate addiction. In addition to my other responsibilities, I led a therapeutic group on Spirituality and I gave free Reiki treatments. I was quickly scheduling Reiki four months out as people asked for this mode of healing for the body and the soul. At the end of my Reiki treatments I always massage the feet of the person so as to help ground them at the end of their treatment. One of my clients told me this was her favorite part of Reiki because "nobody touches me."

Whether we are healthy or sick, our skin is hungry for touch. In an often hostile and violent world, we cherish the safe places to reach out and touch and be touched in kindness and hope. Touch alone can bring about great healing. In a culture that is so often obsessed with looking and appearances, perhaps the only way to really know someone else is by touching them. In the Christian Gospel, Jesus is resurrected from the dead and stands before his disciples who are startled and frightened at the sight of his body. His words are simple. "Touch me and see."[9] Touch me and know that it is I.

Jesus offers his body as the lens through which the disciples must look if they, and we, are to be able to say to our suffering neighbor, "What are you going through?" It is his body, wounded yet living, that gives us the courage to touch one another and to expose ourselves.

Spiritual: A Prayer

You may have heard this one before. How many Lutherans does it take to change a light bulb? None. Lutherans don't change. Now if you didn't know better, you just might assume that when one embraces Christianity, it is because they seek a continual path of transformation. But then again we all know what happens when we assume.

Transformation is about change. It means following Christ in such a way that we die to our old selves and are reborn, not just at Baptism, but over and over again. And frankly, not too many people get really excited about dying.

So we spend most of our time doing religion rather than living our faith. Religion in this culture is by and large about translation and interpretation. It is about rules and doctrine and order. To preserve those rules, that doctrine, and that order, we have developed religious institutions. And of course the very nature and purpose of institutions is stability. The goal of any institution is to *not* change, not transform.

Translation is important. Most of us have heard some really horrible comments made in the name of Christianity that have hurt and alienated us and others that we love. We need to address those teachings and that kind of spiritual violence while offering the life-giving word of grace.

Most of us have also heard a theology of glory: If we have enough faith we will be blessed.

---

9. Luke 24:39 (NRSV).

As we struggle with illness and poverty and broken relationships and discrimination we need to know that the cross is testament to God's presence in the midst of our suffering; that we are never abandoned or outside of God's reach. And in this culture that is so often preoccupied with selfishness and violence and greed we need to be continually challenged by Jesus' mandate to sacrifice, surrender, and love for the sake of others and for the sake of community.

These are undeniably important conversations for us to have, and they are conversations that should bring about deeper spiritual understanding, action, and growth. But at some point we need to recognize that these philosophical and psychological debates, these mental exercises and physical exertions, as necessary as they are, are not ultimately about transformation.

Ultimately, transformation requires us to let go of our certainty and abandon our knowledge in order to experience greater intimacy with God. Transformation is, in one understated word, uncomfortable.

Broken people know this, and they want to be transformed anyway. They know the depth of their need and they long to be changed. We are broken people. Do we know this? Or have we forgotten? At what point do we who follow Christ actually feel comfortable saying the words, "I'm comfortable where I am"?

Perhaps we want too quickly to escape the trials and tribulations of this material world. For most of us it was in deep physical and emotional misery that we began to be transformed. But who wants to invite in physical and emotional misery? It is not a natural instinct.

But what if the sacrifice, the surrender, the death we have experienced is a call to move beyond the material distractions of our world and our self? Without discomfort will we continue on our journey? When the broken bones of our life are healed, will we rest in peace? Or will we continue to seek healing for our broken souls? When we meet each other on the journey, will we be content to help set each other's broken bones or will we find the courage to push against the hidden bruises of each other's souls?

You see, I don't believe we've reached our destination yet, so how can we sit still? You and I are meant to move out of the small self that we instantly and easily identify with to the Self with a capital S—the Self in which there is no longer any barrier between you and me and the Divine, until we realize the ultimate oneness in which we are all held in this world. To realize that all of life is arising right now in the space of our own awareness. To arrive at the day when Jesus tells us, "You will know that I am in my Father and you in me and I in you."[10]

10. John 14:20 (NRSV).

Christian mystics have described this experience as a gift of God that cannot be sought out or earned. They have named it contemplative prayer and described it as a process initiated by God but accepted by one's own self in which we begin to move toward realization of who we really are beyond mere concepts.

This is the kind of prayer Father Thomas Keating believes Jesus is guiding us toward when he tells us to "Go into your inner room, close your door, and pray to your Father in secret and your Father who sees in secret will reward you."[11] Prayer is not something we do but a relationship with the ultimate reality, which we commonly name God. God is the creative presence that holds us in existence in every moment, closer to us than our thinking or even our consciousness. Held by God we are seen by God, and Keating remarks, that the first thing God sees in us is God's self. It is God's self in us that eventually recognizes God, as well.

It is fascinating that in the early church, one was not considered to be a theologian until they had experienced this kind of intimate spiritual communion with God. But in the scholastic period, that expectation changed and the title "theologian" came to be one of academic achievement. So it is not entirely surprising that in Christianity we have a lot of instruction about what things are like at the beginning of the Christian journey and that we can find descriptions from the mystics and from Jesus himself of how things are to be in the fullness of that journey, but we have exceptionally little by way of instruction in moving from one to the other.

In fact, many people leave the Christian faith when they cannot find a path to this reality. They pursue Eastern religions steeped in meditation so that they can draw closer to the Divine. They haven't been taught, as I had never been taught, Christian practices like Centering Prayer. This is a unique form of meditation found in Christian tradition intended to open one up to the potential of receiving the gift of awareness. In Centering Prayer, or in any other meditation, you are not trying to change anything or improve yourself. The purpose of meditation is simply to make contact with what is. Centering Prayer is a contemporary name for the practice that Jesus describes as "prayer in secret."

Jesus speaks of moving away from ordinary psychological awareness to the interior silence of the spiritual level of our being and beyond that, to the secrecy of union with the Divine dwelling within us. As we enter our inner room, we leave behind all external concerns, and by shutting the door, we discontinue even the interior dialogue that usually accompanies ordinary psychological awareness. As we let go, we come to rest fully in

---

11. Matthew 6:6 (NASB).

God. Our only intent is to remain open to the presence and action of God within. This kind of union is not something we have to coerce God into, for God loves us and desires nothing more than to pour that love into us.

We are not called to be comfortable with our self. We are called to allow God to manifest in us and in all that we do. As centering prayer leads us into contemplative prayer, we find our human effort, our offering of our own naked being to God, is met by the Spirit drawing us into even deeper actual experiences of union with God even to the point of self-forgetfulness. This is the place not too clearly identified in Christianity where the spirit and our activity are gently intermingling so that sometimes it is us and sometimes it is pure spirit and we don't always know which is which, and really, we don't need to.

In the Christian Gospel of John, there is a most poignant text, so sad and so beautiful.[12] Jesus has been killed and now Mary has come to the tomb of her beloved friend. You can imagine how she must have felt. Numbness fighting to still the shock still reverberating in her. Going through the motions of preparing the body, the one last way in which she can feel close to the teacher she followed and the man she most certainly loved. Feeling lost and alone and yet finding some comfort in these rites and rituals.

Then even that solace is taken from her. There is no body to touch or to cry over. There is no last time to speak her sorrow while gazing at the face she held so dear. Instead there is the certain knowledge that the joy has gone out of her life, that feeling of hollow emptiness and despair. The sense of being small and insignificant and utterly alone.

Indeed, 2000 years ago, women as a whole were considered small and insignificant. Women were nobodies. Women were property. They had few of the rights of men. They could not be witnesses in court or file for divorce. They could not be taught the Torah. They were to be nearly invisible in public. Public meals were for men only, and if a woman did show up, she was assumed to be a prostitute. Women lived on the margins of society.

For a brief period of time, Jesus elevated Mary and the other women he interacted with to a glorious height of equality. His actions toward women were nothing short of scandalous. He defended them, spoke with them, healed them, ate with them, and even learned from them. Mary was part of the intimate group that traveled with Jesus. She knew personally the warmth of his unconditional love.

And now so profound is her despair that when Jesus speaks to her, she doesn't even recognize him . . . until he speaks her name. When she is named, when she is recognized for who she is and feels again as if she is

---

12. John 20:1–17.

nothing, at a time when she has lost everything, when she is recognized for who she is, she recognizes her Lord. She is filled with new life. In a very real sense, it is Mary who is now resurrected.

So why in this moment of mystical reunion would Jesus torment her further by telling her not to hold onto him? Shouldn't he have swept her into his arms and held her as she wept? Shouldn't he have offered her words of comfort and peace, assuring her of his presence, promising her this was real and that he was there, right there with her?

John wrote the most mystical of our Gospels. In it, Jesus is always using common language to say something beyond the obvious. It is in John that he talks of being born again. It is in John that Jesus stands at a well and speaks to a woman about living water. It is in John that Jesus speaks of the bread of life and the light of the world.

And now he says, "Don't hold onto me." Was his statement as obviously cruel as it sounds or could it be that this man who so often used common language to point to the spiritual is at it again? No, Mary, you don't have to hold onto me. You don't have to cling to me, because everything you saw in me is now in you. My dear sweet Mary, you don't have to look to my physical presence to give you peace, because I am right there with you, in you. That same Divine presence that you sensed in me, I now challenge you to see in yourself. This is what I came to teach and show you. We have the same Father, we have the same God. See in yourself the Spirit you saw in me.

In the Gospel of Mary,[13] which was excluded from the Christian Bible we have come to know, Jesus appears to tell his followers that the son of Man dwells inside them. That should sound familiar as we hear similar words from Jesus often in the Biblical Scriptures. What I am struck by is that Mary responds in this text by saying that Jesus is calling them and us to be fully "human."

So what does it mean to be fully human? Often it seems as if we've been taught it's *not* a good thing to be human. Humanity is fallen, sinful, idolatrous. To be human is to be fallible and flawed. To be human is to be in need of a savior. Why then would we want to be fully human?

Perhaps to be fully human is to recognize that what Jesus says is true. To understand that it is within our humanity that Christ is resurrected. Perhaps it is only in fullness that we regain the knowledge that we are created in the image of God. In fullness that we learn not to belittle ourselves and dismiss our gifts and abilities. Perhaps it is only in fullness that we experience our own resurrection as we realize that the Divine is indeed being birthed in us, and we in the Divine.

13. King, *The Gospel of Mary of Magdala*.

This is foreign, frightening and even heretical talk for some of us who have been raised in the Christian church. Over and over again we have been told that we must always know the difference between the creature and creator, as if we were somehow separated one from the other. Jesus, interestingly, never says anything of the sort. When we are fully human do we finally grasp that we are both the creature and the Divine that infuses the creature with life?

Meister Eckhart said that, "Where the creature stops, there God begins to be. Now God wants no more than that you should in creaturely fashion go out of yourself, and let God be God in you." As soon as we let the image come into our self of being a small creature, "God and all his divinity have to give way. But as the image goes out, God goes in."

"Oh my dear man," he continues, "what harm does it do you to allow God to be God in you? Go completely out of yourself for God's love, and God comes completely out of himself for love of you. And when these two have gone out, what remains there is a simplified One."[14]

Mary of Magdala might use other words. She might say that what remains is one that is fully human. For this woman has allowed the teacher to arise in the heart of her life, growing and taking root in her. In her is the Spirit that will continue to guide her toward fullness.

On Easter Day, 2007, these words became particularly meaningful to me, and that day particularly profound. It was that day that the community I had helped birth, through the guidance and direction of the Spirit, raised me up as their trusted servant leader, called me, and ordained me as an Interfaith Minister.

It was a day I had never thought possible just a few years before. My journey working with the Lutheran Church started out as a fluke. I ran for a position on Synod Council because no one knew me and I'd never get elected. Then I got elected. Suddenly I found myself going to these meetings in Lansing with pastors and church leaders and I was captivated by the work they were doing and the way in which their whole lives seemed to be dedicated to sharing the love of God.

I used to cry on the way home from those meetings. Because I so wanted *that*. I so wanted God to use me to do God's work in this world. I so wanted to do something that important, that meaningful in the lives of others. And I knew God would never, could never use me like that. My life was so flawed. I was so flawed. There was all this crisis and trauma in my life. I knew my history of surviving abuse. I knew I was divorced and struggling to be a decent mother. I knew I was estranged from my father and had cut

---

14. Eckhart, *Meister Eckhart*, 184.

myself off from other relationships. I knew I had failed at so many things in my life. I knew I was unworthy. I was a flawed human being, far too flawed to be used as an instrument of God.

At the same time, I was powerfully interested in at least learning what I could. So when I found out about the Lay Missionary Program, kind of an advanced Bible Study option for people not going to seminary, I applied. If I couldn't be a pastor, at least I could jumpstart my spiritual growth by spending some of my weekends with seminary professors teaching me the core of their classes.

One of the professors was Pastor Rudy Featherstone, a truly incredible man. Retired. African American. Proud husband, father, and grandfather. He was the most joyful person I think I have ever met. We were riding in a car together when he asked me something about my plans and I must have mumbled something about my inadequacies, because the next thing he asked me was if I believed in the Holy Spirit. "Yes," I replied, "I do." "Do you think the Holy Spirit can work in anybody?" A pause—but then, "Yes, of course. The Holy Spirit can work in anybody." "What then," he asked, "makes you so special that you think the Holy Spirit can't work in you?"

Rudy shook me to my foundation that day. I couldn't argue with him. I had to agree that the Spirit could work in anyone . . . even me. Eventually I came to realize that the Spirit not only works in me, but dwells in me. That the kingdom of God is within me. That when I am fully human, when I am fully me, then I have to admit that the package of body, thought, and emotion is not all I am. When I am fully human, I must acknowledge that God infuses me with God's self. When I am fully human I feel the push of the Divine to be ever more all that I am called to be—co-creator of this universe and home of the indwelling God.

These were the words used in our weekly liturgy at Extended Grace. The full liturgy can be found in the appendix of this book. It was a liturgy that made some people uncomfortable and they stumbled or got stuck on the words or didn't say it at all. I took quite a bit of flack for asking that we claim our own divinity and more than once it was suggested that we scrap those words or at least rearrange them to be more palatable.

I understand where that resistance was coming from. As someone raised in the church, steeped in the language of separation, and fully aware of my own sinfulness, there was a time when making such a claim would have felt to me like blasphemy. It would have made me feel like I was losing hold of my faith.

But it is in the certain knowledge of those words that I became more grounded in my faith than ever, and because of that, I need to keep making this proclamation. Moreover, I need to keep extending the invitation for each one of you to make this proclamation yourself—because it is the heart of our salvation. It is the unbelievably refreshing good news that has been proclaimed stretching back throughout the life of the church. It is the life-giving good news we hear in the voices of those who awoke to the startling and glorious truth that we can never be separated from God because we live in God and God lives in us. The voices of people like Meister Eckhart, Mary of Magdala, and Jesus the Christ.

I think when we hear those prophetic voices that the Spirit within us nudges us to suspect it might be true, but we don't dare say it out loud. It was that Spirit within me that led me to cry after council meetings because I wanted to believe God could use even me, and I feared saying so out loud would be an act of arrogance. Of course, now when I confess these words, I feel nothing close to conceit. Instead I find them deeply humbling, to the point where I need to sink to my knees and cry out for help to be what I already am—to see, accept, and acknowledge fully the Divine beauty that lives in me and every one of us.

As Jesus speaks to Mary of Magdala, she becomes the model of all humanity. If it is true, if this Jesus lives and in living calls us by name, then how are we resurrected and how will we proclaim that good news? That question brings us to the challenge of putting the fruits of our Integral Practice into action.

Ethics: Putting Integral Practice into Action

One day I had a conversation with a friend whose sister had asked her for money. Her sister explained that she was in debt and needed the money to pay off important bills. But my friend knew that her sister had been using illegal drugs and had evidence that she was in the midst of a serious addiction. My friend and her husband were financially stable and had money in the bank. Should she use that money to help her sister out?

The 5th pillar of an Integral Practice is Ethics. Morals are standards of conduct and judgment. They are the code of justice or rightness of a person, religion, or group. Service is work done or duty performed for another, an act of giving assistance or advantage to someone else. For an integrated person, one leads to the other. Integral Ethics is the interplay of inward morals and outward action.

When we choose an integral approach, we look at the circumstances of our existence and feel compelled to strive for rightness in the universe. Because we are here, we have to do something. We discern, we seek God's wisdom, and we act. We learn by engaging the world. But what about changing the world? Is that what we as Integral Christians are ultimately to be about?

Well, there is no question that service is one of the marks of true discipleship. But if we are really honest with ourselves, we can admit that part of our service is done out of care and compassion and part of it is usually driven by our own ego. I care and *I* want to make a difference. *I* do. I, me, myself. And so we find the task eternally frustrating because our efforts seem in vain. We didn't get the results we wanted, so we start doing a little less. We come to realize that not only does the world not want us to change it, but in the end we just can't change the world.

There is a Buddhist koen that tells of the monk who in his attempt to fill the dry well at the top of the hill spends his day carrying one teaspoon of water carefully up the steep slope of that hill, dropping the water in and making his way slowly down only to repeat this task the next day and every day after that. I've heard that illustration used in a sermon to show how we must persist in doing all we can even if it only appears to be a drop, because that is the way we make a difference. But this interpretation seems to miss the whole point of the koen. Instead this parable shows us how absolutely crazy it is for us to believe we can change anything, and that even in our surrender to that truth we still continue to do the work.

In that surrender, we admit that we are powerless and utterly lacking in wisdom and understanding. But there is a universal wisdom much greater than us. The absolute truth is that all are one. There is no good and no bad and no division at all. Everything simply is. When we can rest in that awareness, nothing can bother us. There is also relative truth. That truth acknowledges that while absolute truth exists, it is also true that I am here in the midst of suffering and hardship, so I need to respond with compassion.

The more awakened to your oneness with the universe you become, the more you feel the reality of this earthly existence, and the more your pain increases. If one hurts, you feel that pain. Yet at the same time, you realize that Christ is calling you to a union with God in which there is no more pain at all. The pain you endure, even as it grows, bothers you less and less. It is a paradox without resolution.

In the end, we work to alleviate the suffering of others, even though we know waking up to the reality of our union with God ends that suffering. As Meister Eckhart explained, when you have experienced the state of awakening, you voluntarily leave that state in order to offer a cup of soup to one who is hungry.

There are two models of enlightenment within the world religions. One of those is the Awakened Buddha who has managed to get off the wheel of suffering and is now at peace. The other is Jesus the Christ who is the very intersection of the human and the Divine, whose truth is the burden of the cross.

Why should you get involved? Because you made a deep promise in your soul that you would. God grants this kind of blossoming understanding only if you act on it. "Come you who are blessed . . . ; take your inheritance, the kingdom prepared for you since the creation of the world."[15] The absolute we call God. The relative we call compassion. As Christians we are called and challenged to dedicate ourselves to both.

Returning to the conversation with my friend about her sister's situation, she decided not to give her the money she asked for even though she knew it would put her sister in a bad financial situation. Then she warned others about answering these requests for help. She began learning about addiction and the kind of compassion we call enabling. She started talking to other family members about how to confront their loved one with the truth she was denying. This woman knew her sister would be hurt and angry. She knew other members of the family would also turn on her. But she loved her sister enough to act with genuine compassion.

The nature of compassion itself is often confusing. Chogyam Trungpa Rinpoche makes a distinction between compassion and what he calls idiot compassion.[16] Idiot compassion claims that no view is really any better than another and therefore all views are to be cherished equally. To embrace this kind of compassion is to be equally likely to adopt the morals of Christianity or the morals of Nazi Germany.

Idiot compassion also fools us into thinking it is being kind when it is really being cruel. If you have an alcoholic friend and you know that one more drink might kill him and yet he begs you for a drink, does real compassion say that you should give it to him? After all to be kind you should give him what he wants, right? Who are you to impose your views on him, right? So giving him a drink would show compassion, right? Well, no.

Real compassion includes making judgments of care and concern. It requires us to say some things are good and some things are bad and I will choose to act only when my actions would be wise and caring. Giving a severe alcoholic a case of whiskey because he wants it and you want to be "kind" is not being kind at all.

Eastern religions call it real Zen as opposed to grandmother Zen. Real compassion is genuinely unpleasant sometimes. And Jesus is really good at it. Jesus demonstrates this kind of compassion when he proclaims, "Depart

---

15. Matthew 25:34 (NIV).
16. Trungpa, *The Pocket Chogyam Rinpoche*, 73–74.

from me you who are cursed."[17] Go away, you who did not offer me food or water or clothing or comfort.[18] In the year 2014, what might Jesus have to say to us? He doesn't mince many words. If you're not ready for his fire, then you might want to find a new-age, sweetness-and-light kind of teacher who will allow you to wallow in you. Someone to tell you it is enough to take care of yourself and your own needs while giving your ego some really spiritual-sounding name. But stay away from Jesus because he will (in the ever-subtle words of Ken Wilber) "Fry your ass, my friend."[19] He will challenge you and make you squirm. What most people mean by compassion is: "please be nice to my ego." But our ego is our own worst enemy and anybody being nice to it is probably not being particularly compassionate to us.

Jesus offers us an invitation to experience eternal life today, through our suffering and through meeting the needs of others who suffer. What then is the practice of integral ethics as we add this final pillar to our Integral Practice? It is about cultivating our understanding, awareness, and commitment toward the world around us while also letting go of our own self-fascination in order to see Christ in the stranger.

Vidyuddeva, one of our speakers at the Integral Institute, shared his story of learning martial arts in order to be able to survive on the streets where he was raised. As he learned more and his confidence grew, he became more cocky and reckless, even intentionally walking through bad areas daring anyone to touch him. One night he was walking with his girlfriend. They were all wrapped up in each other's arms, when they passed a huge, angry, drunk who muttered something at them as they passed by. Vid sized up the guy and decided he'd better let this one go. But his girlfriend felt offended and wanted to know what he said. Despite Vid's attempts to silence her, she wasn't letting it go. The giant of a man turned around in a rage and Vid's heart jumped into his mouth. Wondering how on earth he was going to survive the beating he was about to get, he found himself a minute later still standing and hearing the words the man spat at him echoing in his ear. "I said I hate you. I hate you because you look like you're in love and nobody loves me."

To be an integral spiritual seeker is to recognize the intrinsic value of the human condition. It is to never underestimate any human being. It is to meet someone where they are and know that you would be where they are if you had followed their path. It is to let go of the burden of believing

---

17. Matthew 25:41 (NIV).
18. Based on Matthew 25:42–43 (NIV).
19. Wilber, *One Taste*, 93.

we can do anything at all while embracing the heartbreak and joy of doing everything we can.

I could tell you that taking care of your family is enough. That being a good citizen is enough. That living a quiet life and not disrupting others is enough. That prayer and meditation and seeking union with God is enough. I could tell you all that. But Jesus wouldn't. He would tell you that as long as there are people in need you have a responsibility not to pat yourself on the back for what you've already done. We are not charged with solving all the world's problems, but to meet the needs right in front of us.

Mother Teresa said we might wonder, "Whom can we love and serve? Where is the face of God to whom we can pray?" The answer, she tells us, is simple. That naked one. That lonely one. That unwanted one is my brother and my sister. "If we have no peace, it is because we have forgotten that we belong to each other. In the end it's not enough that someone died for your sins."[20] There comes a time when you need to start dying for others.

Jesus tells the parable of sowing seeds. Parables were meant to shock the listeners, challenge their assumptions and lead them into new perspectives and understandings. As Jesus addresses his peasant audience, they would know about the need for wise farming practices. They would know the care that must be taken to sow seeds so that they are not wasted.

But here is Jesus painting a picture of God the Farmer who is wildly, recklessly throwing seed all over the place. With risky abandon he takes a chance that some of it will actually land where it can grow and produce a crop. What a beautiful image of a generous God. What a contrast for us in a world where we make almost all of our decisions based on efficiency and effectiveness. What a challenge in a world where our primary motivation is to make good use of our money and our time and eliminate what is simply a waste.

James Boswell, the biographer of Samuel Johnson, often referred to a special day in his own childhood when his father took him fishing and imparted much wisdom to him. In his father's journal, however, the entry for that date reads, ""Gone fishing today with my son; a day wasted."[21]

Today as then, we experience the joy of a wastefully extravagant God. And that was the point—for Jesus to describe God, to describe the kingdom. But we Westerners aren't particularly content to rest in an image of God. We usually are more interested in figuring out who we are in the story and what the implications for our life may be.

---

20. Teresa, "Brainy Quote," lines 1–3.
21. Larson, *Illustrations for Preaching and Teaching*, 83.

As a result, we sit and wonder what kind of soil we are. As I was growing up in my home church hearing these words from Matthew,[22] I wasn't shocked or shaken, but grateful. Oh thank goodness, I must be good soil. I must be, or I wouldn't be here today. Thank you God that I am not like that neighbor of mine that's always so crabby and irritable—talk about seed falling on a pathway! Or like that family that came to church and got real involved in everything right away—but their faith obviously wasn't deep enough to grow roots. Withered away and disappeared as fast as they came. And that weedy soil, God. Here was the precautionary part of the sermon. I've seen that happen before God, please don't let that be me. I just want to be good soil.

That was a helpful translation at the time and it provided a spiritual baseline. But as I reflect on such a perspective now it seems self-serving and deterministic. Because ground is, well, ground. Knowing about different kinds can help explain why I live and act and believe the way I do and others don't, but in a pretty fatalistic and arrogant manner.

I propose that this parable is not meant to label the type of believer someone is or isn't. Instead, I believe this parable about God points to a broader truth about our selves, as participants in God's grand creation. This is a parable about our relationship to and interaction with the Divine.

Imagine that the seeds of the Spirit are continually strewn upon us. Sometimes seeds fall upon the rich, fertile soil of our souls and we blossom and bloom! People see a difference in us; they hear a difference in us. We have been touched by the Spirit of God who now moves and lives and breathes in us, just as we now live and breathe in God.

Sadly, even when we have experienced the wonderful gift of freely given grace, we rarely spend the rest of our lives rolling in clover. So it is that other seeds fall where and when they cannot take root. They fall on the pathways where we have been trampled over by life, by cruelty, and oppression. They land where parts of us have been assaulted with such ferocity that only a barren, hard crust of soil remains and nothing can grow.

Other seeds fall where our soil is shallow and we know the rockiness just below the surface. We desperately grasp at those seeds and will them to burst open now, quickly for we are excited about the promise they bring. But in the end we cannot maintain our momentum, the rocks protrude and there is not enough nourishment there to sustain the life we have tasted.

Then there are the seeds that began beautifully enough, but we did not foresee the worries and the hardships to come. The joy was choked out of us by crisis and loss. The fear and the worry and the striving of the world

---

22. Matthew 13:18–32 (NIV).

began to preoccupy our minds and turn us away from tending this new and tender growth.

It's not about being good soil or bad soil. It's about recognizing that we are composed of all of it. We are fashioned of the dust of the ground. Dirt into which God breathes life. Dirt onto which God casts God's own seed. Our lives are a topography of all kinds of terrain, our faith a journey across all different kinds of ground. Yet all the while God is extravagantly throwing the seed of the Spirit, God's self, upon us, inviting us to surrender to the sun and the rain so that God can awaken that seed within us. Sometimes such surrender takes a very long time.

ABC News Online announced in 2005 that researchers in Israel had succeeded in growing a date palm from a seed that was 2000 years old. The seed was unearthed during an excavation of the ancient fortress of Masada 30 years before and is the oldest seed ever germinated.

We don't have to wait nearly so long. God has already awakened within you the seeds that have brought you this far on your journey, wherever that may be. God has invited you to be a co-creator of a beautiful landscape showered in the generous seeds of grace. Now you can choose to prepare and cultivate the soil to support a whole host of seeds and saplings.

This is the reason for creating an Integral Practice, a plan for your own growth and development. A tool that requires you to think for a moment about what is truly important in your life, what you want to nurture and grow, and what can go by the wayside. An Integral Plan isn't meant to be a strict, formal, regimen of behaviors. Thomas Merton talks about the gift of God being the only thing that can teach us the difference between the dry outer crust of the Church and the living inner current of Divine Life. An Integral Plan can also become a dry outer crust if we fail to remain sensitive to the movement of the Spirit within.

An Integral Plan is first and foremost an intent. It is a conscious choice to increase our mindfulness and expand our awareness of our self, of our world and of God in the midst and at the center of it all. We spend time in silence listening to God in order to discern and deepen a vision. Then we decide what we will do in each of the pillars to move toward that vision.

- What will you do to learn something you don't already know?
- What will you do to strengthen interpersonal relationships and to become emotionally whole?
- What will you do to be healthy physically?
- What will you do to move toward union with God?
- What will you do to put your morals into action?

We end up with a "to-do" list that is balanced and structured, but held with an open hand and a loose grip. "Doing" requires commitment and accountability, but it also recognizes that seasons change. So we forgive ourselves when we fail in our commitment to a particular practice and we release ourselves from accountability when we are called to move in a different way. We approach "doing" with joy, recognizing that sometimes joy is in service to our ego and that as followers of Christ we are also called to the practice of sacrifice, discomfort, and surrender.

Our practice of doing serves our practice of living; the moment-by-moment experience of existence in which we seek, even in the midst of our shortcomings and mistakes, to be more and more aware of God within us, within our neighbor, within the stranger. This is the fruit we are called to bear: to serve not our own needs, but to find our own needs met through service to others. "Doing" leads us to this kind of "living" which ultimately leads us to the practice of simply "Being." To being exactly who we have always been called to be—which is exactly who we have always been.

God keeps throwing seeds upon the landscape of our lives, until we look out upon the glorious pasture of our self—complete with barren paths, which just happen to be perfect for walking; rocky patches that require effort to maneuver but also offer a remarkable view once climbed; thickets of brambles and weeds that offer protection for all that struggles to live below; and flowers, beautiful blooming flowers, and decorative grasses and bushes and trees that provide shade, and growing there on vines and stems and branches are fruits—the actions we take, the things we do, the words we speak that help to nourish and sustain this amazing creation—this living creation in which there is both life and death.

And still God is throwing seeds.

> *Be patient toward all that is unsolved in your heart*
> *and try to love the questions themselves*
> *like locked rooms or books*
> *that are written in a foreign tongue.*
> *The point is to live everything.*
> *Live the questions now.*
> *Perhaps you will then gradually,*
> *without noticing it,*
> *live your way some distant day*
> *into the answers.*[23]
>
> —RAINER MARIA RILKE

23. Rilke, "Goodreads," lines 1–5.

An Invitation for Reflection:

1. What is your practice?
   a. How are you intentional about your Mind, Body, Shadow, Spirit, and Ethics?
   b. What are the obstacles that get in your way?
   c. How will you overcome those obstacles?
2. Instead of answering the question, "What do you believe?" answer the question, "What difference does it make that you believe?"

3

Faith in the Midst of Pain

A Lenten Journey

*God is not found in the soul by adding anything,
but by a process of subtraction.*[1]

—MEISTER ECKHART

Physical Pain

EVERY YEAR ON FEBRUARY 1st, I take time to intentionally sit with my pain. It is the anniversary of the date my son Malachi Aaron was delivered stillborn. He was a perfect little boy with 10 fingers and 10 toes, my chin (poor kid) and my oldest son Jackson's nose. And his umbilical cord wrapped tightly around his little neck, twice. It was horrible in every sense of the word, including the physical pain of it all. We began inducing labor at 1:00 in the afternoon. I was hooked up to an IV for hydration and given prostaglandin to induce labor. The side effects of the drug included diarrhea, nausea and vomiting, fever and cramps. By 9:00 at night I had developed a severe headache and had experienced three bouts of aggressive vomiting and dry heaves. The contractions were unrelenting until finally just before midnight Malachi arrived.

---

1. Eckhart, *Treatises and Sermons*, 194.

Still the placenta wouldn't come so I was given IV Valium so I wouldn't remember the pain of the curettage. Thank God.

I journaled the experience and keep the journal in a Baby Box with ultrasound pictures and other odds and ends. This year I was surprised as I read my journal at how much of the physical pain of the experience I had actually recorded. I think it was the first time I really spent time experiencing that part of the memory. On reflection it turns out that this was truly an experience of holistic suffering!

Life is hard. And life is hard because we hurt. We experience pain—all kinds of pain. We hurt physically, we hurt emotionally, and we hurt spiritually. And we can experience all of these dimensions at the same time—as Jesus certainly did as he was killed on a cross. There is a period in the Christian calendar called Lent. It is the time we spend preparing for the death and resurrection of Jesus that culminates in the celebration of Easter. Good Friday is the day in which we focus on Jesus' suffering, for he endured very real physical pain as he was beaten, crowned with thorns, and nailed to a cross.

Jesus experienced physical pain the same way you and I experience it. Pain is present from the very beginning of our life until our last breath. First we are pushed and shoved out of the warmth and security of our mother's womb into a cold and uncertain world. Our mother bleeds and aches as her body first forces our departure and then reacts to the trauma of our arrival into the world.

From that day on, we will know pain as an unavoidable aspect of life—as we cut our teeth, as we learn about gravity, as we realize why we were told not to touch the stove or play with knives. As we stretch ourselves to learn new skills and, in the process, fall flat on our face. Pain accompanies our journey as we maneuver our way through the sicknesses and injuries of life and keeps us company as our bodies age, reminding us that we are mortal after all.

Pain is also our body's alarm system. Without its warning signals, we would all be in serious trouble. The need for such pain is obvious when you consider silent killers like cancer and high blood pressure or when you think of a disease like leprosy. The major symptom of leprosy is that nerves die. Without those nerves sending messages of pain, the brain cannot mobilize its defenses. Unfelt and ignored, burns don't heal, infections fester, and sores turn ulcerous.

Pain has also played a profound role in all of the world's religious traditions—from the torture of the martyrs to the voluntary self-mortification of monks. Whether by the stabbing of a Hindu bed of nails, the blows of

Islamic iron chains, or the relentless raw scratching of a Christian hair shirt, pious believers have endured the kind of pain that makes us shudder—and have often done so while experiencing a kind of bliss that transcends our 20th century understanding.

Why would anyone invite flogging or crucifixion, sleep on spikes, or walk across miles of scorching desert sand with bare, bleeding feet? In his book *Sacred Pain: Hurting the Body for the Sake of the Soul*, theologian Ariel Glucklich concludes that pain is part of the journey to redemption.

Glucklich recognizes the transcendental nature of pain. "The goal of religious life," he writes, "is not to bring anesthesia but to transform the pain that causes suffering into a pain that leads to insight, meaning, and even salvation. This is the essential paradox of sacred pain: that the hurting body does not suffer silently. It offers a potential voice, if one has the tools to make the soul listen."[2] Glucklich also recognizes ritual pain as a form of sacrifice that enhances the religious community. The painful rituals of initiation are not only understood to increase the power of the tribe, but also to strengthen the initiate's commitment to the community.

Indeed, many of the mystics found sacredness in physical pain. Dorothee Soelle in her book *The Silent Cry* quotes Nisargadatta Maharaj, an Indian teacher of wisdom, who said, "Pleasure lets you go to sleep, pain wakes you up. Through blessedness alone you cannot come to know yourself, for it is your true nature. You have to look the opposite in the face, into what you are not, in order to find enlightenment."[3]

Christianity brings a unique emphasis to suffering. If God became incarnate in Jesus Christ, then Jesus' suffering necessarily meant that God was not a distant observer but a fellow sufferer. And if God is one who suffers, then suffering is not simply something bad that we must either surrender to or try to resist. It becomes instead a reality that has something to do with God and that fits into God's incomprehensible love. The way of suffering is not just tolerated, but freely accepted. The way of the passion becomes part of the disciple's way of life.

Far from separating us from God, suffering may actually put us in touch with the mystery of reality. Hence, many serious seekers practice fasting or frugality or celibacy, intentionally denying earthly pleasure in order to be drawn more fully into God. Soelle says, "It is the place of encounter with God where we make the gift of a sacrifice and God invites us to God's self by bearing the suffering with us. . . For many pious mystics, it was more

---

2. Glucklich, *Sacred Pain*, 16.
3. Soelle, *The Silent Cry*, 138.

important to behold the man of sorrow and embrace the bloodied bridegroom than to meet the risen savior."[4]

Every form of religious suffering, however, must face critical questions. Within Christianity, those questions are particularly sharp because the tradition has fostered an extreme, often pathological obsession with suffering. It is important that suffering never be understood as something necessary for salvation. It is not virtuous to invite suffering into our life. Indeed, Jesus never advises anyone to suffer physically nor postpones his own healing works to allow the ill to first suffer enough.

One extreme embrace of pain in Christianity took the form of hermits who in the Middle Ages had themselves walled in for life, usually next to a church. One recluse was Margareta Contracta. Suffering didn't bother her. What concerned her was that no suffering could satisfy her. This kind of craving for suffering no longer distinguishes between fruitless, avoidable, and self-inflicted suffering and that which is accepted for the sake of the community. At worst it takes delight in acts of masochistic substitution. In a horrendous example of such obsession and dependency, Mechthild von Hackeborn scattered glass shards on her bed "for repentances' sake" and then tossed and turned "until her whole body dripped with blood so that she could neither sit nor lie down because of the pain."[5]

In contrast, compassionate suffering arises in the immediacy of innocent suffering and from solidarity with those who have no choice but to endure it. It is not suffering that people bring upon themselves through extreme acts of asceticism.

But what do we do with a mysticism of compassionate pain in a world where we are taught that pain is not something we must bear, but something to avoid, treat, and excise? It is indeed interesting that as we began developing ways of relieving pain, resistance to such treatment arose from physicians, patients, and theologians alike. As physical pain began to be seen only as a physical malady, and as physical maladies could be relieved, there was a simultaneous increase in diagnoses of hysteria and an expanding role for psychiatry in defining an ever-widening array of neuroses. The use of anesthesia managed to promote the status of the physician while reducing the autonomy and power of the patient.

Glucklich believes that "The role of pain, before it was displaced, was rich and nuanced." Pain "served humanity in a variety of constructive religious and social ways." Anesthesia and pain relief have, perhaps, robbed us

---

4. Ibid., 137–8.
5. Ibid.,139.

of the ability to understand how pain can be valuable "for mystics, members of religious communities, and perhaps humanity as a whole."[6]

Is there a vacuum left when pain is removed as a necessary part of our very existence? A growing phenomenon in our culture today is that of cutting or other self-inflicted personal injury. Ruth Davis, a psychiatric nurse on the staff at Pine Rest, explains that self-harm is a way of coping with overwhelming feelings or situations. Self-harm is defined as deliberate harm or alteration of one's body tissue without conscious intent to commit suicide. The most common methods of self-harm are cutting, burning, scratching, skin picking, hair pulling, and interference with wound healing.

Self-harm is often viewed as senseless and irrational in a culture that avoids pain so diligently. But such a view only serves to make people who do self-injure feel frightened, isolated, and helpless. The truth is that self-harm can be an important coping mechanism. It is a way to feel and express emotion or to tolerate distress. There are four reasons commonly given for self-harm:

1. Self-harm is one way to regulate the mood by calming overwhelming, intense feelings. Physical pain is used as a distraction from emotional pain or to end feelings of numbness.
2. Self-harm is also a way people try to communicate anger and pain that they cannot speak.
3. Some people use self-harm as a way to punish themselves.
4. For some, self-harm is self-nurturing through the self-care they are able to give themselves afterwards. By making an internal wound external, there is an attempt to heal oneself.

The reactions of family, peers, and others to self-harm behaviors tend to include shock, frustration, sadness, guilt, revulsion, anger, and fear. None of this is helpful, and so education is critically important. Self-harm is not to be condoned or ignored. It is a serious cry for help and it is important to address the underlying issues that lead to this behavior. But at the same time, it is vital that we do not compound the situation by adding shame to the burden of those that practice it. Self-harm is a way to cope. If there had been another way to cope at that time they most likely would have used it.

In fact, it is through self-harm injuries that many people have been able to survive. The scars are testimonies to this survival. In *Scarred Soul*, Psychologist Tracy Alderman notes that the courage it takes to survive the difficult times in our lives is something that can eventually become a source

---

6. Glucklich, *Sacred Pain*, 201.

of pride. Stopping the behavior is possible, but only after the person is ready and has developed new skills for coping.

Self-harm speaks loudly of the emotional and spiritual pain an individual feels long before they have the words to express it. Our own intense reactions may very well come from our own deep fear of pain. How many times have I said, "I'm not afraid to die, I just don't want it to be a painful death."

Kajal Basu and Dipankar Das of Life Positive conclude: "There is no way to paint a pretty picture of pain. It both creates and thrives in a devastated landscape. All your life, you walk through its domain, more and more gingerly as you get older and less able to emerge whole at the other side. The irony is that it is not pain itself that shadows you doggedly—it is the fear of pain, a terror that transcends all other fears. Pain becomes even worse when it is accompanied by the fear that it will continue unabated."[7]

It is when I am sitting with friends who live in chronic pain that I realize the absurdity of my own claim that "This headache is killing me," when it is doing no such thing, when I have not even begun to know the kind of unabated, unrelieved, and unrelenting pain that really is killing people. Twentieth century mystic Simone Weil wrote, "Nothing is worse than extreme affliction which destroys the 'I' from the outside, because after that we can no longer destroy it ourselves."[8] But even for those whose lives are now defined by pain, there is grace. When we can meet pain head on, embrace it as our own and impose meaning onto it, pain can be a path of transcendence.

Either way, pain will surely come. And when it does, we can choose whether we will protect ourselves with the diverse and increasingly improving means of numbing that pain, or voluntarily enter into our own pain and the pain of this world. To choose numbness is to invite apathy; to choose agony is to engage in compassion.

Emotional Pain

The physical pain I endured when my son Malachi was stillborn was horrible. But of course, there was much more to it than the aching and heaving of my body. There was an emotional pain that seared right through me. That pain began early in the day, in the doctor's office when she couldn't find a heartbeat and I was sent for an ultrasound. It grew worse when the pictures of my baby were too still and the technician was too quiet. The intensity only

---

7. Basu, "Pain—Experiences of Pain," para. 52.
8. Weil and Miles, *Simone Weil*, 80.

increased when I was admitted to the hospital to induce labor. At that time, they did not have a separate area in Labor and Delivery for those who know they will never hear their baby cry.

When everything was ultimately confirmed with the arrival of my son, I felt my heart break. I had lost something more dear to me than words could express. And that sense of pain was only made more acute by the fact that my husband at the time could not find the strength to suffer with me or acknowledge his own pain. So I was alone when Malachi was delivered and I knew I would be the only one (other than medical personnel) to ever hold him or gaze upon his precious face.

Emotional pain crushes us and brings us to our knees faster and with more efficiency than any broken bone ever could. As we are emptied of everything else—hope, dreams, desires, belief—it is the pain that comes into the void and fills us to overflowing. It arises in times of crisis, trauma, and loss and serves as a cruel reminder of our own powerlessness and lack of control. And it is universal. None of us can participate in this world and not know its sting.

Returning to our Lenten image of Jesus' suffering, we encounter a man bearing a message of love and peace, compelled to share his vision with this world. He is met with hatred and violence. One who sought to bring God's word of mercy and grace is treated with scorn and ridicule. The man who welcomed everyone to come and eat and see is rejected by the very people he longed to embrace, to enlighten, and to heal.

As a man, he surely experiences this as any human would. He hears their words, he sees their expressions, and it breaks his heart. He feels the same pain you and I feel when we are hurt, rejected, beaten up, and cast aside. He knows what it is lose everything and to be utterly alone. Jesus can testify to the pain we bear because he experienced it himself. Then he modeled for us the kind of courage it requires to live in that pain, to resist the urge to strike back or retreat into numbness, and to feel fully the depth of emotional suffering that comes with being human.

Such role models are indeed rare in a world that does not encourage emotional awareness, let alone emotional expression. Instead we are offered a continual array of ways in which we can avoid feeling our pain or any feeling at all. When any glimmer of emotional turmoil threatens to come our way we can choose alcohol, drugs, sex, or food instead. We can distract ourselves from our own emotion by yelling, blaming, or trying to appease somebody else. When sadness, fear, anxiety, or loneliness threaten to descend, we can run away, go shopping, or turn on the TV.

The idea of actually *feeling* our emotional pain can seem strange and even frightening. But the only real way to get through it is to finally experience it. Fully. Unflinchingly. In all of its terribleness and terror. And the truth is: we can. Chaplain and author Dr. Margaret Paul, reminds us that "Until we stop numbing out in the face of our pain, we will never know that we can feel our pain without going crazy or dying, that our pain is not endless, and that it can actually be a source of information and strength rather than weakness."

"In all the years I have been working with people in pain," she assures us, "I have never had anyone die, explode, or go crazy from opening to their pain. I have never met anyone whose pain was unending. Nor do people kill themselves from feeling their painful emotions when they are willing to learn how to heal it, and when they reach out for the appropriate help. It is not opening to painful emotions and learning how to manage them lovingly that causes suicidal feelings; it is sitting in pain with no inner and outer help that causes a person to take his or her own life. When you can open up to feeling, learning about and healing your pain, there is no longer a need to avoid it."[9]

So how shall we feel, learn, and heal our pain? In the Big Mind enlightenment practice led by Genpo Roshi, he asks us to speak as the various voices that make us who we are. In the process, he identifies three distinct voices that all have something to do with pain: the vulnerable child, the damaged self, and the victim. All of us have within us the original unhurt, untarnished, vulnerable child who simply wants to be loved. All of us also have a damaged self, the part of us that carries our pain. When the needs of the vulnerable child weren't met, it was the damaged self that took the hit for us. It is because of the selfless courage of the damaged self that the rest of us is able to continue functioning unharmed. There is also the victim. It is the victim who knows what has happened to us, who has seen it all unfold. All three reside within us. The vulnerable child holds the need, the damaged self holds the pain, and the victim holds the story. Being healthy and whole is not about getting rid of any of these parts of our self, but about owning them and welcoming them as part of the whole human being we were created to be.

Even when we are willing to feel our emotional pain, it can take some practice to actually do so. It's so easy for the voice of the victim to drown out the pain of the damaged self. The victim is the witness who carries our story and that is a very important role. There are times we need to tell our story. There are times people need to hear our story told. But our story is not all that we are. And when we choose to be victims, we choose powerlessness.

---

9. Paul, *Do I Have to Give Up Me*, 148–9.

We choose to remain stuck right where we are. We choose to do nothing to help ourselves or to help those around us.

I can easily see myself as a victim—the victim of a dysfunctional family, the victim of an angry ex-husband, the victim of childhood sexual abuse—but what good does that ultimately do? I can cry and rage against my bad luck all day and all night, but until I'm willing to take responsibility for my pain, I will be stuck with that pain forever, and I will never know joy. The same energy I use to avoid embracing my own damaged self, with all of the hurt it carries, is the same energy that keeps me from embracing my own vulnerable child who holds all of my own original joy and wonder and innocence and who patiently waits to be invited to come out and play.

It takes far more courage to listen to the damaged self, which is where the pain truly resides, than to repeat the story of the victim. The difference is the willingness to stay with the painful emotion, explore it, and own it. Living with a victim identity only serves to trivialize our own suffering and the suffering of those around us.

There is plenty of very real suffering all around us, so much so that as we grow spiritually we will find our emotional suffering only increases. St. John of the Cross said that suffering for our neighbor grows as our soul unites itself through love with God. This kind of suffering arises from a relationship to the world that is not immersed in the "I" alone. Instead it is drawn into the anguish of unliberated life, into the passion of painful existence, onto the road of suffering.

As Blaise Pascal put it, "Christ still hangs on the cross; namely in the victims of injustice, every one of whom is to be regarded as a sister or brother of Christ. . . . Every mystical affirmation of love that pursues no ulterior motive includes the acceptance of suffering and the conviction that without compassion there is no resurrection."[10]

It was the sight of pain that jolted the Buddha out of royal complacency and set him off on one of history's greatest spiritual journeys. It was the sight of pain that made Moses give up his privileged status to lead a political and cultural revolution that is called the Exodus from Egypt. It was the sight of pain that stirred Jesus to follow the call of a social activist in such a way that his teachings, his life, and his death would change the world, influence history, and get him killed—over and over again.

Christ cannot be understood and loved without seeing the ongoing crucifixion done to his sisters and brothers all around this world. A mystical approach to the reality of suffering comes from being overwhelmed with the weight of it all and then voluntarily accepting the suffering of the downcast

---

10. Soelle, *The Silent Cry*, 151.

and insulted as one's own. It is in the light of the cross that we can accept our own suffering and the pain of this world.

In the March 2006 edition of the magazine *What is Enlightenment?* there is an article about Mary Clarke who was married twice, raised seven children, and at the age of 50 left it all to sew her own habit and move to an infamous penitentiary in Mexico to help the inmates there. At 80 years old, after 30 years of ministry, she was still living in a small cell without heat or hot water, alongside drug addicts, murderers, and the poor. At times her work was unimaginably painful. Once for three days and nights she cried and banged on the door of an interrogation room where she could hear the screams of a prisoner being tortured. She has walked into riots begging inmates to drop their weapons. She personally buried the bodies of inmates who died and were left unclaimed by family or friend. When asked about her self-sacrifice, Mary who renamed herself Mother Antonia said, "I don't just work for them; I am one of them. I live the way they live. Once you're on the inside, it's so different. Somehow prison was the place where I finally experienced the freedom to be myself, to really be myself. I think prison freed me." Mother Antonia died in October of 2013 leaving behind a powerful legacy.

Emotional pain can, in the end, be a spiritual pathway. Mechthild von Magdeburg's gender was used to deny her an education and to religiously humiliate her. She was scorned, mocked, and despised because of her ecstatic visions, but chose to continue this suffering by submitting herself to the established authority. "It is the hammer of love," she said, "that nails us to the cross."[11]

Spiritual Midwife Cynthia Trenshaw lives in Washington State where she participates in a Peer Spirit Circle. A while back there was a bad car accident near where Cynthia lives. Several young people died. Her Peer Spirit group talked about it and some said they wished there was something they could do. Cynthia said that if they were serious, each person should pick one of the grieving families, contact them, and pledge to walk with them for the next year. This would require that they listen well to what was truly needed and also know well what it was they could offer.

In this rich and beautiful outreach, I see Cynthia and her friends taking action that doesn't require them to "fix" anything, but that does require sacrifice—the kind of sacrifice that results in relationship, the place in which true healing and restoration can ultimately take place. To be able to give to another in this way, we first need to be authentically in touch with our own

---

11. Ibid., 141.

pain so that our giving doesn't come out of our own ego needs but out of a true compassion for the other.

Emotional pain comes out of nowhere, hitting us when we least expect it in the place that hurts us the most. We can choose to see it as a pointless act of fate. We can meet it by sinking into numbness, deadening dullness, and self-destructiveness. Or we can choose to see it as our personal participation in the cross. In what others call "fate," we can find a suffering God and call that God "love." Dorothee Soelle contends that this kind of "acceptance deprives icy meaninglessness of its power because it clings to God's warmth also in suffering."[12]

Either way, pain will surely come. When it does, we are left in the same place we were when we considered physical pain. We can choose agony or numbness. To choose numbness is to feel nothing at all, to choose agony is to live a life infused with passion.

Spiritual Pain

When Malachi was delivered stillborn, I experienced profound physical pain and emotional pain. But pain was present on another level, as well. I also felt profound spiritual pain: the sense that a part of my very soul had been severed from me. This is the feeling I still know when I return to the cemetery every February 1. I am profoundly grateful that I held Malachi and that I continue to feel his perfect presence in my life. But I also experience a deep and abiding ache that I surrender to once a year. There remains a bleeding wound that I take time to expose, to kiss, and to nurture, and then to gently rewrap in bandages of remembering.

In fact, an important part of my healing was in creating a time to intentionally feel the wounds once more. In the midst of my grief there was a part of me that didn't want to be okay again—that didn't want to let go of the pain. I didn't want to simply blink and then pretend that everything had returned to normal. Yet my normal routine was beckoning me, and the time came that I had to return to life. With no real other choice, I returned. I returned not to the same old world I had known before, but to a world where I knew nothing would ever be the same again. I returned having survived something I didn't know I could survive with strength I didn't know I possessed.

In the midst of our spiritual pain, we stand in the absence of God, abandoned and alone. Like Jesus whose Lenten journey we have been following, we cry out in desperation "My God! Why have you forsaken me?!"

---

12. Ibid., 149.

And like Jesus, we hear no answer to our plea. Like Jesus' mother Mary, we gaze upon the pain of the innocent and the inhumanity of humankind and cannot understand why God has left us alone. Like those who witnessed the torture of the cross we think about the abuse we have suffered at the hands of others, and when we ask, "Where was God when this happened to me?" we find our question is left hovering unanswered in the air, until it is finally washed away by the unstoppable stream of our tears.

Darkness, night, and suffering cannot be excluded from the wholeness of God. And those expeditions into the darkness, night, and suffering cannot be excluded from the journey of faith we all walk.

Today spiritual pain is recognized as a very real factor in our total well-being. Healthcare providers are taught to recognize signs and symptoms and to help bring healing. Even the Joint Commission on Healthcare Accreditation requires that routine spiritual assessments be part of every hospital patient's care. Spiritual pain, emotional pain, and physical pain all interact with each other in both obvious and obscure ways.

Spiritual pain is about a separation from God. It can include loss of meaning, loss of hope, and loss of one's own identity. It can include anger, a sense of betrayal and abandonment, and a disruption to one's core beliefs. It can include fear of God and God's punishment, the need for reconciliation and the necessity for forgiveness.

Religions and religious institutions can exacerbate spiritual pain. By fostering guilt or a sense of condemnation or by promoting doctrines of eternal judgment or karmic reincarnation, these faith communities can amplify feelings of rejection from both the church and from God. Spiritual pain is also magnified when the church discourages us from embarking on our own search for meaning that includes the honest expression of our pain and the raising of difficult questions.

In order to find healing for our spiritual wounds, we have to begin by identifying our pain, welcoming it, and dialoguing with it. By experiencing it fully, we can seek to find new meaning and understanding in the midst of it. A faith community that welcomes individual questions and doubts can offer consolation and the promise of building relationships of care. Prayer and meditation can restore in us the assurance of the abiding presence of a God of unconditional love and grace.

Even in the presence of healing and wholeness, there can come the kind of spiritual pain that arrives as a dark blessing, and a potent potential pathway for spiritual growth. Those who come new to faith can arrive with a radiance that comes with thinking they have entered into a blissful world of near-perfect human beings, instant answers to selfish prayers, and a life forever free from pain, heartache, and suffering. Neither life nor faith will meet such expectations. In fact, as one's spiritual life deepens, the opportunity for spiritual pain only increases.

Kahlil Gibran said, "Your pain is the breaking of the shell that encloses your understanding."[13] Not only might spiritual pain be a necessary part of the spiritual journey, surrendering to such suffering may be the very doorway to a more profound relationship to God and a more complete understanding of reality. For precisely that reason, and because most people are unwilling or unable to open to and accept pain, a genuine spiritual life has never been and never will be particularly popular.

In Dorothee Soelle's powerful and poetic words, "Mystical love for God makes us open to God's absence: the senseless, spiritless suffering that separates humans from all that makes for life. The eclipse of God ought at least to be felt and suffered. The nausea caused by this world of injustice and violence ought to at least be perceptible; it ought to increase to the point of physical vomiting. That kind of nausea is compassion."[14]

St. John of the Cross called deep spiritual suffering the dark night of the soul. In the midst of his exile, humiliation, and imprisonment, John never sought to tear apart light from dark, fulfillment from denial, losing oneself from being found. He prayed to Christ for cross, suffering, and contempt, and he received all of them in all their bitterness, to the end of his life.

For John of the Cross, the night became a symbol of purification. Having had the senses stripped of all pleasure, deprived of everything the ego relies upon, he came to understand the dependency on worldly things he had fallen into. In his suffering, he came to understand that there was a first step he could actively take to purify his own desire but that the next step had to come from beyond him. It is when we are finally passive, when we cease to be at work and to analyze, that God can accomplish the most within us. When we have nothing else, we fall into emptiness. Finally free even from our defenses, we are delivered into the dark night.

To thrill in God's embrace is a good thing, but love is not measured in tingles or sensations but in laying down one's own life. Authentic love is marked by pain endured in the valley, not the sticky sweet feelings in the afterglow of mountain ecstasy. Love does not make darkness harmless through religious chatter. Instead it deepens the darkness and makes it even more unbearable. For the sake of this unbearableness, some mystics have preferred hell to heaven.

According to Simone Weil, "When you, steadfastly clinging to love, sink to the point where you can no longer suppress the cry, 'My God why

---

13. Gibran, "Think Exist," lines 1–2.
14. Soelle, *The Silent Cry*, 140.

have you forsaken me?' but then hold out there without ceasing to suffer, you will finally touch something that is no longer affliction and not joy either, but the pure, supra-sensual, most inward essential being common to both joy and suffering."[15]

Mysticism is concerned with the soul's transformation into God as the ongoing dynamic movement of the spiritual life. Our task is to set the faith of powerlessness against the unfaith of power. Our challenge is to remain in inconsolability as a way to listen to the silent cry of God. For this task the Christ who suffers with us on earth may be more helpful than the one who has risen.

Such a Christ might help us to embrace Dietrich Bonhoeffer's exhortation to hold firmly onto agony against every possibility of escaping into numbness—not because doing so will finally guarantee God's comforting us, but because in doing so, we stand with God in God's suffering.[16]

We start by seeking help from God, but as we are caught up in the way of discipleship, we find that we are brought into the messianic suffering of God in Jesus Christ in which human beings share in God's impotence. This is the complete opposite of everything religious people typically expect from God. Nevertheless, humans are called to share in God's suffering, to suffer with God the godlessness of the world.

As with physical pain and emotional pain, we can be assured that spiritual pain will come. Again we have to choose. To choose numbness is to be content with a superficial faith. To choose agony is to embrace the way of the cross. Reinhold Schneider came to the conclusion that, "It is much better to die with a burning question on one's heart than with a faith that is not quite honest anymore; better in agony than in numbness."[17]

> *Our hearts are too attuned to the shimmering beauty of God's presence to transcend the world's tragedies, pains, and sorrows. We have to bear them, enclosing them within the womb of mercy and inexhaustible ocean of peace until they, too, are transformed.*[18]
>
> —BEVERLY LANZETTA

---

15. Ibid., 151.
16. Bonhoeffer, *The Cost of Discipleship*.
17. Soelle, *The Silent Cry*, 152.
18. Lanzetta, *Radical Wisdom*, 204.

An Invitation for Reflection:

1. When have you voluntarily experienced pain (piercing, childbirth, sports, tattoos, etc.)? Why?

2. What idiotic things have people said to you when you were in emotional pain? Why do you think they said it?

3. What is the source of your strength? What gives meaning to your life?

4. What do you do to relieve pain? When have you endured pain? Has pain influenced your spiritual growth?

4

A Compassionate Response

Some people when we talk about compassion and love, think it's a religious matter. Compassion is the Universal Religion. The whole purpose of religion is to facilitate love and compassion, patience, tolerance.[1]

—DALAI LAMA

Moving Beyond Guilt

THERE ARE TWO UNDENIABLE facts in our world today. One is that there is a whole lot of suffering going on. The other is that you and I can't "fix" it. How we choose to live with that reality says everything about our capacity for compassion.

Many people around the world observe Rosh Hashanah. This is a ten-day period of repentance in the Jewish faith that ends with Yom Kippur, the Day of Atonement and forgiveness, the holiest day in the Jewish calendar. Rabbi Michael Lerner urges us not only to take advantage of this Jewish custom for individual soul-searching, but also to participate in social repentance as a nation.[2]

There is much to lament, but that is not enough. Repentance calls us not just to reflect on the situation at hand, not just to consider the suffering in the world, but also to repent—to measure our own actions against the

1. Dalai Lama, *Ethics*, 230.
2. Lerner, *The Left Hand of God*.

things we say we value, and then to turn back, to return to God, to change our ways and to call on our country to do the same.

According to the latest statistics from www.globalissues.org, 40 percent of the world's population survives on less than $2 a day, leaving 1 billion children (one of every two) being raised in poverty. As a result, every day 22,000 children age 5 years and younger die of illness related to malnutrition and curable disease. That means that this very day before you go to sleep, at least six times more children will die of preventable causes than the number of people who died in the World Trade Center on 9/11. Meanwhile war continues, and the environment is still being damaged. At home, millions are living in domestic violence, while millions more experience homelessness.[3] This in what is considered by many Christians to be a "Christian" nation. A nation, those same Christians say, that was founded on the ideals of Jesus of Nazareth. A man who taught kindness toward strangers and told us, "If you have two coats give one to the person who hasn't any." A man who said, "When you cared for the least, you cared for me."

What would the Nazarene think of our professing to follow him in light of the stark reality of the poverty, violence, and apathy we live in and support by action and inaction every single day?

Our need for repentance is not limited to our participation in global injustices. We also know that we have missed the mark more times than we care to admit in our own personal relationships. Musician Stuart Davis explains the genesis of his song *Someone Else's Ear* as "a very special apology to someone who helped me through an immensely difficult time in my life. Later, when this person reached out to me for support I didn't want any part of their suffering because I was too consumed with the superficial gratification of my career."[4]

One common reaction to witnessing suffering is denial and avoidance, to cut off from other people in order to protect the self from feeling pain and suffering. There is too much to be done, and much we would rather do, so we don't do anything at all. We turn inward and allow our own needs and desires to overwhelm our conscience so that there is no space for the hurt and despair of others.

We do it on a global basis, refusing to acknowledge the cries of hunger, disease, genocide, and exploitation being screamed around this world. We do it locally, refusing to hear the cries of poverty, violence, and despair being screamed throughout this country. We do it personally, refusing to consider

---

3. Shah, "Poverty Facts and Statistics," updated January 7, 2013.
4. Davis, *Self Untitled,* CD Jacket.

the cries for love and acceptance and understanding being screamed, sometimes silently, in our own communities, families, and homes.

It is far too easy to fill up on our own damn selves and squeeze our capacity for concern—to nothing.

Another reaction is to hear the cries and to feel pretty miserable about the way things are. As a result, we pray that God will do something about it. We complain that our leaders aren't doing anything about it. Meanwhile, we never consider the fact that we *could* do something about it. Making noise and turning to others for solutions might get us a little closer, but feeling bad or even righteous outrage is not compassion.

Neither, by the way, is feeling guilty. "You're right. I could be doing something and I'm not—now I *really* feel bad." In fact feelings of guilt just suck what little air was left in that space for compassion right out of us—until all we are is one big contraction, powerless to do anything but conserve precious energy—because frankly, nothing is going in and nothing is coming out.

Compassion can't happen until we let go of the self-contraction, the turning in on our self, and allow Divine energy to enter us. Compassion arises in the space that holds our capacity for concern. This space is where we integrate both our love and our hate for other people.

I'm going to stop there because this is difficult to grasp right away. When I have the capacity for concern, I am able to integrate both my love and my hate for other people. If I can't do this, I end up with guilt. So the first thing we need to admit is that we don't always love everyone. If you have successfully cultivated universal love for everyone, then please consider that there are still people you just don't like.

All of us have someone that gets under our skin, a personality type that brings out the worst in us. Feelings of resentment and anger are simply part of our human condition. When we can own that, when we can admit the struggle inherent in the words, "Love your neighbor" then we begin to pump air, literally the breath of the Spirit, back into that collapsed space in the center of our soul that holds our capacity for compassion.

Creating and expanding this capacity takes intentionality, practice, and hard work. But opportunities for doing the work are all around us—even though they often take us by surprise.

I had such a surprise when I was working as an Assistant to the Bishop in the ELCA. I mentioned that I am a survivor of childhood sexual abuse. One Sunday I traveled to a church to provide the message. The pastor was there, so I didn't lead Communion. When I went to the railing to kneel for the bread and wine, I realized the person kneeling next to me was the father of my abuser—and that the man kneeling next to him was undoubtedly the very person who had abused me so many long years ago.

It was rather surreal to realize there was this sordid and painful history between us that no one knew about, no one could see or hear or perceive. It forced me think about what Communion is supposed to be all about. It made me think about my own new ministry and the assertion I have always made that all are welcome at the table.

It took a lot of soul searching, but I did find the space inside of me to know that I meant it—that I could welcome anyone to the table—because it isn't my table. Not only that, but I realized that the human being kneeling just a few feet away from me was also carrying scars that I could not begin to see or perceive. It was the Dalai Lama who said, "Compassion makes one see the picture clearly; when emotions overtake us, the lack of seeing clearly clouds our perception of reality and hence the cause of many misunderstandings leading to quarrels."[5]

American Buddhist monk Bhikkhu Bodhi wrote: "Compassion supplies the complement to loving-kindness. Whereas loving-kindness has the characteristic of wishing for the happiness and welfare of others, compassion has the characteristic of wishing that others be free from suffering. Compassion arises by sharing the interiority of others in a deep and total way. It springs up by considering that all beings, like us, wish to be free from suffering, yet despite their wishes continue to be harassed by pain, fear, and sorrow."[6]

One of my most prized possessions is the Compassion Buddha I brought back from my trip to Tibet. I am particularly drawn to the Compassion Buddha because of all the Buddha images, it reminds me most of Jesus. I don't mention Jesus' name a whole lot because I don't think that's what he would have wanted. When I read about Jesus and when I read the words and wisdom attributed to him and when I read about how and when he chose to act, I don't discover a man whose life was meant to bring him glory or fame. I don't find a man who lived on lofty words and fed himself and others on platitudes and promises. I find a man who lived compassion, whose entire life was a statement of solidarity with the oppressed and active resistance to social injustice.

Matthew Fox said, "Compassion is not sentiment but is making justice and doing works of mercy. Compassion is not a moral commandment but a flow and overflow of the fullest human and Divine energies."[7]

5. Dalai Lama, "Define Compassion," §4.
6. Bhikkhu, *The Noble Eightfold Path*, 42.
7. Fox, *A Spirituality Named Compassion*, 4.

Jesus was the embodiment of Divine compassion. He saw needs and dared to not look away. He reached out and touched people that no one else would touch. He fed the hungry. He healed the sick. He welcomed the stranger. He saw his people and had compassion on them.

He understood in a way that we are just beginning to understand that we are all connected, and that when one suffers, all suffer. As Thomas Merton would write 2000 years later, "Compassion is the keen awareness of the interdependence of all things."[8]

But Jesus also teaches us that compassion is not always warm and fuzzy. We can learn from this man the marks of true compassion and accept the challenge to forsake our own desires in order to act compassionately toward others, especially those who suffer. And in embracing the model and guidance of this Jesus, who urges us to claim the Christ in each other as well as our self, we can find within the depths of our own humanity the spark of Divine compassion.

Idiot Compassion

I wanted to be a social worker when I entered high school. Then I changed my mind. I decided that there would be too many people that I wouldn't be able to help. I didn't think I could live with that. I didn't think I could take into my self the pain of others without being able to solve their problems and relieve their hurt. I didn't know it at the time, but I had narrowly escaped the trap of idiot compassion.

Idiot compassion is a term coined by the Buddhist teacher Chogyam Trungpa Rinpoche. It comes out of our desire to help other people, but involves acting without wisdom or discernment. And in the end, despite our good intentions, it tends to perpetuate the suffering we hoped to resolve. The relevant question is "Am I a part of the solution or an I part of the problem?"

To have genuine compassion we need to develop the capacity for concern. This space inside us gives us room to admit and integrate the fact that we both love and hate people. When we don't take time to develop this capacity, we get stuck in the middle of guilt. Now, there is a useful role for guilt. We should feel guilty and convicted when we ignore the needs of those around us or when our actions cause someone pain. But guilt can also lead us into unhealthy behavior.

When we get stuck in guilt, we never make it to concern. We never shift the focus from ourselves and our feelings to the other. We get wrapped

8. Merton, *Choosing to Love the World*, 30.

up in over-functioning. Overwhelmed with the need to do something, we can't just be *with* people. Instead we want to do, and mostly we want to fix. In fact, if we can't fix it, or at least feel like we're helping, it feels like we're not being loving—which suggests that maybe we're being hateful. Appalled at the very notion, we begin with even more vigor to help and fix. And we, out of the best of intentions, end up not acting with compassion at all, but with Idiot Compassion.

Idiot Compassion makes us act without first discerning whether our advice or energy is appropriate. It drains us of energy and robs others of the opportunity to move through their own experiences in order to become empowered.

The fact is, I can't do anyone else's work for them. I can only create a healthy space for others in which they can choose to do their own work. Helping people all the time may be balm for my own guilt, it might help me feel better about me, but it doesn't really help anyone else. People are in the end responsible for their own choices, and the best we can do is allow them the opportunity to make healthier decisions for themselves.

Idiot Compassion is not a kind and gentle term. No one wants to think of himself or herself as an idiot. But I like the phrase because it stops me short and makes me really think about what I'm doing or trying to do. Pema Chodron describes idiot compassion as "the general tendency to give people what they want because you can't bear to see them suffering."[9]

Either way, you're not giving people what they need. You're trying to get away from your feeling of not being able to see them suffer. In other words, you're doing it for yourself. You're not really doing it for them.

This was one of the important lessons I had to learn in ministry, and I learned it the hard way. I have Kurt to thank for challenging me to move beyond idiot compassion. Kurt had a pattern of severe under functioning. He preferred asking for advice to thinking things out himself. He often acted irresponsibly, losing and leaving jobs and then wanting the people around him to pick up and repair the pieces of his life. I knew that if I let him, Kurt would drain me dry, so I immediately established clear boundaries with him, even though they sometimes made me feel like I was being too cold.

Meanwhile, Kurt continued to under function and make poor decisions. As a result, he ended up with no place to live and he refused to spend time at the Mission. I continued to offer spiritual and emotional support, but did not offer physical assistance because it was clear such enabling would do more harm than good. I continued to encourage him to make healthy decisions, but let him live with his own choices.

9. Chodron, *"Idiot Compassion,"* line 10–11.

Until I fell into my old trap. First, I got a call from the director of another social service agency that Kurt had approached, and who suggested, without knowing the full history, that I should be doing something more. I allowed that conversation to flip my concern into the unhealthy sphere of guilt. Next, my husband at the time decided to give Kurt enough money to pay for a week in a hotel. The timing seemed right as he was about to begin a new job and this would allow him to clean up for his first day at work.

But in order to find a hotel that Kurt would deem acceptable, I ended up in several telephone conversations with him on my Sabbath, the only day of the week I really tried not to work. At the same time that I was researching every hotel in Muskegon, Kurt was spending the money elsewhere. By the end of the day, I felt truly resentful of this impingement on my time and angry at being lied to and taken advantage of. Idiot compassion didn't solve anything. But it did manage to damage a relationship and leave me feeling like an idiot.

Recognizing my mistake, on the other hand, allowed me to return to a concern-centered approach in which I could admit both my love and my hate for Kurt without feeling guilty, without enabling him to continue underfunctioning, and without taking on the responsibility for his choices and well-being.

We can use the illustration of a violent relationship to make a similar point. If someone is violent towards you, it's not the compassionate thing to keep allowing that abuse to happen, no matter how much you love them or they love and need you. Allowing someone to feed their violence and their aggression does not help them. Of course, if you decide to end the relationship, they are going to be extremely upset and it will be quite difficult for you to go through the process of actually leaving the situation. But that's the compassionate thing to do.

It is the compassionate thing to do for yourself rather than stay in a demeaning, destructive, abusive relationship. It is also the most compassionate thing you can do for them. Clearly, they are not going to thank you for it, and they will certainly not be glad. But you may be gifting them with the only chance they will have to wake up and start working on their side of the problem.

Another dimension of idiot compassion is giving people not what they need, but what *we* think they need. Even given the vast depth of wisdom that I possess, I continue to be amazed that other people know what they need better than I do. In his book *Cross-Cultural Connections*, Duane Elmer retells the story of the monkey and the fish.

A typhoon stranded a monkey temporarily on an island. In a secure and protected place, while waiting for the raging waters to recede, he saw a fish swimming against the current. It seemed obvious to the monkey that the fish was struggling and in need of assistance. Being of kind heart, the monkey resolved to help the fish. A tree precariously dangled over the very spot where the fish seemed to be struggling. At considerable risk to himself, the monkey moved far out on a limb, reached down, and snatched the fish from the threatening waters. Immediately scurrying back to the safety of his shelter, he carefully laid the fish on dry ground. For a few moments the fish showed excitement, but soon settled into a peaceful rest. Joy and satisfaction swelled inside the monkey. He had successfully helped another creature.[10]

Compassion is not simply giving someone what he or she wants, nor is it simply giving him or her what you think they need. True compassion involves acting in a thoughtful and responsible manner around what other people really need. True compassion balances loving-concern with clear wisdom.

When I traveled to Honduras to install water filters it was a successful experience because we worked hand in hand with Honduran Rotarians who were able to direct our work where it was needed. We were also scheduled to spend one day helping clean up at a hospital that was in need of new water pipes. We arrived and were given a tour. Then we were told that they did not want us to volunteer our help. They did not have systems in place to ensure that we would not contract an illness or that would provide security against our endangering the patients who were already struggling in substandard, third world conditions. Instead of spending the day working, we learned about Central American Medical Outreach (CAMO), an incredible organization dedicated to improving medical services in Central America.

One of our group leaders asked me if I was disappointed that we didn't get to work at the hospital. I told her: "Absolutely not." The most important thing about providing service is to listen to what people need and not to impose our will to help where it is not welcome or even safe.

Compassion is not always warm and fuzzy. It does not enable and it does not nurture people's addictions. Compassion does not always give what is asked for, nor does it ask nothing in return. Compassion works in ways that keep the dignity of others intact.

A sense of guilt kept me from pursuing social work many years ago. My own overdeveloped sense of responsibility urged me to stop this quest before I let someone down or caused another pain. But a healthier, more fully integrated capacity for concern guided me back to ministry and to service work. It allowed me to let others take ownership of themselves and

10. Elmer, *Cross-Cultural Connections*, 14.

their decisions, and to put away my own problem-solving tools and ready-made solutions in order to create space for others to grow.

Yin and Yang Compassion

A couple of years ago I was visiting with a friend who just completed her training as an LPN. She had spent the day giving immunizations to little kids. In response, these little kids screamed and confronted my friend with tears streaming down their round little cheeks. But despite the pain she was inflicting, she kept stabbing needles into youthful flesh. Not only needles, but needles that contained a strain of virus that would produce pain and swelling where it had pierced precious skin.

Standing next to each child was another adult. A mother, father, grandparent, guardian who would hold this little child as they screamed and wipe their tears and kiss the owie. Someone to offer comfort, warmth, and reassurance in this world that can suddenly be so unkind.

Which of the adults in this situation was being compassionate?

We will attempt to hold *together* love that knows pain is necessary *and* love that wishes it was not so. This is the yin and the yang, the feminine and masculine aspects of compassion.

According to Buddhist tradition, the savior-goddess Tara was born out of the tears of the bodhisattva Avalokiteshvara, the first Buddha and the one reincarnated as the Dalai Lama. It is said that he wept as he looked upon the world of suffering beings, and his tears formed a lake in which a lotus sprang up. When the lotus opened, the goddess Tara was revealed. Tara is the goddess of universal compassion. Born of a tear, it is said that her compassion for living beings is stronger than a mother's love for her children.

There are two major forms of Tara. One is the white Tara. This is the image that I brought back from Tibet. She has seven eyes (one each in the palms of her hands, the soles of her feet and her inner eye) because she sees all suffering and cries for help for all human beings. There is also a Green Tara. She is fiercer, more wrathful, and always ready to spring to virtuous and enlightened action for the sake of compassion. Together they are Tara and they symbolize the birth of compassion—a birth that takes place when the mind and the heart meet in wisdom.

Yin compassion is probably the one you think of first. It is the one that feels warm and fuzzy. Feminine compassion feels the pain and seeks to nurture, hold, cradle, and comfort. Yang or masculine compassion on the other hand, knows that pain and death are sometimes necessary, and it is willing to kick butt when it needs to.

Yin compassion cries because the children of Jerusalem refuse to gather under the wings of a hen, a loving protective God who longs for their suffering to end and for their joy to be complete. Yang compassion cries out against the acts of vipers and hypocrites and dares to will their undoing.

Yin compassion is gentle, caring, soothing, and serene. It is compassion that flows and loves like a mother, holding the entire universe in its womb with uncritically embracing, unconditional love.

Yang compassion is action-oriented. It is direct and aggressive. And in the face of ignorance, delusion, and injustice, Yang compassion is capable of ruthlessness. It is tough love, the kind of compassion that knows boundaries are necessary for the self and for others. It is the compassion that seeks to wake us and shake us up when we are lazy and slothful, untrue to our calling, and unfaithful to our spiritual path.

Masculine compassion requires the capacity for concern. It demands space inside for us to hold conflicting feelings of love and hate. The opposite of masculine compassion is not feminine compassion; it is idiot compassion. When we don't allow people to experience their own life or the consequences of their actions because it causes *us* pain to see them suffer, then we are exercising idiot compassion. When we jump to rescue people by giving them what they want or what we think they need, we are exercising idiot compassion.

Allowing loved ones to experience their own pain and suffering is yang compassion. Being with them while they suffer is yin compassion. Integrated Compassion, the kind of compassion we see in the myth of Tara offers tough love and kindheartedness at the same time.

Masculine compassion doesn't accept excuses or half-hearted attempts. It's the kind of compassion you get when a teacher scolds you, a police officer arrests you, a minister preaches to you, or a friend reprimands you because they know you are capable of more. It is the compassion you give when you allow your child to grow up. It is the side of love that won't tolerate destructive behavior in our own lives or in the life of our community.

Feminine compassion is the side of love that seeks to protect and to nurture. It's the immediate impulse to run to a fallen child to see if they are hurt. It is the fervent prayer we raise when we hear of a person in need. It is the hope we send to the universe for healing and restoration and peace. It is the compassion that accepts and encourages and welcomes indiscriminately. And very often it cries.

When our heart and our mind meet in wisdom, we no longer have the option of doing nothing. We can't ignore, excuse, or belittle the reality of the suffering before us and around the world. When our heart and our mind meet in wisdom we no longer have the option of responding with idiot compassion. We can no longer make ourselves the focus so that we act out of our own inability to be with other people's pain.

When our heart and our mind meet in wisdom, compassion is born, and we give vaccines even though we know they make little kids cry. When our heart and our mind meet in wisdom, we find ourselves holding a tissue in one hand and a sword in the other so that we might respond with whatever tool is called for in the situation at hand.

When our heart and mind meet.

> *Those who follow compassion*
> *Find life for themselves,*
> *Justice for their neighbor,*
> *And glory for God.*[11]
>
> —MEISTER ECKHART

An Invitation for Reflection:

1. In our rush to help, how might we do more harm than good?
2. When is it appropriate to "do" and when is it appropriate to "be"?
3. How has God acted in your life in ways that integrate Yin and Yang compassion?

---

11. Simpson, *The Politics of Compassion,* 64.

5

Whining as a Spiritual Discipline

I cry aloud with my voice to the LORD; I make supplication with my voice to the LORD. I pour out my complaint before Him; I declare my trouble before Him. When my spirit was overwhelmed within me, You knew my path. In the way where I walk they have hidden a trap for me. Look to the right and see; For there is no one who regards me; There is no escape for me; No one cares for my soul. I cried out to You, O LORD; I said, "You are my refuge, my portion in the land of the living. "Give heed to my cry, For I am brought very low; Deliver me from my persecutors, For they are too strong for me." Bring my soul out of prison, So that I may give thanks to Your name; The righteous will surround me, For You will deal bountifully with me.

—PSALM 142 (NASB)

Complaint

WE ARE ALL TAUGHT relatively early that whining is a bad thing to do. For annoyance and irritation, you just can't beat a high-pitched, nasal, drawn out whine. Not only that, but whining is an inherently selfish thing to do. Think of a kid whining at the top if his or her lungs in the middle of the grocery store. They cling with one hand to the cart, threatening to collapse on the floor, begging for some purchase they simply cannot live without. Where is their perspective? Can you reason with them at all? Are they thinking about the effects of their whining?

whining as a spiritual discipline 73

Are they thinking about what will happen to you if they get their way? Absolutely not. They are insanely focused. And what they are focused on is themselves. What they want. What they need. Nothing else is more important. Nothing else is even worth considering.

In that regard, perhaps whining is our purest form of direct communication. When I whine, there is no intermediary between what I'm thinking and feeling and what you're hearing coming out of my mouth. It is primal and infantile and utterly beautiful.

It is being impeccable with my word. Being impeccable with my word means being honest and it means telling people what I want and need, because it's not their job to try to figure it out, even if they could. It takes courage to whine. Because once we finally give expression to our desires, we might or might not get what we asked for. In whining, we are vulnerable.

It happens to me just about once a month. Something to do with hormones—or so I'm told. Things that I usually take in stride stand out as affronts that need to be named. I say things and do things that are completely out of character for me.

Of course, it seems incredibly unfair that I should be gifted with PMS just by nature of the fact I was born a woman. Interestingly, it turns out that's not necessarily the case at all. Studies have shown that men also experience fluctuations in mood, energy, and sex drive every four to six weeks. During low cycles they can become apathetic, bloated, emotional, irritable, and angry.

So it seems that all human beings experience fluctuations in their hormonal levels, and these changes affect our moods and behavior. I don't doubt it for a minute. In fact it seems pretty obvious that just as the natural world moves by seasons and cycles, we would also find some kind of rhythm to our moods and energies.

While I never appreciate it at the time, I feel incredibly fortunate to have these moments of sheer exposed truth because they allow me to work through the very things I've been taught not to express: my own needs and frustrations. It is so striking because in giving voice to them I can seem to be so different from who I am.

The surprising gift has been to discover that these mood swings actually allow me to tap into feelings that are very real and very deep about what and who I am. They provide for the breaking through of things hidden deep inside that burst forth in full bloom through tears or anger or a high-pitched, annoying whine. Because these moods are so out of character for me during the rest of the month, I have no choice but to explore them and what they mean. That is what turns whining into a spiritual practice.

Whining has to lead to something else. To simply stop in a state of whining is horrific. We all know someone who has gotten stuck in the whine: someone who never has anything positive to say about their life, who has adopted the language and the vocal pitch of the victim, who is filled with defeat while still expecting the world to change and to make their life better or more complete. To get stuck in the whine is to stagnate, to dry up, to cease to live. And it is to alienate virtually everyone else in our life.

On the other hand, whining that is alive can be a deeply spiritual endeavor. The writers of the psalms understood whining. They understood the danger of the false teachings of a church that suggest there is no place for despair or fear in the spiritual life. It is an illusion to believe that God has no use for our anger or that we must never whine to God. The psalmists understood that we simply cannot have an intimate relationship with someone if we can't speak honestly to them, including using voices raised in anger, trembling in fear, and whining in complaint. Finally, they did not understand religion to be a set of ideas about God, but rather a way to pursue an ongoing relationship with God.

Most of the psalms are words of lament. They are cries of anguish and pain that seem to violate every rule of social propriety. Most of them start with "me." Look at me, God, listen to me. The important thing here, God, is me and my trouble and my salvation. They're not even polite. They accuse God of abandonment, murder, and falling asleep on the job. Some try to bribe God and others tell God to just go away. Most disturbingly, they take a distinctly uncharitable attitude toward the enemy with devout wishes that terrible things will happen to them.

The cycle of monthly whining is a blessing because there is an automatic reset, when our hormones return to normal. We are then able to move out of the whine and into something deeper that includes introspection and genuine self-care. Whether we are susceptible to PMS or irritable male syndrome, we can all use whining as a platform for expressing what needs to be expressed and then turning that expression into something richer, and ultimately far more beneficial, than endless complaint.

At its best, whining is prayer. A prayer of lament. Ellen Davis in her book *Getting Involved with God* assures us, "When you lament in good faith, opening yourself to God honestly and fully—no matter what you have to say—you are beginning to clear the way for praise. You are straining toward the time when God will turn your tears into laughter. When you lament, you are asking God to create the conditions in which it will become possible for you to offer praise—conditions, it turns out, that are mainly within your own heart."[1]

Lament embraces the language of our very real suffering and then moves beyond current reality. Laments have a distinct form. They begin by addressing God, usually in a brief cry for help. Then they make their complaint. God is informed of the problems and all of the anger, guilt, frustration, and disillusionment that it has wrought. There are expressions of self-justification and statements defending the integrity of one's own actions. Next is a confession of trust in God, despite the current circumstances. Having expressed confidence in God, the next step is to appeal to God for help and intervention. This petitioning of God awakens new spiritual energies to overcome loss and suffering. Words of assurance come next, that God will hear the request and provide restoration and wholeness. Finally lament ends with praise and a promise to testify to what God has done.[2]

Lament says, "I am in pain," and then boldly assumes that God cares and can be expected to do something about it.

The psalms move from complaint to confidence, from desperate plea to expectant praise. What they don't do is tell us that anything ever changed for the better. We just don't know what happens on the outside. But on the inside we know. We know that the experience of suffering itself has changed, perhaps only because the whiner dared to break the isolation of silence and believe that God has heard.

There is more. There are two psalms that stop before ever getting to the point of praise. The fact that they are included at all seems particularly important, for they suggest that unresolved despair is itself one legitimate, though tragic, aspect of our life with God. Sometimes the only act of faith that is possible is to name our misery before God and to implicate God in our suffering.

Lament is deeply personal, yet it also voices the distress of the community, and, in giving voice to that distress, seeks to change painful reality. If we are silent about our own problems, we are likely to continue to live with them without experiencing the gift of growth and change. The same is true for our society. Nothing ever happens by keeping silent in the midst of injustice, except that we implicitly or explicitly condone its continued presence and oppression in our life.

When Barack Obama was new in office he did a stunning job of unpacking the whine of racism in this country. Simultaneously, the people of Tibet were demonstrating in order to make public the whine they had

---

1. Davis, *Getting Involved with God*, 15.
2. Hamman, *Reflections on Lament*, 1–2.

been carrying privately. Each in their own faith tradition confessed God's holy name, not because it gave them protection against harm, but because it pushed them and us toward living ever more fully in the presence of God.

So the next time you think about whining and stifle it, think again. No matter what the time of month, remember the psalms of lament and know that they are the Spirit of God speaking through us, helping us to pray when we do not know how to pray as we ought. Empowering us when we feel vulnerable, revitalizing our sense of praise and hope, and granting us permission to grieve and protest. Yes, despite everything our parents tried to teach us, the psalms of lament invite us unmistakably to whine.

Yearning

The psalmists remind us that to have a meaningful relationship with God we have to be honest about what we think and feel. Such whining is deeply personal; it begins with "me" and "my" needs. But those needs are often encased within the cries of the larger community. Lament doesn't whitewash problems. Instead, it proclaims in a voice filled with whine, the bitter reality of injustice and social tyranny. It names oppression for what it is and refuses to capitulate to the abuse of power and authority. Lament is the language of the Sudanese who have never known a country without war, of the Palestinians who have never known life outside a refugee camp, of the Tibetans who have never known life outside exile. In their lament, they not only whine about the current state of affairs, they also yearn for a new day. They yearn for something more holy and life giving to emerge. They yearn for God to intervene and for rightness, hope, and joy to be restored.

One of the greatest speakers, loudest whiners, and most sincere yearners of our age was Martin Luther King Jr. Growing up in the harsh reality of racial oppression, he dared to whine about the way he and his people were being personally and systematically subjugated by white society. Knowing that nothing ever happens by keeping silent, he risked and ultimately lost his life in order to be the voice of lament, daring to yearn for a better day.

On April 3, 1968, the day before he was assassinated, King delivered his final speech. He was talking about injustice felt by city sanitation workers who were striking to protest their low wages and poor working conditions. He told his audience that the question to ask was not, "What will happen to me if I help them?" but "What will happen to them if I don't?"[3] As he spoke, King addressed his own mortality. In Lament we realize, as King knew all too well, our own human frailty. That frailty is not meant to cause

3. King, *I've Been to the Mountaintop*, April 13, 1968.

whining as a spiritual discipline 77

us anxiety and sorrow. It is meant to be a source of confidence and joy. It is exactly our frailty that creates our desire and need to see God's power at work, in ourselves, in the faith community, from generation to generation.

Yearning knows that things are not the way they should be and that rightness must be restored. King didn't get stopped in the whine. Instead he yearned, and in his yearning, he called a nation to something better and more holy. Today, much of King's dream has been realized. Laws that codified racial discrimination have been struck down. The Civil Rights Act of 1964 gave evidence to our country's willingness to listen to the whine and begin to take serious steps toward justice and equality. But much remains to be done.

In this generation, we have heard a new voice offering up his own whine, the community's lament of the ongoing reality of racial division and derision. Barack Obama, in his first term speech on *Race and the Reverend Wright,* gave voice to the pent-up frustration, anger, and despair of blacks and whites alike as they continue to live in a society of all-too-often unspoken racial tension.[4] To not say it does not make it go away. That is the problem with thinking we aren't allowed to whine—that God somehow can't hear us when we use that tone of voice. We have to whine. We have to give expression to what we observe and experience, or else we internalize it and damage our own being while the problem continues to perpetuate itself and even grow in the midst of our silence.

That is what Obama realized as he seized the opportunity to air out loud the internal whine of racism in the hearts and minds of today's Americans of all colors and hues. In speaking of the comments made by Reverend Wright and his own white grandmother, he said:

> The fact is that the comments that have been made and the issues that have surfaced over the last few weeks reflect the complexities of race in this country that we've never really worked through—a part of our union that we have yet to perfect. And if we walk away now, if we simply retreat into our respective corners, we will never be able to come together and solve challenges like health care, or education, or the need to find good jobs for every American.[5]

Understanding this reality requires a reminder of how we arrived at this point. In his speech, Obama paraphrased William Faulkner who wrote, "The past is never dead. It's not even past."[6] We do not need to recite here

4. Obama, March 8, 2008.
5. Idem.
6. Faulkner, *Requiem for a Nun*, 73.

the history of racial injustice in this country. But we do need to remind ourselves that so many of the disparities that exist in the African-American community today can be directly traced to inequalities passed on from an earlier generation that suffered under the brutal legacy of slavery and Jim Crow.

By making public the private lament uttered around kitchen tables all around this country, Obama challenged every one of us not to get stuck in the whine. The challenge is not to determine whether we are the victim or the oppressor, but to understand that we are all suffering, and we all need to experience reconciliation. He took up the call of Martin Luther King Jr. and others who came before him, yearning toward the future, yearning to live in the full presence of God.

To yearn is to lament with a goal, to see and believe in a future even if you won't be around to enjoy it when it finally arrives. It is to trust that God is breaking into this world and will continue to transform it and us into who we are meant to be—one with each other and one with God.

When we see the vision and believe in the dream and then reach forward toward it with yearning and desire, even when there is no indication how or when things might actually improve, we transform our lament into praise, our fear into love, and our surrender to victimization into the courage to be advocates of change.

When we put our whole selves and our whole passion into sacred yearning, we stand on holy ground. It doesn't matter if we know where we are going or not. It doesn't matter if the way seems clear or if we look around and discover we are lost. What matters is that our yearning leads us to finally giving ourselves and our situation over to God. By concentrating our whole self on love and longing for God, we create a path toward the joy we yearn to know, the hope we yearn to claim, the coming of the day in which we shall stand in gratitude and awe.

Anger

I am going to confide in you one of my strongest and longest-lasting fears: the fear that someone, anyone, would think of me as a bitch. It was a crippling fear that left me with no healthy way to manage my anger. Bitches get angry and they let you know it. Nice girls, nice ladies, nice women—don't.

Contrary to what our parents taught us, I have been trying to convince you of the importance of whining without reservation or restraint directly to and about God. Now I hope to unsettle you just a little more by challenging you to take up the challenge of expressing your anger.

Now a lot of us have a reaction right away to that very thought. Heck, a lot of us react to the very word "anger." We've been told and taught that anger is unproductive, unhealthy, and unholy. And, in fact, we can express our anger in ways that are all that.

But anger itself is never a problem. Anger is a natural human emotion that everyone experiences often and that needs to be expressed to maintain health. Anger is neither legitimate nor illegitimate, meaningful nor pointless. Anger simply is.

Anger is a signal, and one well worth listening to. Anger is a secondary emotion, one that follows shock, hurt, surprise, pain, insult, sorrow, or injustice. When we feel anger, that anger exists for a reason and it deserves our attention and our respect. We all have a right to everything we feel, and our anger is no exception. "Anger," writes David Richo in his book *How to Be an Adult*, "is the feeling that says NO to opposition, injury or injustice. It is the indicator that something I value is in jeopardy."[7]

Once again the psalmists can help us to own the reality of our own anger in what are sometimes referred to as the "cursing" psalms. Far from expressing compassion, understanding, or anything resembling love and charity toward the enemy, these psalms cry out for revenge and destruction. Psalm 137 is probably the worst offender of our faith-based sensibilities as it exclaims, "Happy shall they be who take your little ones and dash them against the rock!"[8]

We are not talking about a faceless enemy, either. Psalm 55 offers this: "For it is not an enemy who reproaches me, Then I could bear it; Nor is it one who hates me who has exalted himself against me, Then I could hide myself from him. But it is you, a man my equal, My companion and my familiar friend; We who had sweet fellowship together Walked in the house of God in the throng."[9] These enemies are well known and the call for vengeance is a very personal one.

You probably have never heard these psalms read in church. They aren't part of the Christian lectionary. They tend to cause embarrassment and confusion so that they are dismissed as Old Testament pre-Jesus sentiment, actively avoided or willfully ignored. But by silencing that part of the Biblical witness, we are denied the opportunity to be healed and relieved of our anger by bringing it into our most intimate relationship, our relationship with God.

---

7. Richo, *How to Be an Adult*, 36.
8. Psalm 137:9 (NASB).
9. Psalm 55:12–4 (NASB).

Healing and relief never come from covering up our anger. That comes from acknowledging our anger and then offering it up as prayer. The cursing psalms are particularly helpful in giving us a framework for doing that important work. First, they give us language when in our rage we may not be able to find the words to express our anger and hurt. Next, they teach us that vengeful anger is a legitimate way to enter into relationship with God. Not only that, but they confront us with the responsibility we each have in naming and renouncing evil and injustice.

Finally, the psalms lead us to understanding this cry for vengeance as an appeal for *God* to act. They are not about passing judgment and then taking matters of punishment into one's own hands. Instead, they demand that the enemies be driven into God's hands. And who can say what will happen to them there? For our God is one not of judgment alone, but also, alas, of mercy. The cursing psalms call on us to yield to God our own claim of vengeance. And in doing so, they confront us with one of our most persistent idolatries: the notion that God has as little use for our enemies as we do.

This same movement of anger is what we need to experience in our personal relationships. Just as whining must move us toward introspection, and yearning must move us toward action, anger must move us toward acceptance if it is to be a spiritual practice. If we get stuck in the anger, we never heal or find health in our day-to-day relationships.

It is tempting to view anger as a simple process of cause and effect. If we are angry, someone else caused our anger. If someone is angry with us, we must be to blame. Or if we are convinced of our innocence, then the other person has no right to feel angry. But relationships don't work that way. Anger is not caused by an event. It is caused by our belief about or interpretation of the event.

We begin to use our anger as a healthy vehicle for change when we are able to share our anger objectively without making the other person responsible for it and without blaming ourselves for the reactions people have toward us. We are responsible for our own behavior. We are not responsible for other people's reactions to it. Nor are they responsible for ours. Healthy anger management means taking responsibility for our own feelings, thoughts, and behaviors and handing over to others the responsibility for their own.

If we feel chronically angry or bitter in an important relationship, it is a signal that too much of our identity has been compromised and we are uncertain about what new position to take or what options we have available to us. To recognize our lack of clarity is not a weakness but an opportunity, a challenge, and a strength.

How might we express our anger? Again the psalms offer a wonderful template. Consider going into your room and shouting out loud these horrible curses! These psalms, so full of passionate rage and tragic wishes, model for us the need to be able to say things that we don't mean. We can do that by reading their words. Or we can do it by voicing to God without restraint the first thoughts that enter our mind, without having to think about whether we actually want what we say to happen or not. If we are very fortunate, we have a friend to whom we can vent our frustration and say whatever comes to mind, knowing we will not be judged or held accountable for expressing what we would never in a more thoughtful mood intone.

What the psalms don't do is vent *at* the source of the anger. They don't further damage relationships by telling the enemy to his or her face that their children should be dashed upon the rocks. They don't abuse anybody. Often I have heard (and I suspect you have as well) someone say they need to get their anger out so they don't explode later. Venting is not a way to get our anger out. Venting is about unleashing emotion on another person not for the sake of communication and understanding, but for the relief of one's own internal pressure valve. It is not about identifying the core source of one's own trigger system in order to find a way toward resolution, but a way to actively avoid dealing with one's own issues by blaming another. Anger can be so much more productive for us than simply as a rant and rave. It is a waste of good anger to just get it out.

Anger expressed in healthiness never leads to either physical or emotional violence or abuse. David Richo names such tactics not as expressions of real anger but as drama. Drama is merely ego-centered, manipulative theatrics with a storyline attached. Drama is meant to silence the other, not to enter into communication. It blames rather than taking responsibility for one's own feelings. It is held onto and endures as resentment rather than being expressed, released, and let go. Drama and venting never help the situation at all. And in fact they are most likely to work to keep the patterns of anger and response locked firmly in place.[10]

On the other hand, stuffing anger is also a good way to keep unhealthy systems locked in place. When we avoid anger and conflict, we always do so at a cost. By allowing our anger to be repressed and internalized, we invite it to eat away at our self-esteem and maybe even lead us into depression.

I was always a nice person. When things happened that should have made me rightfully angry, I would remain silent. I would feel hurt and I would become self-critical. In fact, I was so uncomfortable with this

---

10. Richo, *How to Be an Adult*, 37–8.

emotion that if I felt anger toward you, I would likely do something to make you angry with me. I could handle your anger. I couldn't handle mine.

By holding my anger inside and refusing to make clear statements about what I felt and what my boundaries were, I could keep from making someone else feel uncomfortable and I could avoid exposing the differences between us. Because exposing those differences meant calling attention to the ways in which we were different, the ways in which I was separate and alone. Fear took hold—that primal fear known as separation anxiety, and with it the belief that by assuming my own bottom-line position, I was risking losing the relationship.

So my energy went into protecting the other person and preserving the appearance of harmony at the expense of being a clearly defined "I." Now add to this guilt. Guilt is a great way to blot out awareness of anger. If I feel guilty about not giving enough or not doing enough for others, it is unlikely I will be angry about not getting enough. Nothing blocks awareness of anger more effectively than guilt and self-doubt.

I feared expressing my anger because in my past I learned that showing anger was dangerous. I learned as a child that to be angry was to be unacceptable and unloved. And I learned by watching the adults in my life that to express anger, especially as a woman, was to be labeled a bitch.

As we work through our old childhood scars, we discover that love and anger do coexist in authentic intimacy. Anger, like any feeling, cannot cancel out love. In fact, anger is inevitable in any relationship in which people are free and in which they allow one another to get close. John Welwood wrote, "To let ourselves be touched also involves letting ourselves be scraped."[11] Love that does not allow anger is not love but fear.

So anger, like any good spiritual practice, turns our attention inward toward our own transformation. Our anger is not internalized in the process, but introspected. It isn't about you finally "getting it" after I've told you over and over again why I get mad at you—but about *me* finally getting at the core of my anger, as well as the unhealed woundedness it suggests. Anger becomes a tool for transformation when it challenges us to become more of an expert on our self and less of an expert on others.

Anger can be a powerful tool for personal growth and change even if it does nothing more than help us recognize that we are not yet clear about something and that it is our job to keep struggling with it. And in our struggle, the psalmists suggest the holy act of expressing our most bitter feelings and our most offensive curses as offerings of prayer. We have been

---

11. Welwood, *Challenge of the Heart*, 69.

whining as a spiritual discipline 83

challenged to whine, we have been encouraged to yearn, and now we find we are even invited to bitch!

Worry

My husband and I separated in December of 2007. We divorced in August of 2008. During that transitional period we came to understand that we could continue to love each other, but we couldn't live together without needing each other to change—and that's no way to live together. I thought it was a mutual decision to celebrate the marriage we had shared even while moving through divorce. We talked of doing so in a gracious and loving way. We had intended to continue being family even as we no longer defined ourselves as a couple.

One day in the middle of this transition, my son Alex and I were talking about this change. He knew we weren't going to get back together and he was adjusting to that. He realized that everyone was getting along better than ever these days and that he didn't need to worry at that point about losing either his step-father or me. But the word "divorce" unsettled him, so I asked him what he was afraid of. He told me that he was worried that I would end up all alone.

From the heart of a 13-year-old comes the expression of one of our most primal fears. A fear that arises in childhood and is carried into our adult relationships. The fear that we will end up utterly alone.

The 22nd psalm begins with words we have heard before. These words reflect the deep pain and anguish of feeling utterly alone, abandoned even by the Divine. "My God, why have you forsaken me?"[12] Those seven words speak directly and unflinchingly to our deepest dread.

The psalmists do not shy away from worrying about their deepest, most heartfelt fears. And then they move forward. As with whining, complaining, yearning and anger, the need for expression is always followed by not getting stuck in it.

There is comfort in knowing we are not the only ones who have felt the grief of abandonment; that even Jesus cried out in the pain and misery of feeling God's absence as he died on the cross. We ourselves have known that deep anguish of feeling forsaken by everyone, even by God.

But even when our life is not on the line, even when things are going relatively well in our world, there is still plenty we can find to worry about. Worry is a healthy signal that warns us that there is danger or potential danger up ahead. Worry is more than a feeling; it's a reaction. It's what we

12. Psalm 22:1 (NASB).

do when we feel anxiety or fear. Just as we need to whine, complain, lament, and voice our anger, we need to allow ourselves the human response of worry. To not worry about anything at any time is to deny the reality of human fear—and I haven't met anyone yet who never experiences fear.

My son Jackson started driving when he was 16 years old. When he wasn't where he was supposed to be by the time he was supposed to arrive, fear would arise and this mom would worry. My son Alex has been struggling with mental illness and while he is doing great as I write, we don't know what his long-term prognosis will be. I worry about him today and I worry about his future. When we struggle in today's economy, or a loved one becomes ill, or we watch as violence and war continue to escalate around the world, our fear arises, and we worry.

Worry is to our emotional health what pain is to our physical health. Both tell us that something is wrong. Pain becomes a problem when it keeps telling us there's something wrong when there isn't. The same is true of worry. Worry becomes unhealthy when it becomes bigger and more consuming than the problem itself. The key to worry is to use it to understand the underlying fear. When we start peeling back the layers of fear, one after the other, we finally arrive at our core fear. And as Alex knows, one of our core fears is being all alone.

In our culture, the music we play, the books we read, and the movies we watch often present despair as a response to loneliness. They express feelings of loss and being lost. They illustrate sensations of being stranded in a vacant wasteland with nobody to turn to but ourselves. Our culture nurtures our fear of being alone.

But we don't need to live in that fear. While we do have a natural human impulse toward community, we also have a natural human impulse toward solitude. This impulse arises when we feel too restricted, crowded and confined. It is an impulse that leads us to move away from people when we begin to fear we are losing not the other, but our self.

The way to get over our fear of loneliness is to embrace our impulse toward solitude. When we intentionally find time to be alone, we notice that we survive it. By choosing the very thing we fear, we gradually find that we enjoy our time alone, our time in solitude. Gerald May says, "Anyone who faces emptiness becomes contemplative in that very moment, for then the truth is seen—just as it is."[13]

The lesson of the mystics is that when we finally let go of our need to be connected with each other and with God, we realize we can never be separated from each other or from God. We come to experience unity. We

---

13. Schut, *Simpler Living*, 49.

are one. The contemplative saints know the fear and pain, as well as the joy and freedom, of entering emptiness.

In my favorite quote from *The Wisdom of the Wilderness,* May says, ". . . maybe sometimes when we feel most alone it is because that One is so very close to us that we can no longer make the distinction."[14] In these words I hear an amazing invitation: an invitation to move from worry to wonder.

Getting stuck in worry is debilitating. The more we feed it, the more it tends to grow. So one way to begin to move is to ask ourselves, "What's the absolute worst thing that could happen?" We keep asking until we get to the core fear and then ask, "What are the chances of the worst thing happening? How many times?" Then instead of imaging and re-imagining the negative scenario, we picture what we ideally want to have happen. We imagine it and then we develop an action plan to begin moving toward it.

My dear friend Bobbi Sabine was making herself sick with worry about her parents dying. In a wonderful display of synchronicity, something made her stop at a yard sale where she spent one of the best quarters of her life on a book by Dale Carnegie called *How to Stop Worrying and Start Living.* In it she found similar suggestions. First, to ask, "What is the absolute worst outcome?" Assume it happens and ask, "Then what?" The realization comes that life goes on, you are okay, and you survive and keep living.

Richo suggests concrete steps for managing worry. First, admit it. Allow yourself to feel it and then act with it. Acting because of fear is cowardice. Acting with fear is courage. Getting stuck in worry allows us to generate a sense of choicelessness that leaves us paralyzed. But when we act in the midst of our worry, even when we're not absolutely sure we're doing the right thing, we release all the nervous energy of anxiety that keeps us paralyzed and reinvest it in our own sense of personal power and freedom. Rather than being powerless in the face of fear, like a deer caught in the headlights, we find we have a choice, where we had come to believe there was only a dead end.

Again the psalmists offer us a model as they move from worry into wonder. The cry that begins "My God, why have you forsaken me?"[15] finally ends with, "Future generations will be told about the Lord, and proclaim his deliverance to a people yet unborn."[16] Ellen Davis writes, "The psalms of lament are prayers of anguish yearning to be transformed into praise."[17]

---

14. May, *Wisdom of the Wilderness,* xxiii.
15. Psalm 22:1 (NASB).
16. Psalm 22:30–31 (NASB).
17. Davis, *Getting Involved with God,* 30.

Praise is not about fabricated flattery. It is about seeing the world the way it is. It is about setting aside our groundless fantasies and fears and looking through the lens of the Divine. We praise God in order to see the world the way God does. We begin to see the world as the work of God's hands and the object of God's endlessly patient love. We come to see every action that serves the needy and that contributes to the good of all to be the way in which the earth becomes full of Divine love.

To praise is to come to a new understanding, a new perception of our own situation. We do not have to strive continually to find a place for ourselves in this universe. That place has been provided. It is something on which we can rely. Resting in that awareness, accepting the reality of our place in the world, we ultimately find our happiness. We recognize ourselves as people blessed by the very fact that we are in relationship with God. To praise in this way is to enter the realm of wonder.

People who pray are people who live in expectation. They are people who seek to transform their anxious worry into something hopeful and holy. The unknown continues. The mystery doesn't go away. The answers don't suddenly become clear, and the problems don't spontaneously disappear. But there is an embrace of it all, a trusting, a hope, and a belief in something bigger than one's own self. A knowing that everything will continue to unfold and that the world will continue to emerge as it is intended to be. As God intends it to be. A movement from separation to unity. From loneliness to solitude. From worry to wonder.

For Crying Out Loud

It is incredibly freeing to be given permission to engage in all the behaviors our parents and our culture have tried to tell us are wrong. I want to add one more to that list. The song "Don't Cry Out Loud"[18] became my theme while growing up. It was a song that suggested it was important not to let anyone know when you were falling apart. It was your job to hide your tears and maintain a brave front no matter what tragedy might come your way. For a very long time, I thought this was a most important life lesson and I would just have to keep trying in order to master it. Now, fortunately, it strikes me as pretty darn sick and I'm awfully glad I finally gave up trying to reaching that pathetic goal.

Whining, complaining, lamenting, expressing anger, and worrying are essential human expressions. If we fail to admit them, express them, and act with and through them, we risk turning a lot of emotional chaos upon

---

18. Allen and Sager, *Don't Cry Out Loud*.

ourselves and never experiencing health, growth, and change. For we are the ones, when we express our most authentic self, who are ultimately changed and transformed.

The psalms have been our guide. They have taught us that whining is an authentic expression of being impeccable with our word. They demonstrate the courage required to ask for exactly what we want and need—and in doing so to place ourselves and our enemies squarely in God's hands, recognizing that in the end we are not in control of the situation, but we are in control of the choices we make and the way we choose to live.

Startling to our Spiritual sensibilities, the psalms of lament seek the destruction of one's enemies in stunning calls for revenge that seem out of place in the Christian Bible. Not only do they cry out for vengeance against other people, but they raise dark accusations against God. They complain that God's absence is not only palpable, but that it is unexpected, unreasonable, and inexcusable. The psalmists are not timid or tentative as they rail against God as untrustworthy, unfaithful and neglectful, all of which has resulted presumably in the suffering and shame of the psalmist.

The presence of these psalms alone can be a source of great comfort, for they affirm our natural human response to opposition, injury, and injustice. We get angry. And anger is important. It serves as an indicator that something I value is in jeopardy. Healing and relief never come from denying or covering up our anger. That comes from acknowledging it and offering it up as prayer. And in doing so, we hand over to God our own claim of vengeance and the misguided idolatry that God feels the same way about our enemies as we do.

Anger expressed in healthiness never leads to physical or emotional violence or abuse. It is not venting and it is not drama. Dealing authentically with our anger is not about blaming the other, but about uncovering our own reaction of anger and seeking to understand what is at its core. Anger can be a powerful tool for our own growth and change even if all it does is let us know we still aren't clear about something and have to keep struggling with it. In our struggle, the psalmists suggest the holy act of expressing our most bitter feelings and our most offensive curses as offerings of prayer.

Lament is a deeply personal act. It begins with "my" needs, but those needs often exist within, and voice the cries of the larger community. Lament expresses anger at the bitter reality of injustice and social tyranny. It names oppression for what it is and refuses to capitulate to the abuse of power and authority. And it yearns for a new day. It yearns for something more holy and life giving to emerge. It yearns for God to intervene and for rightness, hope, and joy to be restored.

To yearn is to lament with a goal. To see and believe in the dream and reach forward toward it with yearning and desire even when there is no indication how or when things might actually improve. It doesn't matter if the way seems clear or if we look around and discover we are lost. What matters is that our yearning leads us to finally giving our situation and ourselves over to God.

That is when our worry becomes prayer. We all find reason in our lives to worry. Worry is our human reaction to anxiety and fear. And one of our deepest fears is of being utterly alone. So we find comfort in the psalms that speak to the pain and grief of feeling abandoned by everyone, including God.

The witness of the psalms is that when we turn our worry into prayer, we discover that there is another way to perceive our own situation. People who pray are people who live in expectation. When we pray, we seek to transform our anxious worry into something hopeful and holy. Answers don't become clear, but in allowing the world to be in God's hands, we move into embracing that world, feeling that there is something bigger and more mysterious going on here than the current discomfort of our own egos.

To pray and to praise without understanding or clarity is to enter into the realm of wonder. It is only when we finally let go of our need to know that we are connected with each other and with God that we find ourselves immersed in the realization that we can never be separated from the other or from God. We come to experience unity. We are one.

This is what we seek to know and feel underneath all of our life-long struggles. "Our problem," according to David Richo, "is not that as children our needs were unmet, but that as adults they are still un-mourned. The hurt, betrayed, bereft child is still inside of us, wanting to cry for what he missed."[19] Because without that expression and the release it allows, we stay stuck. We don't let go of the pain. We continue to feel stressful neediness. In fact, that neediness tells us nothing about how much we need from others. What it tells us is how much we still need to grieve a barren past that cannot be changed as it urges us to call upon our own inner sources of nurturance.

The psalmists teach us to express and to mourn our unmet needs—and they don't allow us to get stuck there. Instead they call us to move from powerlessness to assertiveness. Assertiveness does not remain silent in the midst of pain and struggle. Assertiveness raises a confident voice that is clear about what we want, how we feel, the choices we are making, and the agendas we carry. Assertiveness means that people can trust that our yes

---

19. Richo, *How to Be an Adult*, 12.

means yes, our no means no, and our maybe means maybe. Because assertiveness requires that we be clear; it doesn't require that we be sure.

When we are assertive, we parent ourselves instead of looking for someone else to parent us. We affirm our own truth and we are willing to receive the truth of others. We ask for what we want and then we honor whatever response we might get. We share how we feel and accept how others feel.

Being assertive means that we take responsibility for our actions, our inaction, and our own health and peace of mind. If there are relationships in which we carry wounds that keep us from being our most authentic self, we are intentional about dealing with that unfinished business, either directly with the person involved or in our own therapy. We admit our mistakes, our oversights, and our offenses. Finally, being assertive requires that we accept the right of others to be assertive with us.

When we do our grieving work, when we admit our powerlessness and express our mourning, when we whine and complain and yearn and yell and then move into assertiveness, we realize that we always have alternatives, no matter what our predicament might be. Knowing we always have choices keeps us from getting stuck in depression, apathy, or the paralyzing stance of the victim. Instead we get on with our lives in powerful and productive ways.

Assertiveness begins with naming and admitting whatever emotion has us in its grasp. Gerald May advises us that we don't need to tame our emotions, keep them under control, or civilize them. We don't need to learn how to cope, how to not cry out loud. We need to experience our emotions. Coping separates us from the reality of our own feelings. Wild, untamed emotions are full of life and energy. The challenge is to be with and in our emotions, not apart from them.[20]

And so we embrace them all—even the ones our parents told us were a problem. We are supposed to whine when we feel there's something to whine about. Then, when we are at our best, our whining becomes a prayer. A prayer of lament. Lament embraces the language of our very real suffering and then moves beyond that current reality. Whining moves us to introspection, yearning to action, anger to acceptance, worry to wonder and mourning to assertiveness. So go ahead and lament. And if anyone tries to tell you not to, just tell them it's your spiritual practice . . . for crying out loud.

---

20. May, *Wisdom of the Wilderness*.

> *If there is a wide gulf between your faith and feelings right now because of the hurt and pain you are feeling, that's not hypocrisy—that's honesty.*[21]
>
> —JOEY O'CONNOR

An Invitation for Reflection:

1. Would you rather feel angry, afraid, or depressed? Why?

2. How do you speak to God? Are you comfortable complaining and whining to God? Being angry with God?

3. When have you exercised assertiveness? What keeps you from doing it more often?

---

21. O'Connor, *Children and Grief*, 48.

6

Who's to Blame?

Revisiting the Book of Job

> *Our human compassion binds us the one to the other—not in pity or patronizingly, but as human beings who have learnt how to turn our common suffering into hope for the future. May our suffering draw us into compassion for our neighbor as it unites us with God.*[1]
>
> —NELSON MANDELA

Job: Exposing the Lies

JOB IS A STORY found in the Old Testament. It is part of the sacred Scriptures in both the Jewish and Christian tradition. It is a work of dramatic fiction set in Uz, an unreal place, so far as we know. But the story of Job is very real. Job is your story. Job is my story.

> There was once a man in the land of Uz whose name was Job. That man was blameless and upright, one who feared God and turned away from evil. There were born to him seven sons and three daughters. He had seven thousand sheep, three thousand camels, five hundred yoke of oxen, five hundred donkeys, and very many servants; so that this man was the greatest of all the people of the east. His sons used to go and hold feasts in one

1. Mandela, *Notes to the Future*, 84.

another's houses in turn; and they would send and invite their three sisters to eat and drink with them. And when the feast days had run their course, Job would send and sanctify them, and he would rise early in the morning and offer burnt offerings according to the number of them all; for Job said, "It may be that my children have sinned, and cursed God in their hearts." This is what Job always did.[2]

Things are going along just fine. You're taking care of yourself and your family. You're obeying all of God's commands. You're even making burnt offerings on behalf of your kids just in case they did something wrong. OK, so maybe you're not big on the burnt offerings—but you're still doing everything you think you're supposed to do. And then for absolutely no apparent reason, the bottom falls out of your world.

Your spouse wants a divorce. Your child gets in trouble with the law. You get laid off from your job. Someone dear to you dies. You get cancer. Things go from bad to worse. In fact, you can't imagine things could possibly get any worse than they are. And then they get worse still.

One day the heavenly beings came to present themselves before the LORD, and Satan also came among them. The LORD said to Satan, "Where have you come from?" Satan answered the LORD, "From going to and fro on the earth, and from walking up and down on it." The LORD said to Satan, "Have you considered my servant Job? There is no one like him on the earth, a blameless and upright man who fears God and turns away from evil." Then Satan answered the LORD, "Does Job fear God for nothing? Have you not put a fence around him and his house and all that he has, on every side? You have blessed the work of his hands, and his possessions have increased in the land. But stretch out your hand now, and touch all that he has, and he will curse you to your face." The LORD said to Satan, "Very well, all that he has is in your power; only do not stretch out your hand against him!" So Satan went out from the presence of the LORD.

One day when his sons and daughters were eating and drinking wine in the eldest brother's house, a messenger came to Job and said, "The oxen were plowing and the donkeys were feeding beside them, and the Sabeans fell on them and carried them off, and killed the servants with the edge of the sword; I alone have escaped to tell you." While he was still speaking, another came and said, "The fire of God fell from heaven and burned up

---

2. Job 1:1–5 (NRSV).

the sheep and the servants, and consumed them; I alone have escaped to tell you." While he was still speaking, another came and said, "The Chaldeans formed three columns, made a raid on the camels and carried them off, and killed the servants with the edge of the sword; I alone have escaped to tell you." While he was still speaking, another came and said, "Your sons and daughters were eating and drinking wine in their eldest brother's house, and suddenly a great wind came across the desert, struck the four corners of the house, and it fell on the young people, and they are dead; I alone have escaped to tell you."

Then Job arose, tore his robe, shaved his head, and fell on the ground and worshiped. He said, "Naked I came from my mother's womb, and naked I will depart. The Lord gave and the Lord has taken away; may the name of the Lord by praised."[3]

A word needs to be said about Satan. Satan in this story is not a red devil with horns and a pitchfork, but a character used to show the problems that arise when our religious convictions don't match our lived experience.

By the time Job was written, God had become predictable to the Israelites. They had come to believe that if you were doing well, it was a sign of God's favor. If things were going poorly, it must be because you had done something wrong.

The character of Satan stirs all of that up by playing the role of God's Adversary, the one who challenges God by claiming that the only reason people listen to God is because they know they will get something in return. No one, proclaims Satan, is really motivated by love. To test this claim, we have the character of Job: a good man to whom bad things start happening. He loses his animals, his servants, and even his children. And Job manages even in the face of such unimaginable loss to bless the name of God.

We also know loss. As we try to cope with our grief, along come our friends with all their helpful advice. They try to explain. They try to make sense of it all. Which leads them to wondering just what it is you did wrong. Really, what *did* you do wrong? Aw come on now, there must be something! Just turn around and make it right! But there is nothing you have done wrong. Nothing at least to deserve this kind of suffering. And so at last you shake your fist at God.

Finally, Job is covered with sores that make him a social outcast and cause him incredible pain. It is at that point, that Job says nothing at all.

---

3. Job 1: 6–21 (NRSV).

The silence is more than Job's wife can bear and she offers Job this helpful advice, "Why don't you just curse God and die! Get it over with, Sweetheart. It just isn't worth living like this." But Job refuses.

For seven days Job's friends sit with him in silence. So profound was his grief that they had no other way to respond to it. Silence is an amazing gift if you are able to give it to someone else. When we are truly silent with each other something astounding happens. We are completely within our self and yet at the same time, we become exquisitely aware of the unspoken needs of the other. In silence we are uniquely and completely present to each other.

Nothing is going the way it's supposed to go. Yet Job, like his culture, like many in our own culture, believes that good deeds are rewarded and bad deeds are punished. It used to make a lot of sense. Until it doesn't any more. Until there are no more easy categories of right and wrong, good and bad, just and unjust. Until we realize that much of life is an enigma and the logic with which we want to figure it all out, just doesn't work.

For most of us, however, silence doesn't come easy. Ellen Davis says, "Silence comes to us in grief as a comforter and we are afraid of it, for it invites us more deeply into ourselves, into the dark places in which doubts emerge and pain becomes fully perceptible, where loss can no longer be denied."[4] Silence challenges us to be healed when we wish simply to be soothed.

Out of the silence Job finds his words:

> Why did I not die at birth,
>   come forth from the womb and expire?
> Why were there knees to receive me,
>   or breasts for me to suck?
> Now I would be lying down and quiet;
>   I would be asleep; then I would be at rest
> with kings and counselors of the earth
>   who rebuild ruins for themselves,
> or with princes who have gold,
>   who fill their houses with silver.
> Or why was I not buried like a stillborn child,
>   like an infant that never sees the light?[5]

Out of silence Job learns to admit to his pain. Silence pushes Job to confront God. When Job finally finds words, he demands that God enter into the abyss of his loss and be revealed to him there.

4. Davis, *Getting Involved with God*, 127.
5. Job 3:11–16 (NRSV).

Unfortunately, Job's words are met with perhaps the worst blow of all—the reactions of his friends. No longer able to be present in the pain, no longer willing to remain silent, they begin to speak. In long, droning monologues they argue for the sake of their own tightly held convictions, unwilling to move beyond them even when confronted with the reality of a friend's pain. Foolishly they think their explanations can somehow offer relief for Job's suffering.

Sadly, all of their explanations require blame—they need someone to be responsible. These friends are so intent on affirming their own beliefs about life and how God works in it, that they lay that blame right at Job's own sore covered feet.

Job doesn't disagree. But he does demand that he be shown what it is he has done wrong. What evidence is there to convict him? Eventually he gives up trying to communicate with his friend and directs his argument squarely at God. Job dares to declare God unjust, a dishonest judge who condemns the blameless. And it is in this ranting against God that we see the clearest proof of Job's faith. Despite all that has come before, Job holds on to the hope that someone will hear his words.

The acute paradox at the heart of this book is that Job rails against God, not as a skeptic but as a believer. Job moves from lying in the fetal position wishing he had never been born, to opening his eyes to realities he has never seen before. He discovers that his agony is not unique. He finally notices that the suffering of the innocent is rampant. His eyes are opened at last to that which he never really noticed when he himself was fortunate.

It is the depth of Job's commitment to his vision of a just and ethical God that makes his rage so fierce—and that will finally compel an answer from God. For rage and blame directed at God are valid moments in the life of faith. In fact, we may stay in that moment for a very long time.

Job shouts and rages and then he falls once more into silence and he will not speak again until God has answered him. When that answer finally comes, it comes in the whirlwind . . .

> Who is this that darkens counsel by words without knowledge?
> Gird up your loins like a man,
>   I will question you, and you shall declare to me.
>
> Where were you when I laid the foundation of the earth?
>   Tell me, if you have understanding.
> Who determined its measurements — surely you know!
>   Or who stretched the line upon it?
> On what were its bases sunk,
>   or who laid its cornerstone

> when the morning stars sang together
> and all the heavenly beings shouted for joy?
>
> Or who shut in the sea with doors
> when it burst out from the womb? —
> when I made the clouds its garment,
> and thick darkness its swaddling band,
> and prescribed bounds for it,
> and set bars and doors,
> and said, 'Thus far shall you come, and no farther,
> and here shall your proud waves be stopped'?
>
> Have you commanded the morning since your days began,
> and caused the dawn to know its place,
> so that it might take hold of the skirts of the earth,
> and the wicked be shaken out of it?
> It is changed like clay under the seal,
> and it is dyed like a garment.
> Light is withheld from the wicked,
> and their uplifted arm is broken.
>
> Have you entered into the springs of the sea,
> or walked in the recesses of the deep?
> Have the gates of death been revealed to you,
> or have you seen the gates of deep darkness?
> Have you comprehended the expanse of the earth?
> Declare, if you know all this.
> Where is the way to the dwelling of light,
> and where is the place of darkness,
> that you may take it to its territory
> and that you may discern the paths to its home?
> Surely you know, for you were born then,
> and the number of your days is great![6]

God doesn't take the side of Job's friends in this argument. God doesn't support the notion that worldly rewards are dispensed in accordance with our goodness or lack thereof. In fact, God never even answers Job's question. The most remarkable part of this whole drama is the complete mismatch between Job's demand and God's response.

It seems that God is simply not interested in answering the question that has perhaps always perplexed the human heart. In the end, all of our

---

6. Job 38: 2–31(NRSV).

moral calculations are irrelevant, because this world cannot be reduced to simple morality.

If that's true, then maybe suffering is, after all, not a theological necessity. As David Bentley Hart so eloquently states, "For even though God can bring good out of evil, the wisdom of the Biblical faith is that suffering, death and evil have no ultimate value or spiritual meaning at all. The cross of Christ represents not the validation of pain and suffering, but their ultimate overthrow."[7]

God's answer doesn't explain the reason for suffering in the world. Instead God seems to say: "Look away from yourself, Job. Look just for a moment through my eyes and see this world in all its intricacy and wild beauty. The beauty is in the wildness, Job. You cannot tame all that frightens you without losing the beauty. So take your place in a ravishing but dangerous world, where only those who give up their expectations can live in peace." The great question out of the whirlwind is: "Can you love what you cannot control?"

Having heard God, Job returns to silence. Not the silence of frustration or disgust. This is the silence of having desire fulfilled. Job has seen God. God has entered into the abyss with Job and has responded to his cries. And as a result Job has a new appreciation for the human condition and his own place in the world.

Conclusion

The book of Job looks at first glance like it wrestles with the question of whether or not God is just. But the true focus of Job is on human pain. How Job endures it, cries out, lashes out at God, and ultimately transcends his pain and is transformed by it.

According to Davis we find in this book the theology of a sufferer—one who has passed through a door that only pain will open and who is qualified to speak of God in a way that others, whom we generally call more fortunate, cannot speak.

And what of us? Well, we have been to the theatre. It's a happy ending. We are told that the latter days of Job are filled with more blessings then the beginning. He has more livestock and goes on to father seven more sons and three more daughters. When he finally dies, he is old and full of days.

Of course, we know that these new children can never replace the ones Job has lost. We realize that the question of justice has been asked and

---

7. Hart, *The Doors of the Sea*, 69.

has been left unanswered. We can never again pretend that we know the answers, that we can totally predict or control the experiences of our lives.

We will continue to ponder the question. But in the end, the truth of God is amazingly large, mysterious, stubborn, and elusive and it is only when we can give up our need for certainty and embrace the mystery, that we may finally find peace.

> In the end the contemplative suffers the anguish of realizing that he no longer knows what God is.[8]
>
> —THOMAS MERTON

An Invitation for Reflection:

1. When have you felt Job's pain?
2. How did your friends and comforters respond? How did God respond?
3. At the end of the story, the surest indication we have of Job's renewal is his willingness to have more children. How much did it cost Job to become a father again? How could he open himself up again to the terrible vulnerability of loving those whom he cannot protect against suffering and death?
4. How has your own faith been broken and/or strengthened as a result of your suffering?

---

8. Merton, *New Seeds of Contemplation*, 13.

7

Don Miguel Ruiz' *The Four Agreements*

> *Reality is merely an illusion,*
> *albeit a very persistent one.*[1]
>
> —ALBERT EINSTEIN

Exposing the Lie

As the story of Job illustrates, 2000 years ago there was a prevailing belief that if you were wealthy, you were right with God and if you were poor, you were obviously sinful. The lie was that good acts and good behavior necessarily bring earthly rewards. Those who have much are obviously "more holy than thou." Into this paradigm came Jesus, challenging the prevailing worldview, intent on shedding light on the lie. In our own current time, one modern voice trying to expose the lies that shape our lives is Don Miguel Ruiz. Jesus' parable of Lazarus provides an intriguing framework from which to explore Ruiz' book *The Four Agreements*.

> Luke 16
>
> Narrator: There was a rich man who was dressed in purple and fine linen and who feasted sumptuously every day. And at his

---

1. Einstein, "Brainy Quote," line 1–2.

gate lay a poor man named Lazarus, covered with sores, who longed to satisfy his hunger with what fell from the rich man's table; even the dogs would come and lick his sores. The poor man died and was carried away by the angels to be with Abraham. The rich man also died and was buried. In Hades, where he was being tormented, he looked up and saw Abraham far away with Lazarus by his side. He called out, "Father Abraham, have mercy on me, and send Lazarus to dip the tip of his finger in water and cool my tongue; for I am in agony in these flames."

Abraham: "Child, remember that during your lifetime you received your good things, and Lazarus in like manner evil things; but now he is comforted here, and you are in agony. Besides all this, between you and us a great chasm has been fixed, so that those who might want to pass from here to you cannot do so, and no one can cross from there to us."

Rich Man: "Then, father, I beg you to send him to my father's house—for I have five brothers—that he may warn them, so that they will not also come into this place of torment."

Abraham: "They have Moses and the prophets; they should listen to them."

Rich Man: "No, father Abraham; but if someone goes to them from the dead, they will repent."

Abraham: "If they do not listen to Moses and the prophets, neither will they be convinced even if someone rises from the dead."

I want to make my most important point about this parable right away. Jesus was not a literalist. This is not a passage that says the poor will finally get the reward they deserve and the rich will finally know what it's like to suffer. It is not a passage about finally getting justice in the afterlife. It is not a passage to encourage you to wallow in your suffering because one day you'll go to heaven. And it is not a passage meant to make you gloat that someday the people who treated you poorly are going to burn in hell.

What this passage is, is Jesus exposing the lie. Remember Job? As soon as things started going poorly for him, all of his friends—even his wife—believed the lie. They believed that if bad things were happening to Job then he better get himself right with God. It had to be his fault. There had to be something wrong in his heart or in his mind. But they were wrong. Job didn't fit their social conditioning or the dream everyone was living in.

Now Jesus speaks and, in his story, reinforces the same lesson. Lazarus isn't suffering because he's a bad person. The rich man isn't rich because he is godly. The importance of this declaration is that it means there is no justification for a two-tiered social system of haves and have-nots. Jesus challenges the entire social structure of the time and exposes it as a lie.

But that exposure didn't mean the lie went away. Today we still feel that lie somewhere deep inside of us. It is a cultural lie, a collective lie that on the surface we deny, but deep down we too often believe, especially as we consider those who suffer. It's easy to find reasons to blame people for their circumstances. Conveniently, when we bring judgment to other people's situations, it allows us to continue perpetuating the injustices of hunger and poverty. But perhaps there is no place where our judgment is harsher than in relation to our own life. When things aren't going well, we blame ourselves, beat ourselves up, and spiral into a hell of our own making.

Believing this lie makes it so much easier to believe the other lies we've been told as well. And we have bought a whole boatload of lies, hook, line, and sinker. It's not our fault. We didn't know any better. But all of our lives there have been people telling us lies. Telling us what we could or could not do, what was acceptable and what was not. Parents, teachers, politicians, and religious leaders. It's not their fault either—they were only passing on the same lies they had been told. As a result, here we are living lives full of lies.

Here is an example. I grew up in the Lutheran church. It was a good church. I learned a lot there and am grateful for that background and my roots. But one of the lies I absorbed was that as unworthy and miserable and undeserving as I was, God still loved me.

Now think about that. I was taught to be grateful that God could somehow love me. If I was so miserable and unworthy that it would take God to love me, how could I ever expect that anyone else could love me at all?

Now the church thought it was proclaiming a good message—one of God's love—but it was also telling me I was worthless and essentially unlovable. Not a good message for a kid to absorb. Not a good message to try to live with.

Recognizing those lies and giving them up is the subject of *The Four Agreements*. Ruiz maintains that we are taught what to believe. When we go along we are rewarded for being "good" and when we don't go along, we are punished. Eventually we become our own law enforcer. We create a Book of Law that includes all of the things we have been told to believe, especially about ourselves. Then we become our own Judge who rewards us when we're "good" and punishes us when we don't follow the rules of our own Book. Another part of us becomes the Victim. That's the part that carries all of the blame, the guilt, and the shame for never being able to live up to our own image of ourself.

Ruiz makes a point early in his book about mistakes. How many times, he asks, do we pay for our mistakes? The answer, he concludes, is thousands of times. Human beings are the only animals that don't pay for a mistake once and move on. We make a mistake, judge ourselves, find ourselves guilty, and punish ourselves. But because we have such a powerful memory we don't stop there. We remember the mistake, find ourselves guilty once more and punish ourselves over and over again. If we're really lucky, we have other people in our lives to remind us of our mistake so we can pay for it yet again.

We suffer because we believe the lie that we are supposed to suffer. In fact, this is another lie the traditional Christian church, even with the best of intentions, easily propagates. That is the lie that venerates suffering. The most obvious example is the suffering of Jesus that is horrifically glorified in Mel Gibson's movie *The Passion of the Christ*. The Christian tradition is awash in pictures and iconography of saints whose faces reflect suffering and pain. We can all too easily internalize and interpret these images: "Oh, I get it! To be perfect, I am supposed to be like them. I am here to suffer in patience and then when I die I can receive my reward in heaven. Maybe then I'll finally be perfect!"

It's using the story of Lazarus and the rich man in a way Jesus never intended—to support a lie of suffering that keeps us trapped in our own hell on earth.

The truth is that no one judges us more harshly than we judge ourselves and as a result no one abuses us more. As a survivor of more than one abusive relationship in my life, I resonate strongly with Ruiz' observation that if we are with someone who abuses us slightly more than we abuse ourselves, we will eventually leave. But if we are with someone who abuses us just a little less than we abuse ourselves, we're likely to stay forever.

We stay because we believe we deserve it, that we aren't worthy of love and respect. We believe we aren't good enough. We stay because we believe the lie. We believe the image of perfection we have in our minds for ourself and because we can't ever be that image of perfection, we reject ourselves. We don't accept ourselves as we are and we don't accept others. But when we discard the lie, when we can begin to love and accept ourselves just as we are, we begin to climb out of hell and toward heaven.

Ruiz doesn't have anything to tell us that we haven't heard before. The wisdom he shares is ancient and is found in the teachings of spiritual leaders throughout the ages. As Jesus told us 2000 years ago, we can trade in the old agreements and start living a different life today. We can be reborn. We can live in happiness and joy.

Ruiz suggests we do that by living with four new agreements. The first of those agreements is to be Impeccable with Our Word. I introduced the concept of being impeccable in our speech earlier in the book and now want to expound on that ideal.

The word is a powerful force. In fact, the Christian scriptures testify that the Word calls creation into being. Just as God spoke creation into existence, the word we speak also creates. With our word we have the power to create great beauty, and we have the power to destroy. The word can imprison us or, as our scriptures celebrate, the Word can set us free.

All of our life people have used their words to share their own opinions. When we believe those opinions, we give other people the power to create our world. When my grandfather was a young man, someone told him he couldn't dance, and he never danced again. He never once danced with his wife. In fact, it broke my heart that at his 50th wedding anniversary grandpa was still refusing to dance a single dance with grandma—because he believed that ridiculous lie. He believed that he couldn't dance.

What does it mean to be impeccable with our word? It means that we never use the word to speak against ourself. We talk to ourselves all the time. What kind of things do you hear yourself say? Are you more inclined to congratulate and console yourself or to recount what you see as flaws and failings? Do you remind yourself that you are beautiful and holy or berate yourself for being fat or stupid? Being impeccable with your word means that you never use the word against yourself. It means you take responsibility for your actions, but you don't judge or blame yourself. You don't reject yourself—you don't reject who you are.

Being impeccable with our word also means that we don't gossip or use our speech to judge or blame anyone else. In our culture, gossip is a sickness that infects nearly all of our communication. We talk about other individuals, other groups, and other countries all of the time. We form opinions about people we don't even know and then we share them with others, passing along a generous dose of emotional poison as we do. We use the word to keep other people down and to make other people feel as badly as we do.

We use our word against others because we don't love ourselves. If I don't love myself, I will use my word to express anger, jealousy, envy, or hate. If I use my word to send my emotional poison to someone else, that poison will return to me. If I love myself, I will express that love in all of my interactions.

I'll give you an example. When my first husband and I divorced, I worried about what people would think of me. So in my defensiveness, I would make sure when my divorce came up that the reason did too—and that reason proved conclusively, of course, that the divorce was entirely my ex-husband's fault. People would listen to me and agree with what I said, not even knowing this man. I was spreading poison for no good reason at all. Not only that, but I believed I was pursuing justice with my word. He had done something wrong and he had not adequately paid for it. Of course, all of this regularly came back to haunt me as he responded to my emotional poison with anger and hatred of his own.

But the more I love myself, the more I am overwhelmed with the desire to love others—all others—well. So I can recognize and admit my role in a broken relationship without beating myself up about it. And I can recognize his role in the breakdown and forgive him for it. We will never be best friends, but today I experience a wonderful freedom from the prison of fear and anger in which I voluntarily stayed for so long.

We can use new agreements to replace the agreements that make us suffer. Being impeccable with our word is the first agreement. We all seek to transcend lives of hell in order to live today in heaven, to live a life infused with freedom, happiness, and love. A first step is to acknowledge that the integrity of our word is directly proportional to our level of self-love. Then we can decide to use our word toward truth and love, beginning by telling ourselves regularly and often how wonderful we are. Because, my friends, that's no lie.

Assumptions

We began by looking at the lies we have believed about others and mostly about ourselves. Lies that make us create an image of ourself that we can never live up to. Lies that make us judge ourselves and blame ourselves and reject ourselves. Then we embraced the fact that we don't need to believe those lies any more. We can trade in all the agreements that keep us in hell and begin living in heaven today.

The first agreement is to be impeccable with our word. The next two agreements are: Don't Take Anything Personally and Don't Make Assumptions. We started unpacking the story of Lazarus and the Rich Man and that's where we will return in order to explore the second and third agreements.

Imagine how you might feel in Lazarus' shoes. How would you react to the rich man and presumably lots of other people passing you by, ignoring your plea for help, not even seeing you as they hurry on their way? I can imagine that bit-by-bit it would have to tear away at my sense of self. I imagine I would feel more and more shame and worthlessness with every look avoided and every need ignored. Don't you think he would begin to wonder why he had been born so flawed, so imperfect, so wrong? Wow. Every day he must have felt a little more of the pain of living in hell—not so much because he was poor or sick—but because he most likely took the actions of others personally—as a reflection not of their own character but of him.

We human beings are fascinating creatures. At the same time that we so often feel small and insignificant, we also think everything is about us. It is our most inherently selfish trait—to think it is all about us. If someone is kind to us, we wonder what we did to earn that kindness. If someone is unkind, we wonder what it is we did wrong. The fact is that nothing anybody ever does—for good or for bad—is ultimately about you. It is really about them and their world and maybe the image of you they carry in that world.

People you see, including you and me and everyone reading this book, live in their own minds. We all have our own opinions. We all see the world a little differently. We are each utterly unique. So what we say and what we do are based on the agreements we carry in our own mind.

Isn't that true? How often do you agree 100 percent with anyone else in your life? You disagree not because one of you is right and one of you is wrong, but simply because you see things differently, you experience things differently, and you live with different expectations about the world around you.

Think about that one person in your life who can drive you crazy, who can bring out the worst in you, who you think needs to change. Have you ever noticed that the whole world doesn't feel the same way about that person? Other people actually like that person! How you feel about anyone else is really all about you.

Let's look at this from the other direction. Other people have opinions about you. It's rare that anyone is absolutely universally loved and admired, so chances are someone thinks you're a pain in the neck, while someone else thinks you're absolutely wonderful. Either way, those opinions really have nothing to do with you.

You see, there is a difference between you and who people think you are. The people in your life have an image of you—and you are not that image. You are always just you, perfectly you. Not only that, but other people also develop images of what they think you should be. When we don't live up to the image they have of us, they are apt to tell us so. We can get really torn up about that and wonder how we can be more perfect, how we can fit an image of perfection held in someone else's mind. As a result we can spend a whole lot of our time living in hell. Or we can realize that we are perfect just as we are and that other people's opinions have nothing to do with us.

I was a football mom when Alex was in middle school. His team played Wednesday nights. One week we played an away game in Newaygo. There was a parent sitting four rows up and one set of bleachers to the right who was verbally assaulting the referees of that game. There were other parents who seemed perfectly content with the calls being made. There was one gentleman who kept talking about the things the coach was doing wrong. There was another who kept noting with appreciation that the coach was doing a good job. And all of that came out of the minds of those parents and had nothing to do with the referees or the coach.

Now if the referees and the coach don't know that, they might spend some pretty sleepless nights worrying about their performance, second-guessing their actions and their responses, getting hung up on thinking they have failed to meet the expectations of their role. But if they know better, they leave each game knowing people carry their own baggage, that they did the best they could do, and that they will not take any of the comments—for good or for bad—personally.

It makes sense, doesn't it? The fact that the rich man kept passing him by and refusing to help had nothing to do with Lazarus at all. It only ever had everything to do with the rich man—with his worldview, with his own character, with the hell he chose to live in.

Which leads us to the agreement to not take things personally. When you are immune to the opinions and actions of others, you won't be the victim of needless suffering. There is enough genuine suffering in this world that we all endure that it just doesn't make sense to take on any needless suffering at all. When we really see other people as they are, we can never be hurt by what they say or do. If someone is causing us pain, if they refuse to treat us with love and respect, then it is a gift if they walk away or if we can find the courage to walk away from them. Walking away hurts for a while, but our hearts are durable and they eventually heal. Ultimately, we will find that we don't need to trust others to tell us about ourself and what we do well or not so well. Instead we need to trust ourself and the decisions we make.

The second and third agreements (don't take anything personally and don't make assumptions) go hand in hand. How often do we make assumptions about what someone else is thinking or feeling? Of course, our most common and immediate assumption is that we take things personally. The problem with assumptions is that we think they are true.

We also assume other people will know what we want and automatically respond. To live by the third agreement, we have to be willing to state as clearly as possible just what it is we need and want. No one will read our minds. We must find our voice and know we always have the right to ask. Now it is also true that everybody has the right to respond with either a yes or a no, but it is up to us to give others that option.

I had a particularly difficult week while I was reading *The Four Agreements*. There were simply too many demands on my time. I had all of my regular work to accomplish, a funeral to lead, in-laws arriving late in the week, and a close relative getting married. I thought it was pretty obvious that I would need extra hours in my office to get everything done. But I didn't say so. I didn't ask for extra time that would take me away from the family. So when my then husband mentioned missing me, I took it personally and immediately became defensive.

Once we talked it all out, it became abundantly clear. Both of us had assumed the other would read our minds and neither of us had clearly asked for what we needed. Neither of us had asked the questions that would have kept us from making false assumptions about each other. Making assumptions can lead to a lot of fights, a lot of difficulties, a lot of misunderstandings even with the people we love the most.

We make assumptions because we want to understand what is happening around us. We want answers. And assumptions give us answers—even if they're not accurate. A much better strategy is to ask questions. Asking takes courage. It requires acknowledging that other people don't see the world the same way we do, that they can't read our minds and that they might not even agree with us. We have agreements inside us that keep us fearful of conflict or disagreement. But the only way to come to understanding and to really nurture our relationships is to stop making assumptions and to start asking questions.

Here's the lie that I think causes us to make the most assumptions: The Golden Rule. Yes, I think the Golden Rule is a great big golden lie. Because the golden rule tells us to treat other people the way we want to be treated. The problem is people don't want to be treated like *we* want to be treated. They want to be treated like *they* want to be treated. The only way to do that is to stop making assumptions and realize that other people just don't feel and think and act exactly the way we feel and think and act, as much as we may wish they did.

So what if Lazarus had this all figured out? What if he knew that the rich man and the other people passing him by were living in their own worlds? What if he didn't assume that they shared the same values and realized that he didn't need to take their ignoring his needs personally? Well then, he probably asked God to bless and forgive that rich man and all the others every time they walked by. Forgive them for they do not know what they are doing, they do not know that they are choosing to live in hell. Then, even in the midst of his poverty and sickness and the kind of life none of us wants to romanticize or wish for, in the midst of his pain, and in the midst of all those unhappy people hoarding their wealth and living in fear, Lazarus would still have been living in heaven.

We can too. No matter how bad the circumstances are in which we find ourselves, we can live in heaven in the midst of it all. When we stop assuming that everything is about us, when we stop taking the things other people say and do personally, when we ask questions to better understand the people around us, when we find the courage to ask for what we need, and when we finally recognize our own inherent value, our own perfection, *then* we also live in heaven on earth today.

Do Your Best

The last agreement recognizes how hard the first three can be. Oh, they sound simple and straightforward enough, but once you try to live by them, you'll find it terribly difficult to do. At least I do.

The fourth agreement is to Do Your Best. Your best will vary from day to day and even from moment to moment. Some days you will be feeling healthy and strong and confident. You will feel yourself excelling at the agreements. At other times, you will feel your breath taken away by life's circumstances, and you will realize how hard it is to live in heaven when all around you people are convinced that we all should be living in hell.

The Four Agreements are meant to be tools—ways of thinking and processing what is happening around you so that you can stay grounded and centered in the midst of chaos. They are not meant to be another set of rules that you must comply with at all costs. The most obscene use of the four agreements would be to add them to the list of things you expect your perfect image of yourself to be able to do all the time. The four agreements are not a new standard by which to judge yourself and find yourself coming up short when you don't keep them perfectly.

Some days you'll be really good at it and some you won't. As much as you try to avoid it, there will be times when you get caught up in the drama of the lives around you. Life will throw you a curve ball and you'll find yourself struggling in the grips of anxiety or fear. Your confidence will slip and the old agreements will come back to you with a vengeance. From time to time you will feel the pull of envy, jealousy, anger, and hate. And that's okay, because really you're only human.

Being human is not, however, an excuse for not doing your best. Even when you are consumed with negative emotions, you have choices about how you will react and respond to them. The four agreements are among your choices. One of those choices is to recognize that you are doing your best. Doing your best allows you to stay in the game, to keep trying even when it's so very hard to do. If you break an agreement, you get the chance to try to keep it again. When you do your best there is nothing to criticize yourself for. You don't need to judge yourself and you don't need to live with regret.

To live without regret means to live fully in the moment. There is nothing in the past that we can change. There are no do-overs in this life. So we have to learn to live with the consequences of our actions and then let things go. We need to let our grudges and resentments go, let our disappointments and our heartbreaks go, let our mistakes and our failures go. We need to live each day simply doing our best.

To let go of the past is to welcome what Ruiz calls the Angel of Death. He writes that the Angel of Death takes away the past in order to make it possible for life to continue. For every moment that is past, the angel of death keeps taking the part that is dead and we keep living in the present. In the present we can experience Awakening, Enlightenment, Resurrection. We can know firsthand the birth of something new that emerges out of the ashes of the past. When we refuse to let go of the past, when we insist on carrying the past with us, it makes it awfully heavy to be alive and pretty impossible to be alive in the present.

Forgiveness is really the key to letting go of the past and living in heaven today. We have all been given ample experiences and hurts to forgive in our lives. Some we have forgiven easily. Others have taken great effort. Still others we continue to carry with us. And the fact is, forgiveness can sometimes be a dangerous thing to do. When we forgive before taking care of ourselves, forgiveness can be lethal. I'm reminded of the play *Oliver!*[2] in which Nancy sings about loving her abusive boyfriend, staying with him right or wrong as long as he needs her. By the end of the play, he has killed her. Safety must come first and self-protection always takes precedence over quick forgiveness.

Once protections are in place, the important work of forgiveness can begin, and must begin for our own sake. Forgiveness is an essential part of our healing. Forgiveness really isn't something we do for someone else; it is something we do for ourselves. We forgive so that we can move into the future without being burdened by grievances of the past.

People do terrible things to each other. Relationships are torn apart. Sometimes there is abuse, and even when there is no physical harm,

---

2. Bart, *Oliver!* 1962.

the damage done to the psyche can be even more lasting and painful as we struggle to not take things personally. All of us have unfinished business—relationships that are unresolved and which require forgiveness. A relationship is unfinished business if it still makes us feel uncomfortable emotionally or if we still expect something from the other person. We will know we have forgiven other people when they no longer cause a reaction in us. Healing unfinished business is one of our most important spiritual tasks. We have to forgive our parents, our sisters and brothers, our friends, our enemies, *and* we have to forgive God. When we finally forgive God, then we can forgive ourself. We will know we've forgiven ourself when we accept ourself just as we are. We will no longer reject ourself, abuse ourself, or fail to see the beauty and perfection of ourself.

Like many people, I had a more-than-strained relationship with my father. For many years I thought the best option was to simply not have anything to do with him. I figured I didn't wish him any ill will so that meant I had forgiven him. And I reasoned that there was no reason for me to have any contact with him. But whenever he did show up or call, or even become the topic of conversation, I could feel myself clench up inside. All the indicators of stress and anxiety would come up in me and I would get very defensive and protective of myself.

Through a lot of hard work, I finally did forgive my father. But there was more work to do. I realized that I had to forgive God for giving me a father who could never be what I needed him to be. When I did that, I discovered that I had to forgive myself for failing to live up to my image of the perfect child who could have deserved or earned or created the perfect father. Today I don't feel any aversion toward Dad at all. And I have discovered much about my own beauty and strength of character.

Forgiveness allows us to shed our toxic feelings and free ourselves of revenge and resentment so that the original hurt stops throbbing. You may have been terribly wounded, I have been terribly wounded, but those wounds do not have to keep being inflicted upon us, re-inflamed by our own heart and mind. So we journey forward with forgiveness as our destination. Forgiveness is an inner state, not an outer act. Forgiveness is not something we can simply decide to do. It is something that happens once we have struggled with our own feelings, searched for meaning, and healed. Forgiveness is a process that may take one night or many years.

In Buddhism there is a state of compassionate detachment. This state allows one to step outside their self and rise above the human level in order to see the wider scope of humanity. If we try to see our tangle of hurts and emotions from God's point of view, things take on another dimension. God knows all of the hurts that both sides have experienced in their pasts, and how that past pain contributed to the current dispute. God knows how that pain makes each person act out in ways that hurt themselves and others. God doesn't pick sides. God just sees the tragedy of human victims trying to make their way in a difficult world while carrying all of their own wounds and scars.

Heinrich Heine's quote about forgiveness always makes me smile. He says, "I love to sin. God loves to forgive. Really, this world is admirably arranged."[3] Unfortunately, sometimes the most difficult person for us to forgive is ourself. How many of us, having been forgiven, continue to drag our supposed shortcomings, sins, mistakes, and failings with us throughout our life, even when the weight makes us stumble, even when it keeps us from moving forward at all? We who strive to be compassionate toward others also need to learn to see ourselves with compassionate eyes. Can we who ask that others treat us with respect, require the same of ourselves? Can we remove ourselves from the twisted snarls of guilt and past failures so that we can get on with what God has in store for us? Guilt disables us. Forgiveness frees us to live lives of love and grace toward others.

Let's look one more time at the story of the rich man and Lazarus. As I read this parable one more time, something new grabbed my attention. I was stunned that the rich man just doesn't get it. First, he somehow manages to completely ignore Lazarus because he's quite comfortable believing the lie of the world, the lie that says he and Lazarus are obviously each getting what they deserve.

But then he dies, and lo and behold and much to his surprise, he finds himself not in heaven enjoying his riches but experiencing torment in Hades. Even more shocking, Lazarus is in heaven sitting at Abraham's side. Wake-up call? You might think so . . . but what does the rich man do? He tells Abraham to send Lazarus with water on his finger to quench his own parched tongue. Did you get that? He *still* thinks of Lazarus as a servant, as lesser than, as the person who should be ordered to bring the rich man some relief! Incredible!!

When Abraham explains that such a request just isn't an option, the rich man starts asking that his brothers be warned about the fate that awaits them. Surely if someone from the dead tells them they'll listen. But they don't need someone from the dead. They have living reminders around them every single day. We have living reminders around us every single day. Lazarus is the homeless, the sick, the destitute, and he will always be with us.

But there's still one other way, I believe, to understand this story. All of us are pretty good at not seeing the things about ourselves that we don't

3. Heine, "Looking Up Content," line 3.

like. As a result, we project it onto others. The things that annoy us about other people are usually the things we don't like about ourselves. We also are pretty good at admiring people who have the positive traits we have and don't feel we can claim about ourselves. So another way to understand the rich man and Lazarus are as parts of the same person. We all have the capacity for doing good and doing evil and doing nothing at all.

Let's use the images of this story to look at ourselves through another lens. Let's imagine for a moment that the rich man and Lazarus are not two different people, but two aspects of one person. And let's imagine that we are that person. Now let's stand in the shoes of the rich man and let's pretend that Lazarus represents the old, sick, festering agreements that we carry along with us everywhere we go.

If we really want to do our best, the first thing we need is awareness. We have to be able to see the bad agreements that we are living with—the ones that make us treat others poorly and treat ourselves worst of all. We have to be able to *see* Lazarus, and then we have to realize that Lazarus is not separate from us, not lower or worse, but part of who we are. We have to become aware of the lies by which we live our lives. Then we need to replace them with healthy truths about ourselves and the people and the world around us.

When we start to challenge the beliefs we've never questioned before, the things we've been told about right and wrong, the opinions we've been given about what we can and cannot do, we will find that most of them aren't even true. We'll find that we have all done a lot of suffering for nothing. Ruiz writes: "Your life is a manifestation of your dream; it is an art. And you can change your life any time if you aren't enjoying the dream."[4]

You don't need to have it all figured out. Doing your best is about acting without complete knowledge or understanding—because you will rarely have that anyway. Doing your best means you take risks and allow yourself to live knowing you are making the best choices you can with the information available to you. Things won't always work out the way you hoped or thought they would. But that doesn't mean you didn't do your best.

To do your best you don't need to memorize the pages of Ruiz' book and do it exactly the way he suggests or has done himself. You don't have to perfect the agreements in your own consciousness so that you are always impeccable with your word, that you never take anything personally, and that you never make assumptions. Really, all you ever have to do is your best.

---

4. Ruiz, *The Four Agreements*, 44.

Living the Four Agreements

Ruiz' insights are important because they help us understand the way in which well-meaning people have taught us lies about the world and about ourself. These lies make it difficult if not impossible for us to see our own perfection, so we end up spending a lot of time judging ourselves, blaming ourselves, and beating ourselves up. In other words, we spend a lot of time living in hell.

But all of those lies and bad agreements can be traded in for new agreements so that we can live in heaven today. The four agreements give us a pretty solid foundation for pursuing our own individual health as we deal with the chaos that will frequently move around and even within us. But what does living by the four agreements look like in a practical sense?

If we were always impeccable with our word, about half of the things I hear people say wouldn't be said at all. None of us would apologize for who we are or what we bring to the table. None of us would put ourselves down or talk about being inadequate. As a people who are impeccable with our word, we would use our speech only toward love and truth—beginning with ourselves. That means we would use our words to praise and celebrate who we are, and in doing that we would move closer and closer to truly accepting ourselves just as we are.

As we love and accept ourselves, we will more fully love and accept each other. You and I cannot change other people. We either love them the way they are or we don't. We accept them the way they are or we don't. But first we need to accept ourself and love ourself just the way we are. As Four Agreements practitioners, we would love ourselves and love each other, using our word only to build each other up in the interest of love and truth.

What if we lived by the second agreement and refused to take anything personally? Well the first thing we would do is stop interpreting anybody else's actions as having anything to do with us. Let me share with you a really painful example of how it hurts when we as individuals take things personally.

There was a man who was very involved in the Extended Grace community. Then he suddenly stopped coming. It was several months before I was able to get him to share with me his reason for leaving. He said he had not felt welcome when a woman who had been warm to him suddenly turned "cold," avoiding him and his hug of greeting. He thought she was rejecting him. What he didn't know was that just a few days before, while she was walking on her college campus at night, she had been raped. What this man had interpreted as "coldness" obviously had nothing to do with him. How sad for both of them and the whole community that he chose to take her actions personally.

When we stop taking things personally, we stop trying to make ourselves the center of anyone else's lives. We won't interpret anyone else's actions as a sign of something we did or as something being directed toward us. When you and I stop taking things personally we will finally understand that everything is *not* about You and everything is *not* about Me.

The third agreement is to not make assumptions. As individuals who live by this agreement, we will take the time to ask questions for clarification and tell others what we need. When we are feeling burdened and in need of help ourselves, we will trust that we can bring our needs to the important people in our lives and ask other people to support us in our need. We will also understand that there are times we might ask for something someone else cannot give us. Everyone always has the right to choose how they will respond to a request we make. But we won't expect anyone to read our minds. Instead we will replace assumptions with conversation that is open, honest, and full of grace.

The last agreement is to do our best. Living by the four agreements, we will appreciate our efforts and refuse to beat ourselves up when we fail to keep an agreement. We will refrain from judging how well or poorly anyone else is keeping the agreements, knowing that they too are doing the best they can do, and that they, like us, will also stumble now and then. And every time we stumble, we will celebrate that we now have the opportunity to begin living by the four agreements all over again! As Carl Bard said, "Though no one can go back and make a brand new start, anyone can start from now and make a new ending."[5]

As people who live by the four agreements, we will be a people who play with others well! We will see each other and ourselves with different eyes—in fact, we will see the whole world with the eyes of love. Each one of us will know that God is within us and within each person we see. We will see love coming from everyone, even when they are angry or sad.

As people who live by the four agreements, we will be happy, joyful, and free of unnecessary conflict. We will no longer behave according to how others think we should behave because we'll know that we aren't responsible for anyone else's opinion. And just as no one will control us, we will have no need to control the thoughts or actions of anyone around us.

As people who live by the four agreements, we will also weep loudly and often, lamenting the places in life in which love is absent and fear is strong. We will commit ourselves ever more fully to exposing the lies that

---

5. Bard, "The Quote Archive," lines 1–3.

keep people imprisoned in suffering and sorrow, and to spreading a universal message of love and peace.

As people who live by the four agreements, we will lay down our burdens of guilt and blame. Since we no longer have any reason to judge ourselves, we will no longer have any desire to judge anyone else; which means we will simply forgive others and let things go.

As people who live by the four agreements, we will live without fear. We will let go of all our hesitation and truly, completely love one another without expectation or requirement. We will not be afraid to love or to be loved. We will not be afraid to express our dreams and to live them as fully as possible. We will not be afraid to risk, to explore, to experiment, to live fully, or to die.

And we will finally know that we are perfect. We will live in a state of bliss, a state of grace. We will know the promise of heaven. We will know we have a choice to suffer or to be happy—and we will choose happiness.

*When the power, the energy of truth is well released,
then everything becomes good.*[6]

—THOMAS MERTON

An Invitation for Reflection:

1. What is a lie you've been told about what you can't do or should be?
2. When have you been less than impeccable with your word? What will you do to try to be impeccable with your word beginning now?
3. When have you taken something personally and how might you keep from doing so in the future?
4. When have you assumed people know what you want? How do you ask for what you need?
5. What have you let go/forgiven from the past? How has that helped you to live in the present?
6. How do you know when you are doing your best—or not? What agreement is easiest/hardest for you?

---

6. Merton, *A Vow of Conversation*, 111.

8

Real Relationships

The only common factor in all of my dysfunctional relationships is me.

—ANONYMOUS

Redefining Intimacy

ALL OF OUR COMMUNICATION skills and all of our agreements about life come into play in our interactions with others. We are all caught up in the midst of many relationships. They each have their own unique shape and texture. Some feel comfortable, some are scratchy, and some are downright painful. Some fill us with happiness and joy, others with anger and grief. Some bring out the best in who we are and others seem intent on lowering us to our most base and immature instincts. Each one of them has something to offer us, a gift, a lesson, an insight. Some relationships form by happenstance and others by intent. And each of them offers us an opportunity for intimacy.

Intimacy is an important word for us to define because we can all bring lots of assumptions to that word. Often we confuse intimacy with "closeness" or "sameness." We begin to think that intimacy is about agreement. It's hard to "feel" intimate with someone we disagree with. But the fact is we *are* different. A truly intimate relationship requires the ability to understand that we all see things differently, we all manage anxiety differently, and we all navigate relationships differently.

In her book *The Dance of Intimacy,* Harriet Lerner uses this definition: "An intimate relationship is one in which neither party silences, sacrifices or betrays the self and each party expresses strength and vulnerability, weakness and competence in a balanced way."[1]

Simply put, intimacy in a relationship means that we can be who we are and we can let the other person do the same. That means we can talk about the things that are important to us, take a stand on issues we care about, and state clearly what our boundaries are—what limits are acceptable to us and what we cannot tolerate in the relationship. It means we allow, and at our best invite, the other person to do the same. In an intimate relationship we can stay connected to each other without needing to change, convince, or fix the other person.

The truth is that we can't change other people anyway so it's really a waste of precious time and energy to try. Don Miguel Ruiz makes this point in his book *The Mastery of Love* by using animal analogies. A dog is a dog. No matter what you do, a dog is still a dog. You can never make a dog be a cat or a horse. To try to change someone into being more like you want them to be is like trying to change a dog into a cat. It's never going to happen. And the sooner you can understand and appreciate this, the sooner you'll gain valuable insights into your relationships. Because you'll begin to see people as they really are and not as you want them to be.

This awareness also frees you from the idea that you are responsible for anyone else in a relationship. You are responsible for yourself, for your half, not the other. Just as you can't change anyone, you can't make anyone else happy, you can't fill their every need, and you are not responsible for trying. When we feel responsible for someone else's feelings or growth or well-being, we begin to stop being ourself. We start trying to be what other people want us to be, to meet the expectations they have of us. We put on the masks of our false selves and we enter into a false relationship.

To be in an intimate relationship with another person requires us to move between connection and separateness. It means nurturing the relationship, the "we," but it also, and with equal importance, means nurturing the "I." That means that we are responsible for our own self and our own happiness. We can never look to anyone else to make us happy or to complete us. This kind of love and acceptance always has to come from within. It also understands that the same is true for the other. We cannot complete anyone else—and we are not responsible for anyone else's happiness.

---

1. Lerner, *The Dance of Intimacy,* 3.

Developing and maintaining intimate relationships is no easy task. It requires a clear self, relentless introspection, open communication, and profound respect for the myriad of ways in which we and the other are different. It also requires the capacity to stay emotionally connected to others during times of anxiety.

So if relationships take so darn much work, why do we bother at all? Ken Wilber says it goes back to the beginning. Imagine yourself as God, as infinite being, as I AM-ness itself. How enjoyable can that be over the course of billions of years? Simply put, it's no fun eating alone. So God throws God's self into the universe—and creates other beings so that relationships might form and grow.[2]

To use this image is also to fully appreciate the second face of God—the living God that dwells in every other person you know. Every one of them! You simply can't treat people poorly; you can't disrespect them or abuse them when you see them as an embodiment of God. And you simply can't treat yourself poorly, disrespect yourself, abuse yourself, or allow others to abuse you when you see yourself as an embodiment of God.

This hasn't always happened in our lives. People have not always treated us well. In fact, all of us have been hurt and wounded in one way or another. Those hurts and wounds have always happened in relationships. It's no wonder, then, that we need relationships, healthy, life-giving relationships, in order to repair and heal from those wounds.

If we are currently in relationships that are not healthy, not nurturing, that do not promote our own growth and development, in which we are stuck, we need to remember that we can only change and control ourselves. And that we are always responsible for our half of the relationship. No one abuses us more than we abuse ourself. When we choose to treat ourselves with love, respect, and compassion, we will insist that all of the people with whom we are in relationships treat us with love, respect, and compassion.

Finally, we enter into relationships because we want someone to witness our life with us. An unwitnessed life is a tragedy. But a witnessed life is a life fully lived. To be a witness to someone else's life is a remarkable gift. It is what I find so joyful about working in ministry. Over and over again, people actually invite me to be a witness to their life. Not to problem-solve, not to judge, not even to affirm, but to simply be a witness to their life as it unfolds. People are also inviting you to be a witness to their life. Not to problem solve, not to judge, not even to affirm, but to simply be a witness to their life as it unfolds.

2. Wilber, *One Taste*, 194.

Working It Out

One woman nearly drove me crazy when I started working as a barista at the coffee house. She was the matriarch of the coffee shop, having worked there for decades. She was bossy and opinionated and critical. She also felt entitled to take a break whenever a friend arrived or she felt like it. Space was tight and it was impossible not to cross paths even if you could avoid cross words. Then it finally hit me. This woman felt threatened by the new guard. Everyone being hired was young and energetic and had ideas of their own. Times were changing. She was old enough to have retired years ago, but she didn't want to lose her sense of place in the world. When I understood that, when I could see the threat that I represented through her eyes, everything changed. I left the coffee shop with genuine love and respect for this woman.

We began by defining an intimate relationship as one in which you let me be who I am and I let you be who you are. Now we will get a little more specific as we look at workplace relationships. In the workplace, we are apt to settle for something less than intimacy. What we really long for among coworkers is agreement. When we agree in the workplace, we tap into creativity and are able to get things done.

As you think about your workplace experiences, think about separating people into two groups: those you agree with and those you put up with. The people we agree with at work tend to be the people we like and trust. The basis of trust is understanding.

When there is a breakdown in understanding, we usually don't see it that way. We don't go around saying we misunderstand people. Instead we tend to say, "I understand him—he's a jerk!" Or, "I understand her—she's an idiot!" We tend to say strong things about people we don't understand and usually those are not very positive things.

One huge step we can take toward improving our workplace relationships is to seek to understand the people we work with. The basis of understanding is communication. Right away we have a problem because people say things their way and we hear them our way. Communication is based on our ability to listen to the other person and to actually hear what they are saying. It means listening to them from their point of view. This is a huge barrier because nothing affects how we hear things as much as our own point of view.

If my point of view gets control of me, it impairs my sight and blocks understanding. I need to start by getting a solid understanding of why I think and feel the way I do. Then I can strive to understand and appreciate why you think and feel the way you do. The minute I do that, I am going to tear down the barrier. Our goal at work is to see from the other person's point of view to get in agreement and get things accomplished.

When I worked for Mercy Health, I became a certified Management By Strengths (MBS) trainer. The foundation of MBS is very much like the DiSC Profile or Meyer-Briggs Assessment. In brief, the foci of the different personality types are:

> Direct—Focus on getting results, being in control and solving problems
> Extroverted—Focus on people and teamwork
> Paced—Focus on timing, harmony, and cooperation
> Structured—Focus on being right and doing the right thing

Knowing your own point of view and knowing another person's point of view allows you to approach them the way they want to be treated, rather than the way you want to be treated. Knowing these different styles of communication can go a long way toward improving our workplace relationships, but they don't fix everything.

People will still annoy us and there are times we will hold our breath in frustration and bafflement. So the most important thing we can do at work and in all settings is to remember to breathe, deeply and slowly. Breathing keeps us centered, grounded, and focused. Most of us are pretty good at breathing in. What we need to remember is to breathe out, fully and completely.

Self-introspection is another wonderful tool. What is it that annoys me about this person? Usually what annoys us the most about someone else is something we don't like about ourselves. If we can look objectively at our reactions to others and be brutally honest in our own self-assessment, we can discover something about our shadow, truths about ourselves we have been denying, so that we can name and reclaim those parts of us we have tried to get rid of.

As people of faith we have yet another tool. We believe that the Divine lives within each of us. Author and Social Entrepreneur Carmel McConnell offers this advice: "Mentally acknowledge that everyone is in transition to perfection, some further down the road than others. This helps you to let go of the desire to judge, blame, and snipe."[3]

It is a worthwhile exercise to picture in your own mind someone with whom you have found it difficult to work. It could be someone you're struggling with right now or it could be someone you've worked with in the past.

---

3. Deeble, "Don't Let Them Bug You," October 10, 2003.

Picture them and then see in them the Spirit that lives in us all. Take a deep breath, exhale, and then love them with the Spirit that lives in you.

Relating to Friends

Teresa and I worked together at the urgent care center I used to manage. She ran the Worker's Compensation side of the program. We worked well together, respected each other, trusted each other, liked each other. Teresa and I, workplace partners, became friends.

One day while at work I received a nightmare phone call. My three-and-a-half-year-old son had been severely injured. It ushered in for me the absolute worst crisis of my entire life. As I sat crying in my office, there was only one person who I could think of to turn to. That was Teresa. I will always be grateful for her presence in my life and the way she walked with me through that time of darkness and kept me from despair.

A few years later I was downsized and no longer worked with Teresa. After a few feeble attempts to stay in touch, we drifted apart. I have run into her a few times since, usually at one restaurant or another, and we embrace and say things about getting together. But we don't. I guess I've come to think of Teresa and I as friends for a season.

Circumstances produce both friends and comrades. Comradeship is the feeling of empathy that draws people together in times of war or when people have a mutual enemy or even a common goal. Wartime always brings with it this comradeship, which is the opposite of friendship. Comradeship, that ecstatic bliss and exotic glow that comes with belonging to the crowd in wartime, is seductive and intoxicating. As the war ends, or a common enemy recedes, or a common goal is met or no longer shared, comrades return to being strangers, while friendships that form in the same circumstances continue.

Have you had similar experiences? Friendships that formed in a particular place around a particular reason and then simply faded away? Is there someone that was once vitally important to you, and then you simply lost track? Perhaps you moved away, perhaps they did. You know what I think? I think that's just fine. I think we do make friends for a season. I think Spirit does provide people to accompany us on our journey and that the length of that journey is not nearly so important as the opportunity to walk the path side by side with someone who cares.

The fact that I never socialize with Teresa, that we have no common interests, that our lives have taken us far from each other doesn't make what we shared any less authentic. It doesn't mean we didn't care for each other and love each other deeply. It doesn't mean that our friendship wasn't a gift and a blessing. I will forever be grateful to Teresa and I know she will always hold me in her heart as well.

Of course, there are other friendships, too. Those that endure far beyond a season.

If we are fortunate, we have someone in whose presence we can say the things we don't mean. With any luck, we know someone with which we can be our "ugly" selves without worrying about creating a bad image of us in their mind.

I met John when I was working for Habitat for Humanity; he was pastoring a church. We wrote a grant that allowed us to hire a person who would be a bridge between families in the Habitat program and families at the church. When my grandfather died, he conducted the funeral. When I began working for the Bishop, we started talking more regularly about theology and social justice. When I decided to pursue ordination, he introduced me to seminary. And in the midst of all of this, something grew beyond a workplace relationship.

John became a colleague in a time when I began struggling with the traditional religion in which I was raised. When I felt "different" from those around me, he let me know I was not alone. He became a mentor with whom I could discuss the joys and difficulties of beginning a new ministry. He became a trusted confidant and one of the rare people who had witnessed my tears. He was someone with whom I could be my ugly self and say things I didn't even mean and know that he would see behind and beyond all that to the real and authentic me within. John became my friend.

Human beings are meant to be in relationships with each other. There are certain aspects in life that all of us crave. Friendship provides these aspects: trust, support, communication, loyalty, understanding, empathy, and intimacy. We have been defining intimacy as a relationship in which you let me be who I am and I let you be who you are. In friendship it isn't just about letting you be who you are, it's about sincerely liking who you are—not needing to change you or fix you or make you any different than who you are. And it's about knowing that you like me the way I am, even as I seek to grow and develop and mature. It means relaxing into the knowledge that you accept me just as I am wherever I am on that long, long, long, long road toward perfection.

Friendship does not always last forever. Sometimes friendships need to end. Sometimes we discover that we are locked in unhealthy and even self-destructive patterns and that our current relationships keep us there. Sometimes our values change and we need to find support and encouragement to live out the new values we hold rather than slipping back into that which we no longer claim for ourselves.

When we feel more judged than listened to, more criticized than respected, or when people drain us of all our emotional energy and fail to return any emotional investment of their own, it's time to follow our intuition and seek out more life-giving relationships. When we are moving out of our own unhealthy addictions and people seek to draw us back and hold us captive to our old ways of being, we need to trust ourselves and our Creator Spirit and seek out more life-giving, life-enhancing, life-generating relationships.

So how do we go about cultivating life-giving, life-enhancing, life-generating friendships? We start with healthy and bounded self-disclosure. We don't start by dumping all of our life history and emotional angst onto everyone we meet to see who might pick up on our neediness and befriend us. Instead, we start by sharing a few private thoughts and feelings with one person, someone who is our equal and with whom we share similar values, one person whom we might want for a friend. If they are responsive, they will probably share a thought or two with us. If not, don't think of it as rejection. They can't possibly be rejecting you if they don't even know you yet!

Listening to and acknowledging the other continues to build the friendship. Friendship doesn't demand agreement, it simply desires to be heard and understood. You can practice active listening by repeating back what you've heard, not dismissing or invalidating what anyone else feels, and not needing to problem-solve or change the other person.

As your friend speaks, you also find yourself willing to share information in return. Not fixing or problem-solving information, but information about your own experience or observations or feelings. Because talking is just as important as listening in friendship. When only person does the talking, chances are they are lecturing, bossing, or using the other as a counselor instead of enjoying the gift of a mutual friendship.

Friendship, like self-development, moves along in stages of sorts. At each stage, friendship offers exactly what we need in the way we need it.

Our earliest friendships form around the need to fit in, to belong. We look to friends to provide us with the input we need to form opinions and we remain friends with those whose worldviews mirror our own. I remember feeling fierce loyalty to friends at this stage, including the day I defended my friend Carolyn from Bobby's verbal assault on a walk home from elementary school and ended up nursing my own bloody nose after he punched me. At this stage, we are willing to die for a friend.

As we become more comfortable with ourselves as individuals, as we stand on our own two feet and begin thinking and reasoning for ourself, our friendships begin focusing around common interests. In high school all of my friends were in drama. We had a lot of fun hanging out and exploring our own rebellious nature in a world of parents and teachers who sought to confine us to their own interpretations of right and wrong behavior. Eventually these interest-based friendships drifted away, but they made us ripe for the next stage of friendship and its desire for emotional bonding.

As maturity led to greater introspection, my true friendships deepened, and my view of friendship expanded so that in some sense I felt newly connected to people I had not even met before. There was a spirituality behind relationships that added meaning and significance and that called on me to contribute even more than I received.

An important marker in all of these relationships seems to be a degree of harmony and cohesion. Neither harmony nor cohesion is a bad thing and neither should be avoided. But these days I also feel the pull toward yet another way of relating to friends. When my own self evolves and deepens, when I become more whole, I realize that the absence of conflict—in and of itself—is not higher wholeness, but death.

Authentic friendship—where human beings are creative partners, lovers of life, God, and Spirit—requires individuals to be able to come together and conflict with each other in the most creative way possible. It's not necessarily going to be peaceful, but it will be ecstatic. As we harness the spiritual and emotional energy of creative conflict, we are challenged and released into ever-deeper immersion into the great unknown where ultimately we don't know anything and we know everything we ever need to know.

This kind of friendship requires a great deal of individual autonomy and independence. It means embracing and dancing and arguing and fighting in the most creative ways with other people. But for that to happen, we really have to get beyond our egos. Then it isn't egos that are creating friction, but the God impulse itself, manifested in our own authentic self.

We all go into the world to do our best. We put on the appropriate clothes and pick up the proper tools and perform. We experience highs and lows, setbacks and successes, trials and tribulations, and sweet victories. And when all of that work is done, we come "home" to our friends. We relax, we put up our feet, and we let out a sigh. We remember to breathe.

As human beings, we were not created to live in isolation, separated and removed from other human beings. We were created for relationship. We were created in order to find joy and life and play and love, grace and depth and laughter and beauty in the eyes and the touch and the hearts of each other. We were created to find in each other and in ourselves the very presence of the God who makes us One.

Family Ties

Doggone it. Here I was a grown woman with kids of my own. I had done all the pastoral care classes and studied the basics of counseling. I had identified all the scripts and bad agreements I was raised with. I had met with all of my family members and done the hard work of revealing, understanding, and forgiving. I had made peace with my past! And in the midst of the real issues of my life, raising teenagers, working out relationships, struggling to find any time for solitude, dealing with my shadow, I found myself in therapy . . . talking about my father . . . again.

Of all the relationships we form, none affect us more than our family of origin. In fact, nothing will affect all of our other relationships more than the relationships we had and have with our parents and our siblings.

So far we've been exploring the relationships over which we can exercise some control. We get to choose who our friends will be, what friendships we will nurture and which we will let go. Even in the workplace, we can ultimately choose to quit our job and surround ourselves with an entirely different set of people and comrades. But family is family. You get what you get, like it or not.

And like it or not, the way you relate to your family will influence the way you relate to the world, to other people, and to yourself. Let's face it. You live with these people during every one of your most formative years. You are shaped and molded by them, even if your shape and mold is a result of consciously refusing to fit the shape and mold they expect of you.

At their best, our families are where we learn true intimacy, relationships in which each person is accepted just as they are. Period. There is a secret to real intimacy, and that secret is Self-Focus. It might take a minute for that to sink in. It certainly is counter-intuitive. Normally we think that if we are going to be intimate with someone, we need to focus on him or her—sometimes what they want or need, but more often what they should or shouldn't do. And as soon as we know or even suspect what someone else should or shouldn't do, we have moved into the position of judging and out of the position of intimacy.

If we really want intimacy, if we really want to connect to someone else in a deep and profound way, we need two things. First, we have to recognize that we can't change anybody else. Despite our best intentions and our most sincere efforts, we can't make a cat be a dog. We just can't.

Second, and even more humbling, we have to admit that we are not experts on anybody else. We really don't know when another person is ready to do their own emotional work or how they will tolerate change. Let's admit it. We rarely know this much about ourselves! The beauty of it all is that the less we become an expert on the other, the more we become an expert on the self. It is an unexpected move. In order to connect with someone else, we need to start with separation. We need to begin with our "I."

Now here's where that darn family stuff comes in. In slowly moving toward more connectedness with members of our own family, we actually move toward more separateness as a self. Let me repeat that. The more we connect with family—not distance from them—the more we move toward separateness as a self, which allows us ultimately to form more solid and healthy connections with others.

How, you might ask, can that be? Well, it can be because when we have few connections with extended family and one or more cutoffs with a parent or sibling, we bring unresolved tension and reactivity to our other relationships. The degree to which we are distant and cut off from our first family is directly related to the amount of intensity and reactivity we bring to other relationships.

David Deida invites us into an experience that demonstrates this truth. In his book *Instant Enlightenment*, he suggests that we silently offer the most extravagant praise possible to the next person we see. Then he suggests we remember our mother or father as we are offering this praise and see how we feel. He notes that we have probably chosen a career and sought out an intimate partner in reaction to the praise we never got from our parents. Finally, he invites us to take time to remember what we didn't get from our mother and father while pondering what we seek through our career and our most intimate relationship.[4]

I suppose it was the work I did around my dad that week and the topic of family relationships I was studying at the time that led me to make the call. My sister who lives in Muskegon about 20 minutes away from me answered the phone on the first ring. I asked her if she would join me at Extended Grace to "model" sisterhood with me. She wasn't available. She had plans. Then I asked if she'd like to come have dinner some time. She wasn't available. She said this is her really busy time, being bowling season and all.

This little exchange tells you a whole lot about our relationship. I was the only child until I was 18 months old and my sister was born. As I grew, I would have given almost anything to have an older brother or sister. I longed to have someone to show me the ropes and introduce me to cute boys. But my younger sister didn't want anything to do with me. It turns out that as easy as it is for me to blame all of my neuroses on my father, the most recent research coming out of the United States, Canada, and Europe is that it is our siblings more than anyone else who have the greatest impact

---

4. Deida, *Instant Enlightenment*, 45–8.

on how we turn out and who we become—more that our peers, even more than our parents.

If you think about it, it really does make a lot of sense. In terms of sheer volume of hours, we who have siblings spent more time with them while we were growing up than we did with friends, parents, teachers, or even by ourselves.

According to an article in TIME magazine titled *The New Science of Siblings*, our brothers and sisters are our collaborators and co-conspirators, our role models, and our bad examples. They are our scolds, protectors, tormentors, playmates, counselors, sources of envy, and objects of pride. They teach us how to resolve conflict and how not to, how to conduct friendships and when to walk away from them. Sisters teach brothers about the mysteries of girls; brothers teach sisters about the puzzle of boys. Our spouses arrive comparatively late in our lives; our parents eventually leave us. Our siblings may be the only people we'll ever know who truly qualify as partners for life. Closeness often deepens as time goes by. Even siblings who drift apart in their middle years, tend to drift back together as they age.[5]

Because my own two children spent so much of their time growing up in fisticuffs with each other, I was particularly drawn to what the research says about childhood fighting. Turns out that siblings have some sort of conflict practically all the time. Beginning between the ages of 2 and 4, brothers and sisters clash an average of once every 10 minutes. There is, fortunately, good news. As frustrating as these squabbles can be for mom and dad, they offer the ideal classroom for kids to figure out how conflicts, once begun, can be settled. Unlike friends, you're stuck with your siblings. You really have no other choice than to learn to negotiate things day after day. One of the greatest gifts of siblings is that over time, conflicts tend to fade and even the fiercest sibling wars leave little lasting damage. Even those with troubled or self-destructive siblings come away with something valuable. They learn patience, acceptance, resilience, and cautionary lessons.

One of our natural assumptions about siblings might be that they tend to emulate each other—and they do. Younger siblings try to copy their older brothers and sisters while older siblings try new things so a younger brother or sister won't show them up. But the opposite dynamic also happens and it can have important repercussions. These are the situations in which a sibling doesn't mirror the other, but instead differentiates him or herself—a phenomenon called de-identification.[6]

---

5. Kluger, "The New Science of Siblings," July 10, 2006.
6. Idem.

De-identification helps kids define themselves as individuals and it provides for early self-focus. It can even help push some kids away from risky behavior. We all think of an older brother who smokes, drinks, or uses drugs as putting his younger brothers and sisters at risk for doing the same. And this is depressingly true. But the research shows that some kids break this mold for a surprising reason.

One study of teen pregnancy showed that younger sisters who didn't follow their older sister's example didn't do so out of wisdom and practicality, but simply because it was a different choice to make. One teen mom is a crisis. Two teen moms has a "been there done that" feel to it. So the younger sister purposely chooses the other direction. She decides her sister's role is to be a teen mom and her role is to be a high achiever at school and elsewhere. One conspicuous way to set yourself apart from a sibling is to look at their behavior or habits, and then do the opposite.[7]

Some of us experienced true intimacy within the family system. Others of us learned the art of avoiding intimacy. No matter what our past or present relationships with our family of origin consist of, we are all wonderful and beautiful manifestations of Spirit. We are all cherished beyond measure, even if we didn't learn that in the family systems in which we were raised. The good news is that the Divine knows us intimately *and* accepts and loves us just as we are. In fact, we are loved and accepted beyond what we would have ever dared dream for ourself. No matter what our family or any of our other relationships may lead us to believe, we are lovable and worthy and beautiful and accepted just as we are.

At the same time, we are called to take the same love that is poured out into us, and pour it out into others. We are called into relationship, into the great human family, into our own family of origin, knowing that it is only in relationship with others that we ultimately find the healing and wholeness and intimacy we seek.

Significant Other

Most of us seek one person with which to share our day-to-day lives. The traditional relationship was a marriage—a husband and a wife. But there is no requirement that you marry your significant other. In fact, in many states, our gay and lesbian friends don't have that option. More and more people are finding alternative ways to shape their relationship with that one special person in their life.

7. Idem.

Once upon a time, people didn't even get to choose who that special person would be. People were paired to whomever their parents or the community matchmaker deemed as a suitable fit. If a couple was lucky, they might find some day that they loved each other. My favorite scene in *Fiddler On the Roof* is when Tevye asks Golde if she loves him and eventually she confesses that if her experience isn't love, she doesn't know what love is.[8]

By the end of *Fiddler on the Roof,* the girls that Tevye and Golde raised have all chosen their own life partners. We are left to presume that they all lived happily ever after. But is that really how the story ends? What is the epilogue? The fact is we don't have any stories in our culture for what comes next. Those of us in partnered relationships today find ourselves living in the midst of marriage and divorce and options that have not even been explored. We are on the cutting edge of knowing the way we're going about things now isn't working for lots of people—and not quite knowing what the new way of going about things might be.

As insights are gained and doors are opened, we're beginning to discover that our significant other is not only a choice to begin with, but a choice we continue to make. A partner might travel with us through 50 years of shared living. Or they might travel at our side for a season.

Whenever and wherever we feel stuck on that journey, we need to remember that we can only change and control ourselves. It is up to us to be perfectly honest with ourselves about our own identity and that of our partner. We need to see them as they are, not as we want them to be. If we cannot accept them as they are, if we want a dog, and they are most assuredly a cat, then we owe it to ourselves and to them not to try to make them into a dog but to determine if we can really live with a cat—or whether our relationship has served us well and now needs to be celebrated and allowed to take a new shape.

We can only make that kind of choice when we do not *need* the relationship. This is true for all of our relationships. If we are truly convinced that we cannot live without our husband's support, our mother's inheritance, our current job, or the room in our parents' house, our own bottom-line position may be togetherness at any cost. We may not articulate this bottom line or even be conscious of it. But we live it.

Only after we can be confident of our safety and survival can we maintain a position of self-focus with dignity and firmness. We simply cannot navigate clearly within a relationship unless we can live without it. But when we are firmly grounded in our own identity, we can find a healthy connection to one special person to whom we pledge our love.

8. Stein, *Fiddler on the Roof,* September 22, 1964.

Love is something bigger than any one of us. Human love can be a portal to experiencing Divine Love. Love is something more than a feeling or a sensation, even more than something we fall into or out of. It is rather a mystical gift through which we are broken open to experience firsthand the Divine.

That doesn't mean love is easy or simple or even necessarily forever. Our culture makes it far too easy to either minimize or idealize a committed love relationship. Sadly, the failure of love that we see so often in this world of ours often leads to a scaling down of our expectations, visions, and dreams. It is tragic that many expect from the very beginning that in their love relationships there will be no mystical wholeness at all. In truth, there is no perfect relationship or any bond between two people that is without struggle. But when two people know that reality and choose together to willingly embrace that struggle there are immeasurable blessings to reap.

When the struggles come, and they always do, it is time to start practicing love. Just like a musician practices playing their instrument or an athlete practices their sport, we can practice love in order to participate more artfully and to deepen our experience. Practicing love means that when you want to look away from each other, you look more deeply into each other's eyes. It means that when you want to hold your breath, you begin to breathe more deeply with each other. It means that when you want to shut down, you open up. Practicing love means that you will spend less time trying to figure your partner out, and more time working to understand yourself more deeply, so that you might come to experience the presence of the Divine that dwells within you, deep beneath the layers of protective ego.

It is an important insight to realize that any two-person relationship is inherently unstable. Holding each other, we can keep our balance for a while, but eventually that balance fails and we either walk away separately or we crash together to the floor. Just as a stool needs three legs to keep from collapsing, a couple needs a third element to help them stand together for the long term. This stabilizing agent can change along the way. Without ever realizing this dynamic, most couples instinctively find the "'third thing." Sometimes that third thing is positive and nurturing. They may have a child, share a common activity, or take their relationship to a counselor. Other times that third thing is destructive and heartbreaking, coming in the form of an illness, alcoholism, or an affair. These additions are all good strategies for shifting a couple's focus on something else as the "problem" while avoiding working on the relationship itself, even as the relationship continues to disintegrate and decay.

In our culture we often hear phrases like "you complete me" or "the two will become one." We are misled by Hallmark sentiments when we think we are meant to merge into a single person. No such thing happens. Two people remain two people, deeply connected but always separate. We need, instead of merging into another, to become so self-focused and so self-aware that we can be our most authentic independent self. Our challenge is to stay connected to each other while also being our own persons. When we can dance between identifying who we are as individuals and staying connected with each other, then we need never fear losing ourself or losing each other. Then we will be able to help, nurture, and support each other as we live and learn and grow. The best way to celebrate love and experience intimate communion with another is to simply relax into each other and spontaneously offer our deepest gifts.

Two people have to nourish the relationship they share, but they also have to nourish their own being and other important relationships in their life. We all do better with a community of support. When one person decides that one other person will forever fulfill all of their emotional, spiritual, and physical needs, it is just too much weight for any one person or any one relationship to bear. It is not fair of us to expect our partner, who is already our lover and life companion, to also be our therapist, aunt, uncle, parent, teacher, and priest. Especially when we expect to live to be one hundred years old and have decades of time ahead of us. Love for a significant other cannot thrive for long when it isolates the partners from other meaningful relationships.

Martin Buber said, "The other is like you and the other is not like you."[9] We cannot lay total claim to each other. There is a sacredness of the other, untouchable and inaccessible, which plunges us into a kind of powerlessness. To experience mystical love is to come face to face with that powerlessness. From the very beginning we are out of control. And so in our human relationships, at least, we have a choice. Not about the overwhelming sensation of love's energy, but how we will use that energy.

Love is a choice. It is an ongoing decision that we must make every day. When you choose love in every circumstance, then love will forever break you open to Divine love. Then the love you share not only will bring joy to you, your family, and your friends, but it will truly serve to sanctify the world.

Family of Choice

Sixth grade was excruciating for me. I was raised in a family, as most of us were, without having a lot of choice about those relationships. People were

---

9. Soelle, *The Silent Cry*, 130.

just there to connect to or not. School wasn't that much different. The only thing that mattered was geography. Because I lived at a particular address, I attended a predetermined school. Because we moved when I was in second grade, the kids I met at my new school all had previous relationships with each other, and I struggled to find a place I belonged. That only worsened as I got older. By the time I got into sixth grade I wanted more than anything to just disappear or be hit by a runaway train—which would be quite a feat in Fruitport, Michigan! I was desperate for community.

Then in seventh grade I got the courage to try out for a play. And I was cast. And life changed. The group of thespians at Fruitport Middle School became my first family of choice.

A family of choice is a community you belong to because you want to. It is a group with which you feel at home, or in some cases much better than at home. Relaxed, happy, confident. We find we are not alone, that we share similar thoughts or enjoy similar activities with other human beings. If we are lucky, we feel so comfortable that we show a side of us that doesn't normally come out at work or as we negotiate the complexities and demands of our everyday lives. We play.

My former professor Jaco Hamman knows the value of play. In his book *A Play-Full Life*, he maintains that play is essential to experiencing and maintaining physical, emotional, relational, and spiritual well-being. Play is life-giving and enriching. Play invites us to creatively engage ourself, others, and God. Play is an attitude toward life and a family of choice can be the perfect environment for developing such an attitude. So it is that Jaco combined this need for playfulness with the need for community and gathered a group together that met once a month. They were known as Men Eating Animals Together or M.E.A.T.

Experiencing the different dimensions of a family of choice answers the deep, pervading need within us to belong. As we choose to be part of such a community, we receive the gift of being accepted by the community. Unlike our parents, our siblings, or even the people sent to the same school as us, a family of choice receives us not because in some sense they have to, but only because they want to.

Families of choice also come with the same pitfalls as any relationship and may exhibit the same dysfunctional patterns of any family system. I didn't suddenly get self-esteem and emotional healthiness because I was accepted in the community. We carry into our relationships of choice all the things we learned and are in the relationships we didn't choose. There is the same danger of selling ourselves short, living out old scripts, and being less than our authentic selves. There is the same danger of trying to control and change others, of not allowing them to be their authentic selves. Once again, when we do our own work and deepen into our own authentic identity, when we become more whole and integrated individuals, then we naturally seek to bring that same depth and wholeness to our other relationships as well.

Families of choice are nothing new. I think of the group my grandparents met with once a week to play bridge and other card games, or the bowling league my father participated in for years. One of my friends grew up where there were regular neighborhood block parties. My mother found a family of choice by joining Weight Watchers. And all the members of my immediate family went to Sunday morning church. Such families of choice can serve a much greater purpose than simply offering distraction around a common interest. What they can offer us is a way in which to meet our holy desire to experience God.

When Mardie found Extended Grace she was in the process of transition, having lived life as a male she was finally becoming the woman she always knew herself to be. When Mardie's transgender identity could no longer remain secret, she lost her wife. Almost simultaneously, she was downsized from her job. Soon thereafter, she found herself in bankruptcy. Struggling to find her place in the midst of overwhelming change, she found her way to Extended Grace. There she found a community that welcomed her and loved her and supported her through her losses and the celebration of her newfound identity. She told me more than once that this community of choice saved her life.

Because we have been wounded in relationships, it is in relationships that we can find healing. And healthy communities are where this has the best chance of happening. We all seek health and wholeness. That is the original notion of salvation, the returning to or restoration of health and wholeness. Significantly, the Jewish scriptures never talk about individual salvation, but only the salvation of the people, the family, the community, the whole.

This is especially important news in a world where belonging to a family of choice doesn't seem to be assumed anymore. Sociologist Ray Oldenburg explored our proclivity for having three places: the home, the work environment, and one other place.[10] The other place was often membership in a church, but it could be involvement in a local service club, joining a support group, gathering with people around a hobby. Then a few years ago Robert Putnam, another sociologist, wrote the book *Bowling Alone* and

---

10. Oldenburg, *The Great Good Place*, 16.

called attention to the fact that we are becoming more and more isolated in our society.[11]

We might question the obvious contradiction of longing for community and keeping to ourself, but it makes perfect sense if you think about things like growth and development. A lot of us can relate to having been part of a community that wasn't all that healthy. It wasn't all that healthy because it really didn't want us to be who we are or to think like we did. It wanted us to fit a particular box and recite a particular set of beliefs and convictions. Many communities form on the basis of "us vs. them." For instance, imagine joining someone's political campaign and the excitement of having a common enemy. But what happens when "we" start sounding or acting more like "them?"

We are berated, condescended to, or simply kicked out. Many of us have come out of unhealthy communities that didn't allow for freedom of expression or even freedom of being. As individuals we moved through this crisis by focusing on ourself, doing our own work, becoming aware of what we actually thought and believed, of what we questioned and doubted, of what we needed in a new community. But to enter into community again is scary. We want it and we fear it. We know the downside and carry that baggage with us. We live with a certain kind of "been there done that" mentality in which we limit our own options.

Consequently, we immerse ourselves more fully in meeting requirements and responsibilities. In fact, we as a people can get so tied up in what we are "supposed" to do that we can fail to seek out a family of choice as part of a healthy well-rounded life plan. If we can't seek out a family of choice as part of our integral plan, we increase our likelihood of seeking out a family of choice not as an important part of our life, but as an escape from it. This is often the reality that brings people to local bars and watering holes. In a culture where we experience a holy hunger to experience God's passionate love, we discover that such passion has been exiled to places that encourage brief and superficial encounters with others. In a society where we feel a deep and holy longing for God's presence in our human interactions, we have created a pseudo-community—a place in which people gather, but rarely to connect with each other in profoundly healing and restorative ways.

On the other hand, true community can arise anywhere. In those same local bars and watering holes, for instance, regulars can come to have meaningful and long-lived friendships through repeated contact and the opportunity for sharing personal feelings and experiences. My friend Bobbi has come to treasure a whole new family of wonderful people that she met

---

11. Putnam, *Bowling Alone*, 2001.

while hanging out at Fenian's Bar in Conklin, Michigan. This group now does all kinds of things together outside of the pub, including kayak outings, dinner gatherings, attending each others weddings and funerals, and sharing everyday joys and sorrows.

God is present. Unlimited by our ideas of sacred and secular, God is in the midst of it all. Present in all of our relationships. Present where life and circumstance finds us. And present in our families of choice. Drawing us ever deeper into authentic relationship with each other and with the Divine. Leading us into self-awareness and self-focus so that we might know ourselves, and in knowing ourselves, enter into ever more rich and deepening relationships with others.

> *I must get on*
> *with being who I am*
> *as fully as I can,*
> *as unflinchingly as I can,*
> *as accurately as I can,*
> *which is to say,*
> *as gracefully,*
> *as powerfully,*
> *as faithfully*
> *as you have created me to be.*[12]
>
> —TED LODER

An Invitation for Reflection:

1. When is it difficult to be yourself? Do you ever feel you have to conform to the expectations of others to be loved or accepted?
2. What are the responsibilities of friendship?
3. How close are you to your siblings? What lessons did they teach you growing up?
4. What have you learned about yourself from a relationship with a significant other?
5. When has community called you into greater or lesser authenticity?

12. Loder, *Guerrillas of Grace*, 81.

9

Embracing Mysticism

You can kiss the sky, swallow the mountain, they are that close. Zen says "Swallow the Pacific Ocean in a single gulp," and that is the easiest thing in the world, when inside and outside are no longer two, when subject and object are nondual, when the looker and looked at are One Taste.[1]

—KEN WILBER

We Are All Mystics

JUST AS WE ARE all involved in relationships with other people, so too we are involved in a relationship with the Divine. This is a relationship worth pursuing! Mysticism is the direct experience of God. Mystical experiences happen in every culture and every faith tradition, among people of all different backgrounds and every walk of life. A seminal book on the topic is Dorothee Soelle's *A Silent Cry: Mysticism and Resistance*. Soelle's first undertaking is to rid us of the idea that mysticism is reserved for the elite.

In *Grace and Grit*, Ken and Treya Wilber write about a mystical experience Treya had when she was 13-years-old. She was sitting by herself in front of the fireplace when she suddenly felt as if she had become the smoke from the fire. She felt herself begin to rise up into the sky, higher and higher,

---

1. Wilber, *One Taste*, 82.

until she became one with all space. She experienced a complete dissolving of the self that felt very real and gave her a sense of coming home to the place she belonged. This mystical experience, though she rarely talked about it, became the central guiding principle in Treya's living and in her dying.

Soelle posits that the question to ask about mystical experiences is not "Who are these people? How are they special?" The question is "What kind of culture honors these experiences and which destroys them?"[2]

For example, childhood is ripe for mystical experiences of awe and amazement and wonder. Among the Native indigenous people of North America, a mother will begin a conversation with her children by asking, "What did you dream?" In my non-indigenous North American home I was more likely to lead with, "How was school? Do you have homework?" When our dreams and visions are not honored, they tend to become meaningless, embarrassing, or simply forgotten.

The truth is that all of us are mystics, and most of us have experienced heightened sensations of awareness or unity or being grasped by the certainty of God's presence in our life, often at very young ages. But in our haste to leave childhood behind, we may end up labeling those experiences as crazy or silly or the product of an overactive imagination. "The trivialization of life is perhaps the strongest anti-mystical force among us."[3]

We cut ourselves off from our own experiences by thinking of them as irrelevant. But mystical experience is not limited to the spiritual peak of contemplation. Mysticism is present in ordinary experience whenever we rise above the content of those experiences to find the hidden, non-rational, and subconscious aspects of those encounters. As St. John of the Cross writes: "God does not reserve this high calling of contemplation for particular souls. On the contrary, He is willing that all should embrace it. But He finds few who permit Him to work such sublime things for them."[4]

To have a mystical experience is to have an altered state of consciousness from an encounter with the Divine. This state is referred to as illumination, enlightenment, awakening, or the union of the soul with God. Soelle writes, "This union of the Divine-within and the Divine-without occurs in the spark of the soul. There is a fusion of the Divine that resides in every human being's soul with the Divine, who is absolute being and the ground of all that is. This ground and the individual breathing are one."[5]

---

2. Soelle, *The Silent Cry*, 11.
3. Ibid., 13.
4. Ibid., 10.
5. Ibid., 16.

The stunning message of the mystics is that at the very core of your being, you are God. The "you" that is God is not your individual isolated self or ego. In fact, the individual self or ego is exactly what blocks this realization in the first place. Rather, this "you" is the deepest part of you that transcends your mortal ego and directly partakes in the Divine. The Hindu Upanishads call it "subtle essence." In Judaism it is called "ruach." In Christianity it is the indwelling "pneuma" or spirit.

It is in transcending your mortal soul that you discover your immortal spirit, one with All. So that Paul proclaims, "I live, yet not I, but Christ in me." Paul, the Christian mystic, has discovered his True Self, which is one with Christ. It is the heart of the expression "Namaste" which means the Divine in me recognizes and bows to the Divine in you.

Mysticism is no different from the promises many religions describe in the language of being made whole, liberation, the peace of God, coming home, awakening, and redemption. But mysticism deals with these experiences differently, by lifting them out of doctrine and freeing them for feeling, experience, and certainty.

Grace makes us new, but those who experience grace only by belief, cannot feel or taste it. Doctrine is satisfied when it is accepted by belief, whereas mysticism claims that it is in existential experience, in the actual feeling of it, that we finally know what grace is all about.

To feel grace is to know ecstasy. Mystics claim a relationship with God based on love that arises not because of the demands of powerful institutions or of God, but out of utter freedom. Rabi'a, one of the most important figures in Sufi mysticism, walked along a street one day with a torch in one hand and a bucket of water in the other. When asked why, she replied, "I want to put fire to paradise and pour water over hell so that these two veils disappear and it becomes plain who venerates God for love and not for fear of hell or hope for paradise."[6]

In his book *One Taste*, Ken Wilber refers to beliefs about God as "cardboard nutrition for the soul, spiritually empty calories." He points out that usually between letting go of belief, on the one hand, and finding direct experience, on the other, we are carried by faith alone. "Faith soldiers on when belief becomes unbelievable, for faith hears the faint but direct call of a higher reality—of Spirit, of God, of Goddess, of Oneness—a higher reality that, being beyond the mind, is also beyond belief. Faith stands on the threshold of experience."[7]

---

6. Ibid., 35.
7. Wilber, *One Taste*, 292.

And how shall we experience God if not wholly, completely, and with every fiber of our being? It is all too normal for us to do what we do, work, laugh, cry, eat, meditate, touch with only part of ourselves. We are not wholly present in what we experience, we are still watching ourselves. We hang on to self-consciousness that does not allow the self-forgetfulness of being one with all. We do not play as a child can play; losing ourselves in the moment, becoming all ears, all eyes, all hands, all mouth, all body, all soul.

We need then to cultivate a different attentiveness, a different relationship between what we do and who we are. Wilber describes a mystic as one who does not see God as an object, but one who is immersed in God as an atmosphere.

Psychologist and philosopher William James identified four characteristics common to mystical experience:

1. The loss of all worry with a sense that all is well in the universe,
2. The sense of perceiving truths not known before about life's mysteries,
3. The world new and changed as if it has never been seen in the same way before, and
4. The ecstasy of happiness.[8]

Aldous Huxley describes three gates into mysticism: "We can begin at the bottom, with practice and morality; or at the top, with a consideration of metaphysical truths; or, finally, in the middle, at the focal point where mind and matter, action and thought have their meeting place in human psychology."[9]

The lower gate is preferred by teachers like Gautama Buddha and those who focus on practices that increase concentration, like yoga and breathing techniques. Philosophers and theologians who prefer speculative thought seek the upper gate. The middle gate is the way of spiritual religion exemplified by the Sufis of Islam and Christian contemplatives like Thomas Merton, who said we become contemplatives when God discovers God's self in us.

This experience of transcending the self is not limited to cloistered walls, spiritual masters, or people of a particular level of education, social class, or degree of maturity. It is simply the moment when any one of us is overwhelmed with God.

---

8. James, *The Varieties of Religious Experience*, 242.
9. Huxley, *The Perennial Philosophy*, 1.

The Language of Mysticism

There was nearly a violent overthrow of my first class at Seminary. It was a class for first-year students on Spiritual Formation.[10] I know it doesn't seem like the setting of a violent uprising, but I assure you it was. The source of the dispute? It wasn't a debate about women's ordination, or "just" war, or even homosexuality. It was a . . . prayer. Our professor, Dr. Steven Chase, was introducing us to the idea of Apophatic and Cataphatic Prayer.

Cataphatic means God can be found in all created things.

Apophatic means that God is above and beyond all of our knowing.

Cataphatic makes positive comments about what can be known of God.

Apophatic makes negative comments to show the limits of that knowledge.

The prayer understands that these two must be held together, the true and the insufficient. First it recognizes the Divine presence in all things in descending order and then recognizes in ascending order our limitations in trying to define God using human concepts and perceptions. An abbreviated version goes something like this:

> God is love
> God is being
> God is truth
> God is life
> God is lion
> God is sun
> God is rock
> God is not rock
> God is not sun
> God is not lion
> God is not life
> God is not truth
> God is not being
> God is not love
> God is love . . .

First we claim all that we know God is and then we admit that we can't begin to know all that God is.

Well, a lot of those first-year students didn't understand this practice, and in fact were outraged. They said they felt like they needed to ask God for forgiveness for saying anything so blasphemous as "God is not love."

---

10. Western Theological Seminary, Fall Semester, 2003.

embracing mysticism

The next day the mutiny was building in strength and power. Students were organizing a meeting to make an official complaint. We ended up having to devote another entire class period to letting these students unload while the professor tried patiently once more to explain this type of prayer.

I was pretty annoyed about the whole deal, and not a little concerned about whether I belonged in this place at all. While I did eventually conclude that I didn't belong in that seminary, I also came to conclude that their reaction wasn't entirely the students' fault. You see, they were being introduced to something completely foreign to them, coming as they did out of mainstream Christian churches around the country. They were being introduced to the language of the mystics.

As we defined it earlier, mysticism is the direct experience of God. The church is usually really good at doctrine and really good at theology, but it does a pretty poor job of introducing people to experience. We are not told about our own mystical nature. Nor are we introduced to the kind of transformation that is available to us when we cultivate a mystical awareness, attentiveness, and engagement with all of creation.

Despite this shortcoming, it is rare that a Christian mystic will leave Christianity. In fact, mystics in every religion tend to stay in their own lineage. Instead of seeing the teachings as archaic and the language as a barrier, they come to embrace deeper insight from the teachings and greater meaning in the words of their faith. In this way we also can move from those teachings that close us into the arrogance of believing we are among the few people God loves, to the witness of Jesus who opens us up to see the truths that exist across all religions, in the midst of all God's beloved people.

Dorothee Soelle shares an image of all of the world's religions in a circle. At the center of the circle is a giant X—the mystery of the world, the deity. All of the followers in all of those diverse religions are drawn to the X at the heart of the world and they give it names like Allah, Great Mother, Nirvana, and God. As we move away from the periphery of the circle toward the center, the smaller we become and the closer we draw to each other. The closer we come to the center, the less the differences between individual religions matter, until finally in the heart of God, they have disappeared completely.

As mystics we recognize that no person or group owns God. God is common to all creatures. As mystics we know that it is possible for us to be of one will with that God. As mystics we also know that language is utterly incapable of communicating that experience of oneness.

The more we come to know God, the more our language falters. According to Aldous Huxley, "Those who know God most perfectly perceive most clearly that God is infinitely incomprehensible."[11] This is certain: whatever image you have of God right now, whatever words you use to describe that image—that isn't God.

Meister Eckhart asked that God rid him of his idea of God. The God who is known and familiar is a small God, too small for the likes of Eckhart. To leave God for the sake of God is to relinquish a figure of God, a picture of God, or a manner of speaking of God. For us, that might mean finally letting go of the God of our childhood or of our family. In letting go of that which has become stagnant and predictable, we step into the experience of God, which is unpredictable and alive.

When we can say with confidence, "I do not know this God," we will speak not out of ignorance but out of a deeper knowledge than we have ever possessed. The way of the mystic is to forever seek new concepts, words, and images to describe this God; then to discard them as completely inadequate.

That is at the heart of cataphatic prayer. God is not this, not that, not what you already know or have seen or what somebody told you before.

The heart of apophatic prayer is that we persist in trying to find the words to speak so that we might offer up pure praise. Soelle says, "Given its exuberance, enchantment, and immediacy, mystical sensibility can only sound ridiculous in conventional language."[12] Don't travel the way of the mystics unless you're ready to sound ridiculous. Honestly, there will be a lot of people who cannot hear you and others who will be offended by what you say. Witness the reaction of my seminary colleagues to a beautifully mystical prayer.

What are we to do, then, in the midst of people of faith who know their doctrine and can wax eloquent on theology, but have never heard or considered an invitation into experience? According to Ken Wilber there are two functions for religion: translation and transformation. "Translation is the necessary and crucial function for the greater part of our lives and it requires an outpouring of words. But at some point those words, our latest translation, is no longer enough to console us. We find that the only path that satisfies is not a new belief for our self, but the need to transcend the self altogether."[13] For that we are going to need a new language: the language of the mystic.

The language of mysticism is paradoxical and poetic, and at its heart, it is counter-cultural. It is a language without dominance or hierarchy. It is the language not of obedience and separation, lord and servant, but of

---

11. Huxley, *The Perennial Philosophy*, 25.
12. Soelle, *The Silent Cry*, 59.
13. Wilber, *One Taste*, 27.

unity, oneness, and love. It fully embraces all three faces of God and claims access to God that is possible without the mediation of an institution or its appointed authorities. It's no coincidence that women, who in some places still cannot access the centers of spiritual power within the church, provide so many of the voices we hear in the realm of mysticism.

The final paradox in the language of mysticism is that it is a language of silence. Rumi spoke of a silence in which it is no longer we who speak our prayer, but God who speaks within us. Silence prepares us for the prayer that is infused by God. So Rumi advises us: "Do not speak, so that you may hear what cannot be uttered or described."[14] Silence is both a practice and a preparation, a kind of fasting from words. Silence is the way we make ourselves ready to hear the God who speaks in silence. In the silence we let go of all our images, all that our ego wants to hold onto, until we finally let go of our self.

We are all invited to take up our identity as mystics, but it won't be an easy thing to explain. There are no words to adequately speak of God's presence, and there are those who will ridicule or accuse you when you try. On the other hand there are others who will thank you with all of their heart and soul for giving voice to the experiences they have had and have not talked about for fear of being excluded or worse.

Our paths on the road to claiming our mystic identity will vary. I tend to be one of those people who want to get where I'm going as soon as possible. My preferred method of travel is flying. But if that can't happen, and if a long road trip is called for, then I want to make an excursion out of the trip itself. With the end point already established, and the assurance that I will eventually arrive, I enjoy noting the markers of the journey and making interesting side trips. Paying attention to the road signs, watching for oddities and being willing to be taken in by tourist traps along the way, makes the travel itself as exciting as reaching the final destination.

Perhaps that's what intrigues me about the journey of mysticism. It's fine to know the end point. But how much richer to explore all the twists and turns, highways and hazards and roadblocks along the way.

We might begin our trip by asking, "How do we get there from here?" One answer to that question is we don't. Because we don't *go* anywhere. Everything is already here, in the midst of us and we in the midst of it. Sufi mystic Bayezid Bistami said, "For thirty years I went in search of God, and when at the end of that time I opened my eyes, I discovered that it was he who had been looking for me."[15]

---

14. Soelle, *The Silent Cry*, 73-4.
15. Ibid., 77.

But on his way to where he already was, he also went on a journey. There have been many attempts over the centuries to describe as accurately as possible the steps, degrees, valleys, mountains, and stations of such a journey. They are neither rigid nor universal, but they tend to ring true to the expressions of mystics over the centuries. Steps and stages attempt to order, name, and organize that which cannot be ordered, named, and organized but which can only be experienced.

Ultimately the mystical journey leads us from our false self to our True Self. Thomas Merton uses the striking image that we have been turned, spiritually, inside out; so that our ego thinks it is "us." As infants and children we all have the need for security, pleasure, independence, and control. When those needs aren't met we tend to fixate on them as adults. We try to satisfy these needs with false programs of happiness, believing we need to accumulate possessions and influence or an invulnerable self-image. However, Father Thomas Keating, in his wonderful audio series on the *Contemplative Journey*, tells us these strategies are doomed to fail because at the heart of all of our desire is the longing for Divine union and all of these other things only obscure our access to our true Self and our spiritual nature.

But there are ways we can work to override the system of the false self. We can take seriously our own spiritual longing and development. We can cultivate our awareness of God. If this sparks your interest, it may not be your own doing at all. As Thomas Merton says, "It is not we who choose to awaken ourselves, but God who chooses to awaken us."[16] Each step that we take on the journey is not to be credited to our own discipline and achievement, but to be received and used as a gift of grace. We do not set out as those who seek, but as those who have been found.

This path of enlightenment has been traveled not just in this generation but hundreds of years ago, thousands of years ago, forever. People like you and I have always perceived something about the nature of the Divine and our relationship with it. There have been different cultures and different frames of reference, but always people at all different levels of spiritual development longing for union with the unnamed God. They invite us to experience the journey, to seek arrival at a place where we apprehend and rejoice with Eckhart that the highest angel and fly and soul are equal; until we so seek God that we find God nowhere.

---

16. Merton, *New Seeds of Contemplation*, 6.

Mysticism in Nature

When my family moved during my second grade year, I had to come to terms with a drastic change in my surroundings. We had lived in a suburban neighborhood with children in nearly every house around the entire block. Now we were living in a house at the end of a cul-de-sac in a new development. There were no children my age anywhere within walking or biking distance. It was a painful and difficult move for me into a place of isolation. But there was one consolation. We lived on the edge of a dense, rich woods. A creek flowed through my backyard. I never dared to venture very far into the woods alone, but I didn't have to.

On the right side of the footpath there was a tree that you just might pass by without noticing at all. But if you were paying attention and if you happened to be short, you just might notice that the branches of this tree were full and draping, so that if you passed through them you would find yourself standing in a clearing around the tree surrounded by a cascading waterfall of leaves. This became my place of escape—not to solitude—but to communion. For I was never alone in this place.

We've been talking about mysticism as the direct experience of God for which there are no adequate words. But where in our everyday lives do people experience mystical oneness, breakthrough, or wholeness? Simply put, there is no limit to the places of mystical experience. God is just as present to me on a summer day at the beach, in the waiting room of a Methadone clinic, or in the rooms of an art museum. And Dorothee Soelle writes, "To remain faithful to the road without roads means to consider every place, even churches, suitable for God."[17]

Nevertheless, there are places where mysticism seems especially accessible. They include nature, eroticism, suffering, joy, and community. We cannot create and manufacture moments of mystical enlightenment, but we can cultivate our awareness so that we are less apt to dismiss them when they take us by surprise. In nature, we can simply learn to pay attention to what is around us—to notice the birds and the flowers and to take our cue for living from them.

Nature is a place where we can routinely encounter the Divine. There are many stories of nature mysticism: of being taken unexpectedly out of one's normal awareness to a place where everything exists in peace and harmony, and the small self enters into union with all that is. These are experiences of being completely overwhelmed with joy or weeping in the presence of a knowing, a sensation, a light. Mysticism understands creation

---

17. Soelle, *The Silent Cry*, 97.

as the book God wrote. To read it means to bring amazement and thought together in an experience of reverence. In nature mysticism, we glimpse a God that transcends both the world and the soul and holds everything together in love.

Of course, authentic love requires dependency on one another. Today we are becoming increasingly aware that our task is not to master and dominate creation, but to enter into shared dependency. We human beings need the world and the plants and animals that exist here. And this world is dependent upon us. Unfortunately, we have routinely botched that relationship and exploited what we should have loved. Our collective consciousness is finally coming to admit that we have to pay attention to our own contributions to climate change. But long before we began to cultivate ecological awareness, Meister Eckhart was insisting on yet another kind of dependency inherent in the mystical spirituality of creation. He declared that, "without us God cannot be for one moment; if we cease to be, God must by necessity give up the spirit."[18]

Such is a God of everyday miracles. Super miracles have, of course, always gotten a lot of press. People have always been excited by stories about God's overturning or suspending the physical laws of nature. But mystical amazement sees the original miracle in being itself, in creation, in the blooming flower. The mystic also sees the lame walk, the deaf hear, and the hungry fed, but the decisive act is not intervention. It is in the interaction between nature, the yearning for healing, and the inbreaking of grace.

Mysticism in Eroticism

Mysticism is also present in eroticism. All religions witness to the intersection of mysticism and eroticism. In fact, many texts are written so that you can't really tell if they are expressing mystical love for God or human *eros*. The *Song of Songs* from the Old Testament is both a worldly love lyric of erotic longing between a woman and a man and simultaneously a spiritual song of love between God and humans. The human soul is the soul awakened and loved by God. In an old Sunday school song we sing, "We love because God first loved us."

In erotic mysticism there are always two movements—descending and rising. God descends to the rising of the thirsting soul. Or, as Rumi declared, "It is not only the thirsting who seek water; it is water that also seeks the thirsty."[19]

18. Ibid., 107.
19. Rumi, *goodreads.com*, December 5, 2013.

Dorothee Soelle writes, "The soul did not know itself without the You, an experience that many people have in first love . . . The soul is awakened, it becomes free. Erotic life always occurs in the alternation of losing oneself and finding oneself again in others; roaming aimlessly and immersing oneself, existing incompletely, undiscovered, partially only, and being found."[20]

Think about the first time you fell in love—or the last time. God breaks through to us in a variety of ways. Personally, nothing has so broken me open to receiving life, to receiving God as love. In fact, when I came upon the topic of mysticism in eroticism, my mind and my heart and my soul all began whirring around thoughts of love and mystics and God. Something had inexplicably caught in my heart. This spiritual door had opened that I longed to explore.

I thought I was the only one, but it turns out many of us have had a moment when we met and touched another, and felt the earth shift. When he talked to me, I heard my own words in his voice. In his eyes I saw an ancient truth and wondered whom this person was that I had always known. As I explored him and myself, my eyes were newly opened to the colors of the world. This became the single most significant time of my life for mutual love and for spiritual growth. It was then that I began to question the material goals I had set for myself and came to the conclusion that I would have to do work "that made a difference." No longer a passive recipient, I engaged the world as an agent of change, opening myself up to be a channel of love and grace.

Clearly we experience something Divine in the act of falling in love with another person—and it is ecstasy. But ecstasy is not only about soaring thrills and wordless joy. Ecstasy also contains deep terror and painful longing. And it is not especially suited in the long term for even the best of human relationships.

In D.H. Lawrence's book *Lady Chatterley's Lover,* there is a scene in which the woman watches her lover as he washes and dries himself. It reads, "His body was beautiful, his movements intent and quick, she admired him and she appreciated him without reserve. He seemed completed now. She knew him all around, not on any side did he lead into the unknown. Poignant, almost passionate appreciation she felt for him, but none of the dreadful wonder, none of the rich fear, the connection with the unknown, or the reverence of love."[21]

Lawrence concludes his love story by calling it a failure. Having been overcome with erotic ecstasy, immersed in the unexpected, dissolved into

---

20. Soelle, *The Silent Cry,* 118.
21. Ibid., 126.

another world, there comes a point where such ecstatic love is bound to fail. There is a necessary element of the unknown, the undiscovered, of the dreadful wonder, that cannot be held onto in this grand adventure of love. And when this is suddenly understood as something missing by both of the lovers, this lack leaves everything behind destroyed.

But if ecstasy is short-lived or elusive in our worldly relationships, it is the very heart of mystical eroticism. One of the most beautiful names given to God in mystical poetry is *loin-pres,* which means the enrapturing far-near one. According to the mystics, it is this One for whom the soul ultimately yearns—a part of which resides within each human. So this far-near God must include but also transcend any human relationship. Indeed, the state of ecstatic love depends on a farness, a darkness, an unknown and undiscovered contour of the beloved, which is why ecstasy always includes the bitter along with the sweet.

Despite all of the joy and wonder of human love, only the far-near one remains a mystery. Soelle observes that, "Perhaps that is one of the reasons why, in spite of its horrid history of abuse, religion is so irreplaceable, so indispensable: it depicts this otherness, this darkness in the midst of light. Mystical love for God holds together both what causes us to tremble in fright and what never ceases to fascinate us."[22] For this God, closer to us than the water in our eye, cannot be possessed and for that reason will always remain "other," far away, eluding, and ever giving itself anew.

As deeply as we might love, there is a genuine risk to the relationship when we begin to think we know the other person and when that person begins to think they know us. Danger arises when we make assumptions about what someone else thinks or feels with certainty in our own conclusions. My love now for my significant other is deep and abiding and trustworthy. But I am most compelled to recall the ecstasy of falling in love when he shows something of himself he rarely shows or when he gains an insight into himself—a reminder of the unknown that lies within each of us, undiscovered even by ourselves. Part of the unknown is surely our shadow that can be explored and discovered therapeutically. But I am convinced that the unknown also includes the very presence of the Divine that dwells within, revealed and hidden, the far-near God.

According to a mystical understanding of erotic love, the otherness of the other must be preserved, even as two engage in mutual sharing of sacred power, not to rule over or dominate each other, but to participate in the very energy of life. Being loved and loving continually flow one into the other without one being primary and the other being secondary. And much to the

---

22. Ibid., 126–7.

chagrin of patriarchal order, mystical eroticism crosses over the boundaries of time, space, and socially constructed sexual roles.

There is a 13th century book of instruction for women mystics titled, *The Mirror of simple annihilated souls and those who only remain in will and desire of love*. This "Mirror" reflects the soul's way into mystical eroticism. Its pages explore how human love is related to Divine love, how the first might lead us into experiencing the second. And it explains how to become free of dependency on possessions, status, power, prestige, and the "known" God, and boldly claims that the only certainty of life is found in the love that destroys all else.

The book was written by Marguerite Porete, a long-silenced and forgotten member of the Beguine community who continued to circulate it after it was banned as heretical. She passionately lived what she believed, and was ultimately burned at the stake for the sake of her love. Mystical eroticism more than any other mystical expression is, finally, incompatible with the institutional church.

On one hand, Porete's understanding of the immediacy of the experience of God leaves no need for the church to mediate the relationship. The soul can do without the intervention of the church or its agents once it becomes absorbed in the *loin-pres*. Not only that, but Porete concluded that as the soul ascends, it has less and less desire for masses, sermons, fasts, or prayers and becomes more and more free from the rule of virtues. Ultimately, religion itself is utterly unnecessary and superfluous.

In a mystical sense, however, religion is also indispensable. It is religion that espouses our powerlessness, insists on the otherness of God, and reminds us of that power within us that brings us together and heals.

Falling in love is an incredible experience, but what brings the ecstasy is the chance that our love might be reciprocal. The fear and the joy and the nervousness are around the possibility that the one I love might love me, too. There is something in being fallen in love with that makes us see ourselves differently, through another's eyes, so that perhaps we even fall in love with ourselves. We might say, "I love the me that you see," "I love what I am in your eyes," "I love who I am when I am with you."

One February evening I dreamt that I was sitting at a booth—like a restaurant booth, except there's no restaurant, just me and the booth. It is a 1950s-era booth with a seat covered in mahogany-colored fake leather. There is a grayish Formica table. Suddenly, I am filled with that feeling of "falling in love" and I realize this is it; this is what it is to be overcome with falling in love with God. And I'm torn. I want this so badly, but I am scared because I know giving into it will finally change everything completely. As I sit in this indecision I see myself from behind. I watch as my entire left side becomes numb, without any feeling at all, so that I topple over to the left and cannot move.

When I first had this dream, I wondered about my reaction to loving God. Why would I hesitate to fall into this love with the great Mystery? But by the next day I realized that the question in the dream was not whether I would fall in love with God, but whether I had accepted the fact that God had fallen in love with me. And so my divided body was about holding both movements of eroticism within my own person—lover and beloved, loving and loved. May you also embrace the truth that God is in love with you and may we all receive the invitation to fall into the ecstasy of mystical eroticism with this enrapturing far-near God.

Mysticism in Suffering and Joy

This God that calls us into Divine union also offers us every opportunity to experience the suffering and the joy that comes with being human beings. The mystic call to love is not a call to run away, but to come face to face with the deepest of our desires: the yearning to love and to be loved. Psychiatrist and contemplative Gerald May wrote that our purpose for being is to grow in our capacity to endure love's beauty and love's pain. You probably have experienced this longing yourself, perhaps in hoping for a relationship, in searching for meaning, in praying for fulfillment, or even in sensing a destiny.

In *The Awakening Heart,* May asks us to "Remember some moments in your life when you felt most complete and fulfilled; what did you taste there? Recall also feeling very bad, alone, worthless; what were you missing? If you pause and look quietly inside, you may be able to sense something of your desire for love right now in this moment. Sometimes it is wonderful to touch this deep longing; it can seem expansive and joyful. At other times it can be painful, lonely and frightening."[23]

Mysticism of Suffering and Joy calls us to be absolutely in that moment, in this moment, immersed in the emotion whatever it may be. Life is right in front of us wanting to be noticed, to be experienced, to be lived. Yet we so often remain unawakened and asleep, disconnected, distracted, disassociated from our own deep longing, suffering, and joy.

Suffering and joy are both about attentiveness, mindfulness, being in the now. They allow no escape, no muting as they wash over us. Thich Nhat Hanh teaches us that "there are two ways to wash dishes: the first is to wash dishes in order to have clean dishes; the second is to wash dishes in order to

---

23. May, *The Awakened Heart,* 2.

wash dishes."[24] The miracle, he tells us, is not to walk on water, but on earth. Mysticism, experiencing the Divine, is as simple as that.

Suffering and joy mirror each other. If we cannot feel deep pain, we will never feel deep joy. So it is no surprise that the enemies of suffering and of joy are the same. They are distraction, numbness, denial, apathy, and a bland, all-embracing sadness that cannot weep or pray because it has robbed us of the ability to feel. Joy is not about being glad because of things or experiences. When we fully embrace joy, we rejoice in the ecstasy that fills our soul for no reason, cause, or purpose and changes the soul in profound ways.

Alternately, when we fully experience suffering, we can discover that even the starkest reality cannot destroy our being lost in God. God does not will our suffering—but God also does not immunize us from it. Grace allows us to find meaning in it, faith allows us to believe God is present in the midst of it, and love allows us to continue loving without expecting a reward for having endured it. This experience of mysticism opens us up and expands our narrow focus that we might begin to take on the hurt and the joy of this whole world.

In our expanded awareness comes a new appreciation for all that we experience. According to Soelle, "We learn to cry not only through pain but also through life's riches and its beauty. Whenever love succeeds and life turns out well, the longing for wholeness is not really stilled, but grows with fulfillment."[25]

Joy, laughter, and delight are powerful forces. Indeed, they are strong enough to break down what divides us and bold enough to cross the boundaries of orderly, dignified, and proper behavior. In its physical expression, joy takes on the form of dancing or leaping, not simply because it wants to, but because it must.

When Rumi's son Alim was born, the poet is said to have danced for seven whole days. The Beguines would regularly express their joy in loud laughing, enthusiastic hand clapping, daring dancing—behavior that was seen as suspicious and frightening by the established church and other outside observers. Moreover, if dance is the physical expression of joy, then praise is its voice. Much of mystic poetry is written as if we each have two voices—one that broods and one that rejoices. One seems ever prompting the other to get out of itself and look around, and in seeing, to celebrate and to praise.

24. Hahn, *The Miracle of Mindfulness*, 4–5.
25. Soelle, *The Silent Cry*, 185.

Thomas Merton had a friend named James Laughlin. In letters written between the two there is a revealing conversation. Merton gripes about the rules, regulations, and all the other problems at the Abbey of Gethsemane. Laughlin replies by saying, "Well Tom, why, if it gives you this much pain, why do you stay there? After all, you're a brilliant writer, you could go out in the world. You could still do your spiritual teaching; you'd be a very successful writer. Why do you stay there?" According to Laughlin, Merton looked at him incredulously and said, "J., you don't understand. That's where I belong. That's my home."[26] Merton sought no escape from his life, and despite experiencing more than one nervous breakdown, came from this monastic home to love the world.

It is the contemplative saints, May tells us, who know the fear and pain as well as the joy and freedom of entering emptiness; they have chosen to confront that which has to be thrust upon the rest of us. They have stretched and yielded themselves to experience directly and unflinchingly the hunger and brokenness of their own hearts and of our world. They have willingly sought to deprive themselves of anesthesia. They have claimed their desire to be bearers of love regardless of the cost.

May tells us that if we really want to be loving, we must ultimately face our own emptiness. All of us have experienced emptiness, we have lost love or youth or health or compassion for the pain of others. These are expressions of what Rilke called "a great motherhood as a common longing."[27] But some of our experiences are uniquely our own, carried in the secret places of our hearts, touched only in solitude. "Anyone who faces emptiness becomes contemplative in that very moment, for then the truth is seen—just as it is."[28]

Mysticism in Community

Jesus was a Jew. He was a Jew who ushered in a whole new lineage of spiritual teaching. We call that lineage Christianity. But just when did the Christian community begin?

Most often we think of it starting after Jesus was crucified and appeared to his disciples. These small groups of scared followers would gather to proclaim the mystery—what once was dead is now alive. Slowly they grew in number, gathering around a meal, sharing all that they had with

26. Cooper, *Thomas Merton and James Laughlin*, 383.
27. Rilke, *Letters to a Young Poet*, 49.
28. Shut, *Simpler Living Compassionate Life*, 49.

each other, retelling the stories Jesus told, and offering to the community their own experiences of God's presence and love and grace.

But the Gospel of John seems to say something else. According to Professor Donald Capps, the Christian community began before Jesus took his last breath. He points to the foot of the cross as the moment of conception.

Here at the cross those who loved Jesus the most came together in their great pain. Here Jesus told a woman and a man to behold each other. And in that moment they saw what the one on the cross had seen in each of them. The Gospel tells us that he took her to his home. According to Capps, "In that moment, a bond of love was established, a bond much stronger than . . . the death we die daily. By inviting them to behold one another as he was, even then, beholding them, Jesus exercised a new kind of authority, and ushered in a new era in human relating."[29]

We have identified that our deepest hunger and longing as human beings is to love and to be loved. And we have acknowledged that mysticism—the direct experience of God—both satisfies and heightens that yearning by bringing us finally face to face with our own true Self.

We've explored mystical experiences occurring in nature, in eroticism, in our suffering, and in our joy. So far, you might have gotten the impression that mysticism is purely a private and isolated affair. But nothing could be further from the truth. In fact, for mystical communities, the idea of isolating the individual is intolerable. For they understand that God needs the community even when the ego thinks it can become whole without it.

In fact, that same ego can so easily pile on so many layers of self-protection and defense that we can have a nearly impossible task picking up any clues as to who we truly are. Many people will never look, but for those of us intent on self-discovery, we will find ourselves in the midst of a great cosmic treasure hunt. To find the hints that will lead us to ourselves, we need to look to God, but not to God alone. We also need the assistance of others because our true Self is discovered through interaction with others. We learn who we are not just in private introspection, but in the way our own souls reflect and are reflected by others.

Rabbi Joseph Soloveitchik wrote, "A community is established the very moment I recognize . . . and extend greetings to [you]. One individual extends the 'shalom greeting' to another individual; and in so doing, creates a community . . . the individual withdraws in order to make room for the [we]." This recognition isn't just about making a physical identification. This recognition is about identifying someone "as a person who has a job to do, that only he can do properly. To recognize a person is to affirm that they are

---

29. Capps, *The Depleted Self*, 166.

irreplaceable. To hurt a person is to tell them that they are expendable, that there is no need for them."[30]

Community is not a melting away of individuals into a common, lumpy soup. It is the deep valuing of each individual as a unique expression and incarnation of the living God. Jean Vanier wrote, "Communion is not fusion. In a relationship of communion, you are you and I am I . . . We are called to grow together, each one becoming more fully himself or herself."[31]

So often we set up a false dichotomy between the individual and the group, devaluing one or the other. We can assimilate, get along, and lose ourselves, or be defiant, self-centered, and egomaniacal. There doesn't seem to be much space in us or our culture to honor both the individual and the corporate experience. But on the spiritual path, we come to find life continually oscillating between integration and differentiation.

The Society of Friends, or the Quakers as they are commonly called, offer a rare example of a Christian religion without dogma, church buildings, or paid clergy. They worship in silence. This silence isn't about people showing up to meditate individually at the same time and in the same place. Instead, it is a time for turning inward as a way of attuning themselves to each other. One of their primary teachings is that there is only one light and the closer we come to it, the closer we are to one another.

Ralph Waldo Emerson pleads for solitariness as a conduit for entering into real community, encouraging us to gain greater trust in ourselves through intentional acts of self-reflection so that we might affect a "revolution" in human relationships. "The deepening and strengthening of our true selfhood," he advises, "will result in more satisfying, more authentic human associations, expressive of the real convictions and desires of those who come together. Absolute independence results in loneliness, but individuals are even more desperately lonely when they are compelled to misrepresent themselves, to put forth a false self."[32] We need to develop as individuals apart from the expectations and repressions of the group. Then as individuals we continue to grow as we craft together true community.

Hasidic philosopher and activist Martin Buber lived out this transition. In 1914, at a time when he was actively pursuing his own individual mysticism in isolation from society, a young man came to visit him. He had been filled with religious ecstasy. But now, with the interruption and presence of another, he felt his enthusiasm dissipating. It was only after the young man died that Buber learned about his crisis of health and understood that was

---

30. Soloveitchik, *The Community*, 15.
31. Vanier, *From Brokenness to Community*, 17.
32. Capps, *The Depleted Self*, 111.

the reason for the visit. "Since then," Buber wrote, "I have left behind that kind of religiousness which is nothing more than . . . a matter of being taken away . . . or else it has left me behind . . . What help is it to my soul that it can be transported again from this world into that unity when this world has . . . no share whatever in that unity?"[33]

In place of his isolated pursuit, Buber found meaning in the gift of community inherent in the I meeting the You, what he called the I-Thou relationship. The I-Thou doesn't deny that the soul experiences ecstatic union with God, but it goes on to ask about the consequences of that union.

One consequence is that we are given the opportunity, the challenge, and the responsibility of communicating the experiences of our soul to others. In the sharing of experience comes the search and struggle for language. I love the hard questions my most intimate friends ask of me about my inner feelings and unexpressed images because they force me to bring them out into the open where they can be seen, appreciated, and maybe even marveled at by others. In the process, those feelings take on more richness, depth, and meaning.

To remain silent, concluding that nobody can possibly understand our experience, is not only arrogant but an abdication of duty. When I attended the Integral Institute, Ken Wilber voiced his belief that we only receive such experiences and understandings because somewhere deep in the bottom of our soul we made a promise that if we did, we would share them by getting involved with others.

Thomas Merton said, "Any joy that doesn't overflow and help others rejoice in God doesn't come from God."[34] Holy power is that which distributes itself in order to make others strong. When my consciousness expands, my knowledge deepens, and my being changes. This is the beginning of a process with a much greater conclusion than the salvation or illumination of individual souls. Genuine mysticism must move beyond spiritual egoism, into the ongoing creation of the world in which we participate.

In his Gospel, John describes Jesus as a man who saw his followers so clearly that he was able to open their eyes to seeing each other. One summer night at the Extended Grace drop-in center, a man nobody knew came for the first time. The next night he was pouring a cup of coffee when a woman came in for the first time. Seeing him, she walked over and, without being introduced, said his name. He turned around and recognized her as well. It turns out they were brother and sister, long estranged, with no idea how to find each other. In this story there is more going on than the human players.

33. Buber, *I and Thou*, 162.
34. Zielinski, "Mysticism in Community," para. 17.

Martin Buber would use this as an I-Thou experience. There is an I, there is a Thou, and what happens in between—is God.

Mysticism is Resistance

Once upon a time, being a Christian was a dangerous thing. People wanted you silenced or dead. But not because you wanted to pray in school or because you wanted the 10 Commandments posted in your courthouse or the Nativity scene displayed in the public park at Christmas time. In fact once upon a time the risk of being Christian wasn't even about worshiping a particular god, performing a particular ritual, or *even* holding a particular belief. The risk was because you actually *behaved* like a Christian. And that not only made you weird and amusing, it also made you dangerous.

The early church grounded itself in the belief that they could behave as if they were living in the reign of God. These first Christians opted out of the benefits and the requirements of the Roman Empire. They refused to participate in the entertainment meant to divert people's attention away from the real problems that surrounded them. They refused to worship the emperor, swear any oaths, or have anything to do with the military. It is to this model of resistance that Christian mystics have turned for inspiration over the centuries.

The prophets of the Old Testament asked, "What do you want of us, God? Burnt offerings, oil, firstborn children?" And they are told that our religious gatherings, our songs, and our words are meaningless. Only justice is required of us. Only that. You see, purely religious activity is harmless. It threatens no one and changes nothing. It keeps us within safe walls, separated and apart from the way in which the world continues to operate. But when we move beyond religiousness to a relationship with God, we come to understand something about human dignity and freedom. We come to realize that the Divine spark cannot be reduced to a special religious space or shared with only an approved set of people.

Dominican theologian Simon Tugwell points to a distinction between active clergy who risk living in society making the salvation of others the way to benefit your own soul, and monks who live apart from society to cultivate good habits and escape from the temptations of their own frail humanity.[35] Jesus never played it safe. Instead he did justice, loved kindness, and walked humbly with God. And of course, that was all dangerous work. In fact, it got him killed.

---

35. Tugwell, *Early Dominicans*, 1982.

embracing mysticism 157

It's not too dramatic a question to ask ourselves. Will we be bold participants in the creation of the world, risking our own survival for the sake of the All? Or will we play it safe, keeping our faith a private affair that never moves us to act and never touches the life of another?

For Christian Mystics this is not a choice. Thomas Merton proclaimed that Christianity is not merely doctrine or a system of beliefs; it is Christ living in us and uniting us one to another. Merton also embraced the teachings of Buddhism and its call for compassion for all things. But compassion is not merely an intellectual, emotional, or spiritual exercise. True compassion makes it impossible for us not to act for change. In mysticism we experience not only a vertical relationship that leads us to interior awareness of God, but also a horizontal relationship that leads us to communal awareness of God—in, between, through, and among.

All revolutionary movements arise from a deep sense inside us that something is wrong. That this is not how things are supposed to be. We cannot escape looking at the circumstances of our existence, and when we do, we are compelled toward rightness and universal good. But revolutionary movements also require caution. When we identify injustice as something that takes place out there, by those people, we easily become judgmental and malicious toward others.

Mystical revolutionary movements always begin with the awareness that *I* am part of the problem; that all of the evil and greed and violence of the world live inside of me, as does the good, the compassion, and the peace. It requires humility to admit that while I believe I am acting as I should, I don't know all of the ramifications of my actions.

Which means the first thing I have to learn to resist is my own ego. Failing that, I only heap more greed and violence onto a situation in which I now claim to know the problems and to have the right solutions. When I become intent on seeing myself as right and good and holy and the other as wrong and bad and sinful, then I become just as destructive as those whose values I claim to resist.

Mystic resistance begins when I no longer can feel comfortable living according to the standards of the empire. Opting out of the culture of greed and violence leads us to making different decisions about the way we live our lives.

That's when things get scary. It's one thing to stand up when we are downtrodden and have nothing left to lose. But how do we resist in a rich world when we *do* have something to lose? Soelle reminds us that in this country, we are both overeducated and underpowered. We have knowledge that has no consequences for action and which makes us helpless. Knowledge [for us] is not power but impotence. Knowledge doesn't move us to

158 Tension in the Tank

activism. Instead it too often moves us from analysis to paralysis to despair, until in our great hopelessness, we heave a heavy sigh and resign ourselves to the sad conclusion that "there's nothing we can do about it."[36]

Mystic resistance tells us that we cannot do nothing and it brings us together to accomplish in community what we would never be able to achieve on our own. One such community resistance movement eventually ended South African apartheid.

In 1978 a woman estranged for several years from the church and from prayer journeyed to South Africa. While there she found herself surprisingly at home in a worshipping community. What she discovered was that, "The congregation gives as much as I am prepared to put into it." She also recognized that she was part of a large company of fighting, believing, loving, and suffering human beings. "I suddenly realized," she said, "that praying was important for me, that I needed it. Not as a retreat from dreadful reality but much more as a time of holding still to face that reality in its horror and beauty, face it as a part of it, but also to experience at the same time that it is not the last world."[37]

Several years ago after walking through a particularly painful segment on my spiritual path I wrote this in my journal:

> Just done meditating—of sorts.
>
> Images. Disturbing images that didn't upset me. Human condition. Striving for success. Hedonistic sexual frenzy. Betrayal. Then dark. And then I was given a breath. As if resuscitated, this spirit came into me with a start and my lungs took it in and my chest expanded. And I remembered My Spiritual Director asking why my pain had been taken away and the "where was God in all this" question. I had told him I still feel a lot of pain. The pain of others. And I knew that was true. I am emptied of myself that I may take others in.

That's what Christ's essence within does to us. It allows us to bear the pain of others, not so that we can sit in a corner and feel bad for the state of the world. But so that we have no choice but to act for justice. For we cannot be fully who we are meant to be as long as anyone is denied their right to be fully who they were meant to be.

One day a student asked Rabbi Isadore, "How is one to know the precise time when night ends and day begins?" A different student answered, "It is when one can distinguish between a dog and a sheep in the far distance, that

---

36. Soelle, *The Silent Cry*, 204.
37. Ibid., 206.

is when day begins." Yet another student said, "It is when you can tell the difference between a fig tree and a date tree, then night is fully gone." "No, it is neither of those things," said the Rabbi. "It is when you can see your brother or sister in the face of a stranger. Until then, night is still with us."[38]

It may still be night, but we actually believe somewhere deep in our souls, like those crazy mystics that came before us that it will not last forever; that injustice, violence, and greed are not the last word. And so in the darkness we stop grasping for those things that are without depth or truth, and we resist. We become lights of change and lights of hope, behaving as if we were living in the reign of God. Of course, when you become a light in the darkness, you can't help but draw a little attention to yourself. It can be wonderfully dangerous to be a Mystic.

Mysticism Beyond Ego

"Why should I be anxious? It is not up to me to think of myself. It is up to me to think of God. And it is up to God to think of me."[39] These words from Simone Weil, point us to the teaching of the mystics that when we remember God, we forget the ego. When we hold remembering and forgetting together in this way, each the side of a single coin, then we enter into the mystical realm in which to lose our self is to be immersed in the atmosphere of God. Our inner journey has consequences not only for our own being, but also for all of the human community. In mysticism, we let go of the small self and move out of the chaos of an interconnecting web of ego, possession, and violence.

Henry Nouwen identifies the temptations of the ego as being relevant, being spectacular, and being powerful. To resist these temptations is to discover what it truly means to be liberated and free. When forgetfulness of the ego replaces the all-too-common forgetfulness of God, we can join Nouwen in allowing prayer to deepen in us the knowledge that we are already free, that we have already found a place to dwell, that we already belong to God, even though everything and everyone around us keep suggesting the opposite.

Suggesting? I'd say that everything around me is screaming just the opposite. Ego propaganda is pervasive and unrelenting. Small wonder we have become an ego-fixated people, spending untold energy trying to figure out what we want and how quickly we can get it. Our desires are fueled by consumerism that heaps upon us an overabundance of choices and a surplus of

---

38. SPLC, *Teaching Tolerance*, 5.
39. Yaconelli, *Fear, Wonder and Longing*, 50.

stuff. The complexity of options consumes our time. The accumulation of material goods brings with it the need to protect and secure them—by any means necessary.

When the Bishop of Assisi spoke to St. Francis about the poverty and lack of possessions in his life, he was told, "My lord, if we wanted to have possession we would also need to have arms for our defense. But that is where the quarrels and fights come from that so often impeded love for God and neighbor. That is why we do not want to possess temporal things in this world."[40]

Now possessions in and of themselves are not evil things. Social scientist Erick Fromm understands that humans cannot live without having things. But he believes that it has only been since the development of capitalism that *being* human has come to be defined by what we have. If we are only somebody when we have something, then what might have been something enjoyable to own becomes a burden that must be obtained so that we become enslaved to what we own, imprisoned in our own ego's desires.

This imprisonment creates dependency for our ego while simultaneously destroying our identity as part of a larger community. Affluence breeds domination and subordination. It establishes barriers and, because these barriers have to be defended, sets the stage for war. Separation destroys solidarity. And vulnerable people will instinctively seek out weapons.

Mysticism calls on us to live simply so that others can simply live. It invites us to limit and simplify our possessions. It tells us that less choice leaves us with more time and energy for other things. But it also always makes a distinction between voluntary poverty and the poverty that people are thrown into without being asked. Voluntary poverty has always been understood in mystical terms to mean more than owning less. Poverty in the institutional sense means to be excluded from privileges. St. Francis embraced and kissed lepers, not only as an act of humble charity, but because he wanted to liberate them from their exclusion and remove the boundaries that society constructs based on what we own.

In such actions we also come to learn that embracing nonviolence demands much more of us than simply refraining from violent acts in our personal lives. It means that we can no longer ignore the forces of violence that institutionalize poverty, destroy the natural environment, build ghettos of despair, and leave the countries of the third world destitute. To exist free of violence requires that we begin to think and act with other living beings in a common life.

---

40. Soelle, *The Silent Cry*, 233.

In his short story *Man and Master*, Tolstoy tells the story of a powerful master and his servant Nikita. The master is a wealthy businessman. Nikita is a good-natured peasant who is constantly browbeaten by his master. When they find themselves lost in a snowstorm, the master tries to escape the blizzard on horseback, leaving the sleigh and the poorly clothed servant to freeze to death. Failing to find a way out of the storm, the horse returns, bringing the master back to Nikita and the sleigh. When the master sees his servant half-frozen and waiting without complaint to die of exposure, his greedy egomania suddenly vanishes. The master lies on top of the servant, warms him with his fur coat and his body heat, and saves the servant's life, while freezing to death himself in the storm. The mystical conversion in the master is that he suddenly believes he is Nikita and Nikita is he. He dies saying, "Nikita is alive, so I too am alive!"[41]

Howard Thurman said, "It is not only the socialist but also the confirmed mystic or the man seeking the fullness of the vision of God who must say truly, while there is a lower class, I am in it. While there is a criminal element, I am of it. While there is a man in jail, I am not free."[42]

This cannot happen until I own the role I play in creating and sustaining systems of injustice rooted in ego, possession, and violence. In her own reflections, Dorothee Soelle came to the conclusion that her cowardice was complicit in accommodating violence. "First I submitted to external violence, I knuckled under, paid my taxes with which more weapons were produced, followed the advice of my bank, and I consumed as the advertisers commanded. Worse still, I hankered after violence, wanted to be like 'them' in the advertisements, as successful, attractive, aesthetic, and intelligent as they were."[43]

Mystical awareness can help us to finally sever the bond between violence and cowardice, enabling us to let go of the desire to win, the wish to defeat and humiliate those we would call enemies, and the masquerade that we are somehow nothing more than innocent bystanders.

Nouwen reminds us that this is difficult work. "Jesus," he tells us, "has a different vision of maturity: it is the ability and willingness to be led where you would rather not go. Jesus confronts us with the hard truth that we will be led to unknown, undesirable, and painful places. The way of the Christian is not the way of upward mobility in which our world has invested so much, but the way of downward mobility ending on the cross."[44]

---

41. Tolstoy, *Master and Man*, 74.
42. Thurman, *Mysticism and Social Change*, 28.
43. Soelle, *The Silent Cry*, 20–1.
44. Hernandez, *Henri Nouwen*, 79.

Which leads us to an important point. We are not called to succeed in changing the world. Martin Buber says, "Success is not one of the names for God."[45] As soon as we make success the outcome for which we must work, we have re-engaged our ego in the same vicious cycle it knows so well. In contrast, to let go of the ego includes stepping away from the need to succeed in order to go where you are nothing. Without this form of mysticism at its heart, resistance loses its focus and dies before our very eyes.

In 1966 Thomas Merton sent a letter to James Forest, a leading opponent of the Vietnam War in which he wrote: "Do not depend on the hope of results. When you are doing the sort of work you have taken on, essentially an apostolic work, you may have to face the fact that your work will be apparently worthless and even achieve no result at all, if not perhaps results opposite to what you expect. As you get used to this idea, you start more and more to concentrate not on the results but on the value, the rightness, the truths of the work itself."[46]

Mystical spirituality will find us fluctuating regularly between hope and defeat. The religiosity of positive thinking, like the theology of glory, seems void of depth and spirit. The dark night cannot be denied out of existence or made easy by wearing "Jesus Saves" T-shirts or WWJD bracelets.

Nor can we deny the hope of our faith. However small we judge our own power to be, it is certainly greater than we guess. Learning to believe in the Divine as the power of life means that I do not have the last word in assessing success or uselessness. Still, I have a choice. I can let go of outcomes and direct my activities toward truth and justice, simply because I know that is the right thing to do.

Mysticism as Liberation

I can't tell you how delighted I was when I read Thomas Merton's proclamation that to be a Christian, one must be a Communist. I love this! In high school I used to argue (and never found anyone to agree with me) that heaven would have to be Communist. Merton captures the sentiment of my heart exactly when he explains that this kind of Communism is not an act of denying anybody anything, but an act of giving up what is one's own. Everything is ours on one condition—that it is given.

It is our right as human beings to experience beauty and vision. Mysticism is the direct experience of God in which we come to understand the oneness and wholeness of life. Feeling that oneness, celebrating that

---

45. Buber, *en.wikiquote.org*, December 8, 2013.
46. Merton, *Hidden Ground of Love*, 294.

wholeness is the *joy* of the mystic. But as mystical union opens our eyes to the profound interconnectedness of all, it also reveals how deeply fragmented life is. Seeing clearly a world split into haves and have-nots, sick and healthy, powerful and powerless, and finding it all unbearable is the *suffering* of the mystic.

A Mysticism of Liberation occurs when the soul comes to see the world with God's eyes. A soul freed from the prison of illusion sees what otherwise is invisible and irrelevant. In perceiving the world anew, we enter into a new interdependent relationship with God. We come to realize we are the only hands and feet God has in this world. Justice is no longer a goal, but a grounding orientation. That orientation affects how we behave and relate to everything, and that groundedness always begins by understanding that injustice is not "out there." Injustice is not something "they" do. Injustice is born in here. In this heart, in this consciousness, in this human experience.

I was fortunate enough to be in the audience when Arch Bishop Desmond Tutu spoke in Grand Rapids, Michigan on March 25, 2003, on behalf of the World Affairs Council of Grand Rapids. He spoke of the atrocities that were committed during Apartheid in South Africa. Each day they would receive reports of the number of people who had been killed. If there were only three or four people on the list as having been killed that day, they would rejoice. He described the torture inflicted upon victims of the regime in brutal and disturbing detail. It was absolutely horrifying. Then he looked at us, the audience, and told us that we dare not think for one minute that we would not be capable of committing those same acts if we had lived the same experience as those that perpetrated them. He told us that we all have the capacity to do great harm and to do great good, and that we were in no position to judge.

Dorothy Day's life and legacy is the radical movement of mystical liberation. Day's vision continues in the Catholic Worker Movement that she co founded with Peter Maurin. What I find most stunning about Dorothy Day is that she was able to identify herself so completely with others, particularly those who we revile. So she could declare, "I was the mother whose child had been raped and slain. I was the mother who had borne the monster who had done it. I was even that monster, feeling in my own breast every abomination."[47]

What terror to discover the evil that lies within us. And what liberation in being able to see ourselves clearly without our veils of defense and disguise, and lay ourselves bare before the great Mystery that still loves and

---

47. Day, *From Union Square to Rome*, 6.

embraces us and gives us the strength and power to control our basest impulses and channel our awareness into acts of compassion and justice.

Of course such honesty brings with it the burden of ambiguity and the need for our works to be continually reborn of repentance and humility. We cannot know for certain what God is doing in the world, and still we act, claiming that what we will is what God wills. Our best human efforts are intermingled with self-righteousness, vanity, and pride. We need always to be reminded that the alternatives we pursue and point to are not the reign of God. While at the same time, we celebrate that our fallible human attempts to know and implement God's will are honest and noble ways of trying to live consistently with the great I AM.

Our ego will not have the satisfaction of "fixing" the injustices we see and the problems we try to solve. Even someone like Day whose whole life revolved around such efforts didn't finally "fix" anything. Like any human being who hungers for justice and peace, there were times she needed to withdraw and cry. For days at a time, she would sit and weep.

We too must lament. Where people come together to praise God and do not lament, the relationship is one of denial and pretense. Lament forms people. Lament requires us to give name and words to suffering. When we lament, we keep the question of justice visible and legitimate. We will glimpse what this God is doing only to the extent that we allow ourselves to be present in profound solidarity and compassion where people and creation suffer the most. When we recognize social systems of injustice, such love is manifest when we refuse to be silent about it, refrain from participating in it, and seek more just and compassionate alternatives.

Howard Zinn wrote, "'Civil' disobedience is not our problem. Our problem is civil obedience. Our problem is that numbers of people all over the world have obeyed the dictates of the leaders of their government and have gone to war, and millions have been killed because of this obedience. Our problem is that people are obedient all over the world in the face of poverty and starvation and stupidity and war and cruelty. Our problem is that people are obedient while the jails are full of petty thieves, and all the while the grand thieves are running and robbing the country. That's our problem."[48]

Like Day, Martin Luther's life and legacy is also one of radical mystical liberation. When asked if Christians should flee from a town if it were infested with the deadly plague, Luther said that a Christian could flee only if no one needed her or his assistance. As a new merchant class began to emerge, he established norms for economic life, believing Christians should

---

48. Zinn, *A People's History*, 484.

refuse to charge what the market would bear when selling products and that they should not buy essential commodities when the price was low and sell when it was high, because doing so would endanger the poor.

Well, Luther was certainly more influential in religious terms than he was in economics. Living in the United States today, there is little that resembles anything of Luther's economic vision. But there are things we can do, small steps we can take in the interest of true liberation.

Signing petitions, writing legislators, standing in demonstrations, holding vigils, not buying products, participating in social justice activities, investing only in ethical companies, and educating others are all concrete acts of resistance that challenge an economic system that leaves people destitute, and help us to resist finding our security in those economic systems and the military force used to maintain them. Resistance grows from the refusal to reduce life to earning a decent income and consuming without limit. In the midst of community, we are called to love, even when that requires swimming upstream against torrential and dangerous social forces.

The Quakers list the qualities of spiritual life as boundless happiness, absolute fearlessness, and constant difficulty. Mystical resistance requires the courage to face disapproval and conflict and respond to it faithfully and fruitfully, with patience and with humility. It is no accident that Jesus said to pick up your cross and follow me *after* he had been marked as a danger and a threat to the political, religious, and economic powers of the day. This work can be dangerous, even life-threatening, calling for courage beyond what we believe we have.

Every day Beverly would walk to work. She lived in downtown Seattle and her walk would bring her through some of the most despairing sites of the city. Every single day she would walk by faces, hungry faces with searching eyes and fading hopefulness. It was overwhelming. One person could do nothing, except perhaps avert their eyes. Then one day it occurred to Beverly that there was something she could do. She could share her lunch. And so she stopped and gave half of her lunch to one of those starving faces. The next day she left her house with two lunches so that she had one to give away. After a while she left her house with a couple of lunches, eventually she brought 30 lunches with her on the way to work. Today Beverly is the Founder of Operation Lunch Sack, which over the years has provided millions of meals to the homeless living in Seattle. Beverly is also a singer who wrote the stirring lyrics, "Till we all have faces that someone else can see . . ."[49]

---

49. Graham, *Till We All Have Faces,* title track.

We need to support each other. As we take stands, we will need to know that we have friends who have got our back. And more than that. As we begin to look long and hard at the systems of this world, we will more and more discover the seed of injustice in our own lives. Then we will need each other to help us explore that shadow and then to help us embrace forgiveness and grace as we realize the enemy is indeed the person in the mirror. Finally, we will need each other to provide a swift kick in the pants of our angst and tell us to get to work being the only hands God has in this world.

The poet enters into himself in order to create.
The contemplative enters into God in order to be created.[50]

—THOMAS MERTON

An Invitation for Reflection:

1. When have you had a mystical experience? Did you tell anyone? If so, what was their reaction?

2. What need is your false-self still trying to satisfy? Security, pleasure, independence, control?

3. Is it harder to love (God) or to be loved (by God)? What are the challenges of each?

4. How do experiences of suffering enhance experiences of joy? Vice versa?

5. How is your liberation tied to the liberation of all people?

---

50. Merton, *New Seeds of Contemplation*, 111.

10

Advent

The Terrible Journey to Christmas

> *Those who do not understand emptiness
> are not receptive vehicles for liberation.*[1]
> —DALAI LAMA

Week 1: Letting Go of Love

WE BEGAN THIS BOOK by exploring Christmas through the lens of a variety of faith traditions. We return to the Christmas season now with a focus on the time of preparation. The Christian calendar includes the season of Advent. This is a time of preparing for the birth of Jesus, the arrival of the Christ child. In most churches Advent is celebrated as a time of joyful anticipation, growing louder and brighter with each successive week until finally we light all the candles and yell out a cheerful "Joy to the World" on Christmas Day. In its own way, it follows the rhythms of the shopping world as homes are decorated, lights are hung, and gifts begin to pile up beneath the Christmas tree.

But there is another way to experience Advent. It is one of recognizing the changing seasons, the shortening days, and the longer periods of time

---

1. Dalai Lama, *Engaging Wisdom and Compassion*, 37.

we spend in darkness. It is one that understands Advent as a time of transition, a time of darkness and uncertainty. It is a time when we wonder who we are and what we are doing and why—especially when we aren't feeling very joyful at all. It is a time when we look realistically at the world of hurt and suffering around us and admit that we are indeed living in dark times. And we sense in the deepest recesses of our heart that it will get darker still. It is a time of waiting.

That will be our journey of Advent in these pages. Into the dark, into the silence, into the stark emptiness of a world longing for a savior to appear.

We cannot make such a journey if we try to carry with us a lot of extra luggage. And so our journey is also a time for letting go. Letting go of the lies of the world. Letting go of our illusions and the false hopes we cling to. Until finally we enter into silence and wait for a glimmer of light. Together we will walk toward a theology of absence, letting go of even our most basic attachments—love, faith, and hope—so that we might be totally open to receiving the new light and life that awaits our arrival on Christmas Eve.

How shall we prepare the way of the Lord? For me, it happened in 2006 when I finally began letting go of my limited ideas of love.

It was a hard thing to do, because it seemed Extended Grace was doing "love" so well. John the Baptist tells us that to prepare we need to be just and to do what is right. What wonderful news! That was a cornerstone of this faith community. We were a thriving ministry with a service orientation that recognized the needs of those on the margins and acted in tangible ways to be the living Christ to a world that aches. We had always been about inclusivity and justice.

I admit I felt pretty proud about what we had accomplished—until I read the words from John the Baptist who pointed out that we had only done as we should have done. I had to let go of thinking we had "done" love. Because when I think I've "done" love, I realize that I want to receive something back for all of my hard work. I want God to bless my efforts so that I know I've "done it," I have loved God's people, and now God is returning that love to me.

And I realize I have completely bought into our society's lie about love; that it comes in pretty packages and bows. Because usually it doesn't. The real gift of God comes in our moments of death and dying as God greets us. It is in our pain and our suffering that we are gathered as sheep into the arms of God. It is by far the sweetest gift of God that we can come to see even those moments of darkness, even the ratty and gnarled presents tossed at us from the garbage heap of life as signs of God's love, and the very things that have helped us to grow, to mature, to find the strength and the fortitude we never knew we could possess.

I don't want it to be that way. I want to know I am doing God's work by receiving the rewards of this world. I really do. I want to be handed a precious trophy or medal that says, "Well done good and faithful servant. You have accomplished something special, something important."

But reality is something different. It was during that Advent season in 2006 that our parent church decided we didn't fit into their mold for congregational development any more. They said they would support us for a transitional year and then we would be on our own. I was notified that my employment would officially end on February 1. At this time of Advent, Extended Grace itself moved into transition, entering into a journey in the darkness. In a world where worth is equated with income and success is measured in dollars and cents, it was hard to see this news as a gift. So I found myself personally waiting in the dark for the promise of light, the promise that God's love is unfathomable, faithful, and true.

In your own life you just might want those assurances too. You just might want to know you are doing God's work by receiving the rewards of this world. "Comfort, comfort my people,"[2] says God. And we want comfort. We want praise. We want our efforts to be recognized and acknowledged. We want more than anything in this world to be loved.

Nevertheless, we need to admit that often instead of finding such reassurances, we find ourselves living in exile, yearning for God to come, yearning for God to make a shelter for us, remembering that God has delivered us in the past, and at the same time, finding God unmoved by our pleas of today.

This is our Advent journey, and the first lie to let go of is the false promise that God loves us with worldly rewards. We need even to empty ourselves of the notion that we know what love is. For this is a time of subtraction. A time to experience God's inexplicable absence. Until we find ourselves standing with each other in silence, waiting, waiting, waiting for the tiniest glimmer of light to appear.

It's easy to get caught up in the wrappings of the season. Pretty paper and bows and strings can really stir up the juices of desire. Advertisements tell us what we should give to those we really care about and just what present best says "love." But what the world wants to proclaim as the signs of love are often anything but. They are distractions, amusements. They are mere possessions that promise to quench our thirst, but only stir up our greed and our longing.

For some of us, that longing becomes excruciating pain during this season. What does love mean when we feel we have no one to love and no

---

2. Isaiah 40:1 (NIV).

one who loves us? What does love mean when we cannot love someone else or even our self because of the scars and the shame we bear? What does it mean when love is absent from our lives and God just doesn't seem to care?

It means we wait. We have yet to experience the full measure of God's love, we have yet to imagine its depth and its breadth. And so we surrender our preconceived notions to wait in the darkness and the silence, for the glimmer of light, the hint of warmth, the promise of love. And we know one thing for certain: it won't arrive in gift-wrap with an appropriately chosen Hallmark card.

Week 2: Letting Go of Faith

Well, the world is definitely heading toward Christmas! Decorations are everywhere! Lights and sounds and smells bombard our senses. Holiday cards are being mailed and Christmas trees are being put up, hung with lights, bejeweled with ornaments, and draped with tinsel. Which can only mean that soon the presents will begin to pile up beneath the tree.

Our conversation, however, is out of step with society. Our lights are dimmer; the sounds are quieter. Even as we cannot escape Christmas music on the radio and the persistent advertisements that fill up our mailbox, we are moving toward less, as we continue our Advent journey into the darkness. For Christmas doesn't arrive under a fancy Christmas tree, it arrives in the shadow of the cross.

Advent is for us now a time of transition as we wait for God's presence to be felt in the midst of uncertainty and sorrow. It is a time of journeying toward a theology of absence as we let go of our ideas of love and faith and hope, in order to become completely empty so that we might find ourselves truly filled with the new light and life that is Christ on Christmas Eve. First we were challenged to let go of our ideas of love and the way love manifests in our lives. Now we will seek to let go of our ideas of faith.

For some people, "faith" is very simple. It means stating a belief in a creed or a theory or a particular life choice. In the Christian church you often hear the words, "Let us confess our faith in the words of the Apostle's Creed (or the Nicene Creed)." There is an assumption that our faith can be captured in a collection of letters gathered in structured sentences.

There are some people who think that what they believe is also what everyone else has to believe, at least if they want to be on God's good side. But we have come to let go of exclusive "faith" and worship together a God who transcends our attempts to claim absolute possession of truth. In our embrace of Christian mysticism, our journey toward the direct experience of God, we find that the distinctions we draw between religions become less and less important as something to divide and separate us and more and more important as something to raise up and celebrate.

As a Christian Interfaith Community, Extended Grace celebrated together the three persons of God. We would bow to the third person of God before whom we stand in humility and wonder. We would embrace the second person of God with whom we have a personal relationship, even as we await the birth of Jesus who introduced us anew to our Father/Mother God. And we would dare in naming the first person of God to claim our own divinity, the bold proclamation that the incarnation is real, that we are inherently responsible for the state of our world, and that we have no excuse for not recognizing the face of Christ even in the face of the "other" that does not have the name of Jesus on their lips.

As Christian Mystics we move through Advent anticipating the arrival of the Christ child just as it has been heralded for 2000 years. We embrace the deep truths in the story of a virgin mother and a fearful father who had to let go of their faith, the things they had been taught and believed with all of their heart, in order to accept the breaking in of a new reality that shattered their feelings of comfort and security and cast them into a dark and lonely journey to Bethlehem.

We realize that the same is true today. There is much we must let go of if we are to be open to the real presence of God being born in us now. That can feel scary and uncomfortable. As we seek to love God not because the church tells us to or because we think God demands it of us, we experience freedom that can be disorienting. As a result, we intentionally stay engaged in our tradition, while longing to overcome the conflict that so often arises between the mystic's love for God that is too great to be bridled or controlled, and the institution's concern for regularity and order.

We take seriously the challenge of being a Christian who does not summarily reject or dismiss every other possible truth. Sadly, there are more and more people making the painful decision that as they let go of someone else's imposed ideas of what they are to believe and not to believe, that they must consequently abandon their own Christian lineage in order to live out their new understanding of God, even though it was Christ who opened them up to see those truths in the first place.

It is indeed fascinating to watch the flow of the Spirit as we are more and more exposed to God's work in a diverse world. Consider the sweeping growth of Eastern religions in America or the sweeping movement of Christianity in the East. It only makes sense that the predominant religion in any area becomes acculturated, taking on the values, and being made a servant of the society around it. As a result the religion develops a shadow side.

Those who live in the culture see that reality and become disillusioned with a religion that does not seem to live by its own ideals. But when individuals are introduced to a new religion, they are introduced to it in its pure form. They see the light side and are thrilled to at last find a religion with such promise and integrity.

An interfaith approach allows us to understand more rationally the shadows and cultural pitfalls that all religions are subject to, so that we have a more realistic view of our common work in always reclaiming and reforming the life of the spiritual community. But perhaps the greatest promise of interfaith work is that it allows us to hold the light of other religions up as a lantern onto our own that we might reclaim the Good News as Jesus shared it, apart from our own cultural trappings.

Such faith transcends doctrine and creeds in order to grasp the reality behind its own religious symbols, while also acknowledging the symbols of others. Such faith seeks universal justice beyond one's own system. In the big picture, it is this kind of faith that causes the walls between cultures, traditions, and people to crumble, while opening up the believer to radical possibility and wonder. We let go of the shackles of limited faith and pursue an interfaith identity.

Extended Grace was intended by the Evangelical Lutheran Church in America (ELCA) to be a mission start that would eventually organize as a Congregation. But the Spirit had other things in mind. It became clear that what was needed was not another church, but another way of being church. This meant that as Extended Grace was born, our parent church often didn't know exactly what to do with this ministry that refused to fit any of the regular boxes. At the same time, the institution mysteriously failed to do what institutions so often do. It failed to shut Extended Grace down simply because it didn't fit. It even continued to support this ministry as we were pushing the church further and further into areas of challenge and discomfort. For that we can be grateful! Just look at the plant that has taken root because there was enough time to water the seed!

But over time, Extended Grace managed to raise enough anxiety in the system that it caused a crisis in its relationship to the ELCA. This was a dark time for our community as we faced a transition to an uncertain future. It was a dark time for me, a servant who believed I had been faithful to my call. It was dark and ominous and I didn't like it a bit. So I had to ask myself, just what had I put my faith in? In an institution? In a paycheck? That this work was only possible if the people in power "get it?" In the misguided belief that God would somehow reward God's work with worldly rewards? If so, then God needed to help me to let go of my faith.

Psychologist Casmir Dabrowski speaks of positive disintegration.[3] It sounds like a contradiction, doesn't it? Dissolving doesn't sound like a particularly helpful path to growth and happiness. But Dabrowski points to the wisdom of all major religions, mystical literature, philosophy, psychology, and human experience to assert that the journey to maturity and compassion mostly requires us to fall apart.

In fact, Scripture pretty much guarantees us that certain deep things can only happen to the soul when it is helpless and exposed in the desert. Sometimes, like Jonah, we need to be carried to some place we'd rather not go in the dark belly of the whale. Even the promise of the baby Jesus we await was only brought to full compassion as he sweat blood in Gethsemane and then died a humiliating death on the cross. Sometimes in order to grow we must fall apart, go into the dark, lose our grip on our faith, enter into frightening chaos, and be carried in pain to a place where we would never go on our own.

In the dark night of Advent, we don't try to escape the pain by reciting words and calling it faith. We don't try to make ourselves believe those things that we have learned are no longer true. We don't look at the Christmas tree expecting it to bear the savior we seek. We don't turn on the Christmas lights in order to drown out the darkness, nor do we turn up the volume of carols in order to drown out the silence. Instead we weep, we wail, we cry at the foot of the cross. We let go . . . and we wait.

Week 3: Letting Go of Hope

Unlike the world's movement of light and color and sound as it pummels headlong toward Christmas, we have been walking slowly, silently into the dark, watching the nights lengthen and become darker still. This week it is dimmer yet, quieter, starker, slower. Despite the demand for merriment around us, we have not sought to hide the pain we carry or the troubles that burden our heart and our mind. We have looked upon this world of greed and envy and despair and realized that we are indeed living in dark times. We have called out to our God for help, remembering that we have been saved in the past, yet finding God unresponsive to our pleas today. We have begun to let go. To let go of our ideas of love and faith—in order to become virgins—empty of our false notions about our God—so that we might feel the real light and life that is Christ being born in us anew.

Still, we have clung to hope—the hope that maybe we're wrong. Maybe God *does* work the way we want God to. Maybe our good deeds *will* receive

3. Dabrowski, *Positive Disintegration*, 1964.

the world's rewards. Maybe it *is* enough to have faith in the promises of the world. And so tonight we are challenged to let go of even that—even our hope. Surrendering completely to the dark and the unknown, we acknowledge finally that we are not in control. And we do the only thing we can do—we wait. We wait for the savior we so desperately seek in dark and frightening times.

We wait and we look toward the future.

In the church there's a fancy word for looking toward the future—eschatology. It has to do with believing that ultimately God's peace and love will fill this whole earth. It's a different way of looking to the future than much of the world does these days.

Out there, in the hustling, rushing, consumerist world, the future is taking on the shape of a dizzying mix of hope and expectations. Kids hope they will get lots of fun stuff on Christmas morning. Families hope loved ones will be able to journey home for the holidays. Lovers hope they are choosing the right gift and spending the right amount of money to demonstrate their love. The lonely are hoping that this year someone remembers to send a card or call them to say "Merry Christmas." And the very first twinges of panic are beginning to be felt, as people hope that they'll be able to pay their credit card bill when it comes due.

To be eschatological is to live in and move toward the reign of God in the ever increasing span and depth of the life we lead. This Christmas we understand that there are two different futures we can pursue—and we are well aware of the cost. For we know that following the way of Santa will cost us a fortune. Following the way of Christ will cost us our life.

Spirit has offered to us a dream and a wonderful vision of all we are called to be. In that dream we seek to authentically dig deep into the heart of the Christian tradition and discover how it parallels and diverges from other traditions in both superficial and important ways. From this foundation, we are invited to participate in a deeper walk. Those who are committed to their spiritual growth come to realize that such growth does not take place in a vacuum removed from the harder realities of the world, but that a journey toward God also calls us back to the world in order that we serve one another. Spiritual growth is accelerated through integral awareness and intentional development of our mind, body, spirit, and shadow.

The way of mysticism deeply honors each individual's spiritual journey as unique and precious, while also recognizing the deep spiritual need to stand in solidarity with each other in order to resist worldly distractions and gods that interfere with spiritual growth. The journey of the mystics brings us into union with God in order that we might reenter the world transformed, seeking to be agents of transformation as individuals and through common action toward social and ecological justice.

I was asked during this particular Advent season to describe what happens in me through the course of preparing and writing and delivering a sermon. So I paid attention as I wrote this original message so that I could explain it to others. I started the week thinking about hope and how we use the word and what we really mean by it. I read. I talked to people. I began to form ideas and came up with a pithy saying or two. Then I sat down at 8:00 a.m. Friday morning and I started to type. I spoke things as I typed, trying to find the right words and intonation to express whatever was trying to be released. And about 10:00 a.m. at exactly this point in my message, I was overcome with tears and I began to sob.

Because I had no hope. The church in which I was raised was turning its back on me, and I felt so alone. I didn't even know what to call myself if I'm not a Lutheran. I felt the support Extended Grace had been receiving being tugged out of my clenched hands and I just didn't get it.

Still I knew I would stand before my community on Sunday night and I knew how much we loved each other. I heard the words of a Vienna Teng song telling me, "It's the season of scars and of wounds of the heart and knowing we are not alone in fear, not alone in the dark."[4] And I knew that God was with us. I know that the Gospels tell me that if we're doing it right it's supposed to be this way. We are supposed to be misunderstood and criticized and maybe even killed.

So I continued to ask, "What am I supposed to share and what do I need to hear? What do I need to read and listen to in order to share those words with those who will listen? What is Spirit saying to me?"

And what I heard Spirit saying to me and to you was, "Don't deny reality. The reality is that it sucks. It hurts. It really, really does. The reality is that I'm sad and angry and that this fire of pain is transforming us all. Because the reality is also that this is God's. I am God's and you are God's and God's peace and love will ultimately fill this world. In fact, God's peace can fill your little part of the world right now. God's peace can come into our hearts and give us the courage and patience to wait out these long nights of Advent when it feels as if the sun might never rise."

The reality is that the real spirit of Christmas isn't about a blazing collection of brightly colored presents and decorations, but about claiming life that arises out of the ashes.

The reality is that we are all struggling with something. We all feel some kind of loss, absence, emptiness in our lives at some time or most of

---

4. Teng, *The Atheist Christmas Carol*, lines 15, 18–9.

the time. The reality is that there must be an alternative to living according to the belief in scarcity that leads to spiritual bankruptcy. So we will seek that alternative. We will continue our journey and we will do so knowing that our faithfulness just might serve as a witness to others and to an institution that too often operates out of fear and the belief that there just isn't enough to go around.

Beyond hope, beyond faith, and beyond love, beyond any emotion or thought at all, lies the light we seek. Yearning, longing, pressing on in the dark we move against impossible odds daring to hold within our hearts the promise of Christmas. Strip everything away from us—and still something remains. Maybe a story of a young girl and her husband and the terror and fear of being outcast from their own people and everything they held dear only to bear a child who would bring light to a whole world. For that light we wait. Together we wait. Knowing we are not alone in fear, not alone in the dark.

The hope we let go of is that of wishful thinking, unending optimism, the hope that some Prince or Princess Charming will recognize the value of what we do and come rescue us or that some intervening miracle will change the past. The hope we let go of is that someone will pay the price for us—for the cost of following Christ doesn't appear on our credit card statement in January. Instead it compels us, a little more each day, to lay down our whole life.

Week 4: Absurdity

Throughout Advent we have been taking a journey into deeper and deeper darkness. Following the rhythm of the seasons, we entered into a time of transition where the days grew shorter and nights grew longer and darker. We looked out upon this world and our lives and found the courage to say that God often seems to be anything but present. And in that acknowledgment, we began to face our illusions and to let go of our false notions about love and faith and hope.

We do so in anticipation that our silent darkness will be broken as we await the light of Christmas to arise. And arise it will! Christmas Eve brings with it the celebration of the birth of the Christ child into our world and into our own souls. We will find ourselves eating and singing, and roaring with riotous laughter.

So what do we make of this journey and how do we justify arriving at a place of such unbridled celebration?

As we journeyed, I have shared my own struggle in the darkness as my time of employment with the Church ended. I recognized even as we heard John the Baptist tell us that in the desert we are to prepare the way of the Lord, that I needed to spend my own time in the desert.

I went to my dear friend Pastor Reed's cottage on the other side of the state. I wrapped myself up in the buffalo hide draped over a chair in the sunroom and I sat and I waited for hours at a time, feeling a deep sense of being comforted, protected, and embraced. I slept on a cushion next to the chair where I could see the sun rising on the lake. And I experienced the tremendous freedom that letting go allows. With that freedom arose a newfound joy and appreciation for the humor in it all. I felt the assurance that as good as it gets, this is still Samsara, and as bad as it gets, the coming reign of God's love and peace is still closer than ever before.

What finally lies beyond hope and faith and love? The utter absurdity of it all. The fact that despite all evidence that we're crazy, we keep at it. We follow our own individual calls in this world that so often doesn't have a clue what to do with us. And we don't do it because we have cleverly plotted out the advantages and disadvantages and made a careful and refined decision. We do it because we simply have no other choice.

We do it because we follow a teacher of the absurd, whose birth we celebrate every year. This child who would grow to be the Rabbi we know as Jesus, whose first miracle as recorded in John, the turning of water into wine, is the perfect backdrop upon which to celebrate not only Christmas but our coming New Year's Eve.

Jesus was the ultimate New-Year's-Eve-kind of guy. Not only did he not allow the wine to run dry, he did it with amazing gusto. That water didn't turn into the cheap house wine, it became the select vintage kept in storage in the great wine vault. Imagine Jesus showing up at the bar at 2 a.m. not with Mad Dog 20/20 or even a jug of Mogen David, but with Dom Perignon. Imagine the amusement and laughter he would leave in his wake.

In embracing absurdity, we finally relinquish fear. There is nothing to fear—even in the dark. There is nothing to fear in the rising light. There is nothing to fear in endings or beginnings. There is nothing to fear in our own selves.

Beverly Lanzetta in her book *Radical Wisdom* proclaims: "There was a time to fear. But even fear is gone. What use is it anymore? There is nothing else we can do or be, there is no other path to tread, there is no other spiritual life that makes sense—that doesn't leave gaps and holes in our being or hold us hostage to a way of speaking and relating that is a lie. Holy Wisdom has cajoled and prodded, called and sought. She has found us out and left us to lie in our own sorrows and anguish; then she will anoint us and we arise and say Yes. Yes it is!"[5] Together we have journeyed, giving up the known for that mysterious horizon, for the authenticity of Spirit that calls to us today, to God's voice in the wilderness that beckons: Leave all and follow Me.

In the final analysis, there is no reason for hope, there is no rationale for faith, and love simply defies logic. Our Western minds fight against such an obvious truth. We want a solid foundation to under-gird our ideals. We want the strength of evidence and assessment to support us in our endeavor. But the reason they are ideals is that they make no common sense at all.

The incarnate God infuses us with something beyond our ability to construct careful hypotheses and theorems. The incarnate God invites us to laugh and to play, to hope, to have faith, and to love—with free and reckless abandon—embracing the absurdity of it all in this and every moment!

> *My Lord told me a joke.*
> *And seeing Him laugh has done more*
> *for me*
> *than any scripture I will*
> *ever read.*[6]
>
> —MEISTER ECKHART

An Invitation for Reflection:

1. What are you being emptied of? What transition are you experiencing?
2. How do you know when you are loved? How do you let others know you love them?
3. What did you used to believe?
4. What have you given up hoping for?
5. How might embracing the absurd make a difference in your life?

---

5. Lanzetta, *Radical Wisdom*, 213.
6. Eckhart, "Goodreads," lines 1–2.

Epilogue

Creating a New Groove

IT WAS A BIT stressful starting a new mission church, but I trusted that things would work out just fine. So I didn't spend too much time worrying. Instead I prayed, I planned, I carried on. Then after the first two years, I found myself sleeping like a baby: I'd sleep a couple of hours, then wake up and cry for a couple of hours.

Fear had finally seized me. The anxiety, the nerves. Was I a failure? Was this attempt at mission development a failure? I didn't appear to be measuring up. It sure wasn't reaching the projected target numbers like it was supposed to. So what else could it be?

... but then there was the difference. The difference it was making in people's lives. There was the hope where people had given up hope. There was the love where people had believed they were unlovable. There was grace for people who believed they were too far away for God's grace to extend to them.

And that's when the Holy Spirit knocked me upside the head with the proverbial 2x4. There really was nothing to fear. God was at work in this place. This "place" was just a little different than any of us had at first imagined.

Extended Grace started out as a typical mission plant. The demographics were reviewed and all the population projections showed growth. Most churches grow because of births or people moving into the area. We were in position—so to speak—to be a great success.

But the message at EG was so radically about grace and inclusion that people started showing up who didn't know anything about church growth. People came who had no vision of organizing as a church or of building their own facility for worship. They just wanted a place of peace, a place where they could be loved and accepted and fed. They just wanted to experience God.

I realized that EG was not a mission start after all, but a ministry to people on the edge. People who had been part of an unhealthy community (and sometimes that was their former church) and who had been working on individual health and now were on the edge of overcoming their fear and entering into healthy community, but who could so easily retreat the other way.

Have you been to the Grand Canyon? Whether you've been there or not I invite you to go there for a moment in your mind. Close your eyes and picture yourself standing on the very edge—this enormous, vast, beautiful canyon opening up below you. The river cutting its way through layers of rock, solid and steady and true. Feel the temptation to enter into that beauty. And then feel the fear. Standing so precariously at that edge. You could fall, you could be injured, you could be killed.

Take a step back now and relax. Feel your heartbeat return to normal. Take a deep breath.

You have just experienced a moment of living on the edge—the place where most of the people I have encountered in ministry try to navigate their life.

For many of them that Grand Canyon is the church. It is massive and magnificent and beautiful. But it is also terrifying. People have fallen there, they have been injured, a part of them may have even been killed. It is tempting. On the edge they feel the wind and sense the call of the Spirit. But it is so hard. Easier really to take a step away, feel the heartbeat return to normal. Take a deep breath.

So how does one go about ministering to people living on that edge?

By standing next to the Grand Canyon, taking a stick and starting to dig a new groove.

Do you have any idea how much time and effort it takes to dig a Grand Canyon? Oh yeah, it's a great idea, but it doesn't beat any records for speed or volume! It's a lot of sweat and tears and effort, and people wander into the groove who often aren't able to find a stick to help you dig—people who don't have the ability to offer anything but themselves. And there is no greater gift in the world.

So what might a new canyon look like? For Jesus' earliest disciples, it included sharing dinner with tax collectors and sinners. For Extended Grace, it meant meeting in a bar right next to Wicked Ways as a community made up of Christians, Buddhists, Hindus, Pagans, Agnostics, Atheists, and the utterly confused.

The new groove takes Jesus seriously when he says, "This is my command: Love each other."[1] Love the tax collectors and the sinners. Love the skeptical and the doubtful and the faithless. Love those with body piercings and tattoos, those who are gay or lesbian, those who struggle with addictions. Love those who are poor and dirty, the mentally and physically challenged, the voiceless and the powerless.

That's something all of us need to be about no matter our setting. We might be ministering in a place with all the majesty and grandeur of the Grand Canyon or we might feel like we're struggling in a drainage ditch. Wherever we are, we are called to cut a new groove. Every prayer, every invitation, every action you take for people on the edge deepens and enlarges the groove in the path we are cutting into tomorrow. The path that Jesus walked and that God calls us into. This is how we join God who with us and in us and who, through us, is turning this world around.

There's an added benefit to joining in this work. What with all that digging, you just can't help but get a good night's sleep!

Namaste

---

1. John 15:17 (NIV).

Appendix A

EG Worship Template

Extended Grace Liturgy

Prelude: All Are Welcome—come into the circle
Focusing Meditation

Calling the Circle:

We come together celebrating our unity with all human beings and with all creation.
For God has created us and all that exists.

We come together celebrating our diversity.
For our differences can lead us into conversation about our faith and the way we live in the world.

We come together to worship.
Knowing that God is present here and that all are welcome in this sacred space.

We Celebrate the Three Faces of God:

We celebrate the third person of God: the face of the one God who is in and beyond all that exists . . .
I bow to the Great Mystery that transcends all that I am and all that I could hope to be.

We celebrate the second person of God: the face of our beloved, our friend, our Jesus . . .
I return the embrace of my divine friend and companion who shares with me all of my joy and all of my sorrow; who knows me intimately, accepts me completely and loves me unconditionally.

We celebrate the first person of God: the face of our own true Self . . .
I claim my own divinity as an embodiment of the incarnational God, knowing I am finally me when I am fully infused with Spirit and Christ consciousness knowing myself to be Co-creator of this universe and home of the indwelling God.

The river is flowing, growing and flowing, The river is flowing back to the sea
Mother carry me, a child I will always be, Mother carry me back to the sea
The river is flowing, growing and flowing, The river is flowing back to the sea

Reflection/Prayer/Reading
Silence

One Minute Check In: What do you need to share to be fully present?
Prayers of celebration and concern as we care for each other and the Community
Silence

The river is flowing, growing and flowing, The river is flowing back to the sea
Father walk with me, a pilgrim I will always be, Father walk with me back to the sea
The river is flowing, growing and flowing, The river is flowing back to the sea

Cognitive/Mind Piece
Shadow Piece

We Struggle With the Three Challenges of God:

We struggle to love God above all else . . .
I commit myself again to placing God at the center, not just in the words I speak, but in the way I live my life and the way I use the gifts I am given.

We struggle to love our neighbor . . .
It is easy to be annoyed by other people, by the reflections of my shadow I see in them and have not yet been able to claim as my own. My relationships

are better when I am impeccable with my word, when I don't take anything personally, and when I don't make assumptions. I commit myself again to seeing the living Christ in the face of all so that I am moved not just to words of acceptance, but to acts of peace and justice.

We struggle to love our self...
When I do my best I don't need to fall into the traps of self-judgment, self-abuse, and regret. When I move out of isolation I find the healing and restoration offered in community. I commit myself again to being who I really am.

Spirit Piece
Time for silent meditation/contemplation
Body Piece
Unity Feast/Dinner

Promises:

My faith transforms me and opens me up to see that God is also at work in the faith of others. I claim the gifts of God's mercy and grace and the promise of salvation that is mine to share with the world. Amen.

The river is flowing, growing and flowing, The river is flowing out from the sea
Spirit transforming me, healing me, sustaining me,
Grace and mercy go with me, Out from the Sea
The river is flowing, growing and flowing, The river is flowing out from the sea

Ethics/Putting it All Together
Checkout/Feedback and Evaluation
Planning/Announcements

Dedication/Releasing the Circle:

We bow to the great mystery
We embrace our beloved friend
We claim our own divinity
We go in peace . . .
Namaste

Appendix B
Integral Practice

What to Include

Picture yourself one year from now
What are your hopes for yourself?
What do you need to do to fulfill those hopes?
Include at least one element in each category

- Cognitive (ex. Reading, Coursework, Brain Teasers, Audiobooks)
- Psychodynamic (ex. Journaling, Therapy, Dream Work, Support Group)
- Physical (ex. Weight training, Diet, Yoga, Tai Chi)
- Spiritual (ex. Meditation, Sabbath Keeping, Prayer, Labyrinth Walking)
- Ethical/Service (ex. Volunteering, Donating, Activism, Teaching)

Tracking Progress

Right brain people don't necessarily like to track. They often feel that their life is their practice and they don't need a checklist or accountability people. Left brained people generally prefer to track everything. Tracking one's practice can be a practice in itself. Whichever category you fall into, if you are beginning or changing your practice it does help to break it down, analyze, and track it when you first begin. Increasing mindfulness alone is a good reason to track your progress for a while.

What works?

Begin with an inventory of all the things you already do. Chances are you are already doing something in at least 2 or 3 of the categories. Build on what you're already doing.

> Synergize through skillful combinations (integral cross-training).
> Decide what you can realistically commit to—Daily? Weekly? Monthly?—to support one practice.
> Anything you do less than once a month is not practice.

Intention

Be explicit about what you intend to do without being attached to it.
Share your intention with others—give voice to it.
Be realistic—you want to slowly build momentum toward your vision. Start with small frequencies and increase them when you have traction, while also allowing yourself to ramp down when life requires it.
Establish and deepen your vision.
Balance—focus on what changes or supports your vision.

Integral Design

Commitment—write a statement of commitment to yourself.
Decide what you want—if it is on the list because you think you "should," remove it from the list and see what happens.
A "should" is never as fun as a "want."
A "should" can become a "want" once you experience the consequences.
Follow through—be consistent, accountable, and realistic.
Overcome obstacles—commit to just one minute, reduce frequency or duration.
Add something you want to do, someone you want to spend time with, or a ritual you enjoy.
Reward yourself.

Appendix C

Chat Ground Rules*

1. Honesty

We are not here to debate who is right and who is wrong. We are here to experience true dialogue in which we strive to communicate honestly with one another. Dialogue is never an opportunity for proselytizing. We invite you to open your hearts and minds to experience new ideas, feelings, situations, and people even though, at times, the process may be uncomfortable.

2. Equality

Our leaders are not experts. Their role is to provide a structure and process by which we can better communicate with each other. Everyone at the table is an equal and valuable contributor to the discussion.

3. Respect

We recognize that we might have preconceived assumptions and perceptions about topics being discussed and about other people. Some are conscious; some are unconscious. We invite you to be aware of how they influence the way you listen and interpret others' words and actions. We also invite you to be aware of how these assumptions affect the way you speak and act in the group. In doing so, we can better maintain our respect for and acceptance of self and others as valuable human beings.

4. Listening

We invite you to listen intentionally. We hear at a rate of 400–600 words a minute, but most people speak at a rate of about 125 words per minute. That makes it easy to start thinking about other things—our response, for example—when someone is talking. We can expand our listening sense to include not just words but also feelings being expressed, nonverbal communication such as body language, and different ways of using silence.

5. Responsibility

We invite you to take responsibility for what you say and for your own feelings as they surface. Most of us have "hot buttons" that set us off, often without our fully understanding why. When that happens, it's difficult to enter into open discussion and truly consider opposing views. Hot buttons can cause such deep emotional reaction that even the most open-minded person becomes uncharacteristically close-minded. We sometimes mistake our hot button reactions for conviction. But hot buttons are about feelings, not careful reasoning or examination of the facts. Dismantling them isn't easy, but the barriers that come down and doors that open make it worth the effort. When your buttons are pushed, simply communicate the feeling without blaming others. In doing so, members of the group can hear and learn constructively the consequences of our words and actions.

6. Confidentiality

We invite you to hold the personal information shared here in confidence because only in this way can we feel free to say what is in our minds and hearts.

*Based on the work of Eric Law, *The Wolf Shall Dwell with the Lamb: A Spirituality for Leadership in a Multicultural Community*, Danvers, MA: Chalice Press, 1993.

Bibliography

Alderman, Tracy. *Scarred Soul: Understanding and Ending Self-Inflicted Violence.* Oakland: New Harbinger, 1997.
Allen, Peter and Carol Bayer Sager. "Don't Cry Out Loud." Song performed by Melissa Manchester, 1978.
Bard, Carl. "The Quote Archive." No pages. Online: http://tinybuddha.com/wisdom-quotes/though-no-one-can-go-back-and-make-a-brand-new-start-anyone-can-start-from-now-and-make-a-brand-new-ending.
Basu, Kajal. "Pain—Experiences of Pain." No pages. Online: http://www.lifepositive.com/body/body-holistic/pain/eliminating-pain.asp.
Bhikkhu, Bodhi. *The Noble Eightfold Path: Way to the End of Suffering.* Onalaska, WA: Pariyatti, 1994.
Bhikkhu, Phra Santikaro. "The Way of Giving." *The Dhamma Times,* March 28, 2004.
Bonhoeffer, Dietrich. *The Cost of Discipleship.* New York: Simon and Schuster, 1995.
Buber, Martin. *I and Thou.* New York: Touchstone, 1996.
Capps, Donald. *The Depleted Self: Sin in a Narcissistic Age.* Minneapolis: Augsburg Fortress, 1996.
Carnegie, Dale. *How to Stop Worrying and Start Living.* New York: Pocket Books, 1985.
Chodron, Pema. "Idiot Compassion." No pages. Online: http://www.shambhala.org/teachers/pema/qa5.php.
Coolidge, Calvin. "Brainy Quote." No pages. Online: http://www.brainyquote.com/quotes/quotes/c/calvincool121116.html.
Cooper, David, ed. *Thomas Merton and James Laughlin: Secret Letters.* New York: W.W. Norton, 1997.
Dabrowski, Kazimierz. *Positive Disintegration.* Boston: Boston, 1964.
Dalai Lama. "Define Compassion." No pages. Online: http://compassionate.askdefine.com
———. "Engaging Wisdom and Compassion." Conference hosted by Jewel Heart. Ann Arbor, MI, April 19, 2008.
———. *Ethics for a New Millennium.* New York: Riverhead, 2001.
Davis, Ellen. *Getting Involved with God: Rediscovering the Old Testament.* Cambridge: Cowley, 2001.
Davis, Stuart. *Self Untitled.* CD Jacket. Oarfin Records, 2000.
Day, Dorothy. *From Union Square to Rome.* Madison: Arno, 1978.
Deeble, Sandra. "Don't Let Them Bug You." *The Guardian.* October 10, 2003.

Deida, David. *Finding God Through Sex: Awakening the Spirit Through the Two of Flesh.* Boulder: Sounds True, 2005.

———. *Instant Enlightenment: Fast, Deep, and Sexy.* Boulder: Sounds True, 2007.

Eckhart, Meister. "Goodreads." No pages. Online: https://www.goodreads.com/quotes/29260-my-lord-told-me-a-joke-and-seeing-him-laugh.

———. *Meister Eckhart.* Classics of Western Spirituality. Mahwah, NJ: Paulist, 1981.

———. *The Essential Sermons, Commentaries, Treatises and Defense.* Mahwah, NJ: Paulist, 1981.

———. *Treatises and Sermons.* New York: Faber & Faber, 1958.

Einstein, Albert. "Brainy Quotes." No pages. Online: http://www.brainyquote.com/quotes/quotes/a/alberteins100298.html.

Elmer, Duane. *Cross-Cultural Connections.* Downer's Grove, IL: InterVarsity Press, 2002.

Faulkner, William. *Requiem for a Nun.* New York: Vintage Books, 2004.

Fox, Matthew. *A Spirituality Named Compassion and the Healing of the Global Village: Humpty Dumpty and Us.* New York: HarperCollins, 1979.

Fromm, Erick. *To Have Or To Be?* New York: Harper & Row, 1976.

Gafni, Marc. *Soul Prints: A Journey of Mystical Discovery.* Chicago: Atria, 2001.

Gibran, Kahlil. "Think Exist." No pages. Online: http://thinkexist.com/quotation/your-pain-is-the-breaking-of-the-shell-that/1573317.html.

Glucklich, Ariel. *Sacred Pain: Hurting the Body for the Sake of the Soul.* New York: Oxford University Press, 2001.

Graham, Beverly. "Till We All Have Faces." *Till We All Have Faces.* Seattle: Beverly Graham. CD, 2000.

Hafiz. "Good Reads." Translated by Daniel Ladinsky. No pages. Online: http://www.goodreads.com/quotes/95754-not-only-the-thirsty-seek-the-water-the-water-as.

Hahn, Thich Nhat. *The Miracle of Mindfulness: An Introduction to the Practice of Meditation.* Boston: Beacon, 1999.

Hamman, Jaco J. *A Play-Full Life: Slowing Down & Seeking Peace.* Cleveland: Pilgrim, 2011.

———. "Reflections on Lament: The Writing of a Psalm of Lament." Empowering Christian Education and Pastoral Care, Fall 2003. Holland, MI: Western Theological Seminary, 2004.

Hart, David Bentley. *The Doors of the Sea: Where Was God in the Tsunami?* Grand Rapids: Eerdmans, 2005.

Heine, Heinrich. "Looking Up Content for John 14:15–21." No pages. Online: http://cep.calvinseminary.edu/thisWeek/viewArticle.php?aID=505.

Hernandez, Will. *Henri Nouwen: A Spirituality of Imperfection.* Mahwah, NJ: Paulist, 2006.

Huxley, Aldous. *The Perennial Philosophy.* New York: HarperCollins, 1944.

James, William. *The Varieties of Religious Experience.* New York: Modern Library, 1929.

Keating, Father Thomas. *Contemplative Journey.* Vol. 1, Audiobook. Boulder: Sounds True, 2005.

King, Karen. *The Gospel of Mary of Magdala: Jesus and the First Woman Apostle.* Santa Rosa: Polebridge, 2003.

King, Martin Luther Jr. "I've Been to the Mountaintop." April 13, 1968.

Kluger, Jerry. "The New Science of Siblings." *TIME Magazine.* July 10, 2006.

Ladinsky, Daniel. "Goodreads." No pages. Online: http://www.goodreads.com/quotes/112764-the-great-religions-are-the-ships-poets-the-life-boats.

Law, Eric. *The Wolf Shall Dwell with the Lamb: A Spirituality for Leadership in a Multicultural Community*. Danvers, MA: Chalice, 1993.

Lanzetta, Beverly. *Radical Wisdom: A Feminist Mystical Theology*. Minneapolis: Augsburg Fortress, 2005.

Larson, Craig Brian, ed. *Illustrations for Preaching and Teaching From Leadership Journal*. Dartmouth, MA: Baker, 1994.

Leong, Kenneth. *The Zen Teachings of Jesus*. New York: Crossroads, 1995.

Lerner, Harriet. *The Dance of Intimacy*. New York: Harper and Row, 1989.

Lerner, Rabbi Michael. *The Left Hand of God: Healing America's Political and Social Crisis*. New York: HarperCollins, 2006.

Liar Liar. Shadyac, Tom, director. Universal Pictures, 1997.

Loder, Ted. *Guerillas of Grace: Prayers for the Battle*. Philadelphia: Innisfree, 1984.

Mandela, Nelson. *Notes to the Future: Words of Wisdom*. New York: Atria, 2004.

May, Gerald. *The Awakened Heart*. New York: HarperCollins, 1991.

———. *Wisdom of the Wilderness*. New York: Harper Collins, 2006.

Merton, Thomas. *Choosing to Love the World: On Contemplation*. Boulder: Sounds True, 2008.

———. *New Seeds of Contemplation*. Gethsemane: New Directions, 2007.

Merton, Thomas and Naomi Burton Stone, ed., *A Vow of Conversation: Journals 1964–1965*. New York: Farrar Straus Giroux, 1999.

Merton, Thomas and William H. Shannon, ed. *The Hidden Ground of Love: The Letters of Thomas Merton on Religious Experience and Social Concerns*. New York: Farrar Straus Giroux, 1985.

New American Standard Bible. The Lockman Foundation, 1960.

New International Version Bible. Grand Rapids: Zondervan, 1973.

New Revised Standard Version Bible. Division of Christian Education of the National Council of the Churches of Christ in the United States of America, 1989.

Newburg, Andrew, et al. *Why God Won't Go Away: Brian Science and the Biology of Belief*. New York: Ballentine Books, 2002.

Nouwen, Henri. *In the Name of Jesus*. St. Louis: Crossroads, 1992.

O'Connor, Joey. *Children and Grief: Helping Your Child Understand Death*. Grand Rapids, MI: Baker, 2004.

O'Reilly, Sean, et al. *The Road Within: True Stories of Transformation and the Soul*. Berkeley: Publishers Group West, 2002.

Obama, Barack. "Speech on Race." March 8, 2008.

Oldenburg, Ray. *The Great Good Place: Cafes, Coffee Shops, Bookstores, Bars, Hair Salons, and Other Hangouts at the Heart of a Community*. New York: Marlow & Company, 1999.

Oliver! Bart, Lionel, composer. Broadway Debut, 1962.

Paul, Margaret. *Do I Have to Give Up Me to Be Loved by God?* Deerfield Beach, FL: Health Publications, 1999.

Porete, Marguerite and Ellen Babinski. *The Mirror of Simple Souls*. Classics of Western Spirituality. Mahwah, NJ: Paulist, 1993.

Putnam, Robert D. *Bowling Alone*. New York: Simon and Schuster, 2001.

Richo, David. *How to be an Adult: A Handbook of Psychological and Spiritual Integration*. Mahwah, NJ: Paulist Press, 1991.

Rilke, Rainer Maria. "Goodreads." No pages. Online: http://www.goodreads.com/quotes/717-be-patient-toward-all-that-is-unsolved-in-your-heart.

———. *Letters to a Young Poet*. New York: Penguin, 2011.

Roshi, Dennis Genpo. *Big Mind DVD*. Integral Life Practice Ver. 1.1. Boulder: Sounds True, 2006.

Ruiz, Don Miguel. *The Four Agreements: A Practical Guide to Personal Freedom (A Toltec Wisdom Book)*. San Rafael, CA: Amber-Allen, 1997.

———. *The Mastery of Love: A Practical Guide to the Art of Relationship: A Toltec Wisdom Book*. San Rafael, CA: Amber-Allen, 1999.

Schut, Michael. *Simpler Living, Compassionate Life: A Christian Perspective*. Denver: Earth Ministries, 2008.

Shah, Anup. "Poverty Facts and Statistics." No pages. Online: http://www.globalissues.org/article/26/poverty-facts-and-stats.

Simpson, Dick W. *The Politics of Compassion and Transformation*. Athens, OH: Swallow, 1989.

Soelle, Dorothee. *The Silent Cry: Mysticism and Resistance*. Minneapolis: Augsburg Fortress, 2001.

Soloveitchik, Rabbi Joseph. *The Community*. New York: Spring, 1978.

Southern Poverty Law Center. *Teaching Tolerance Magazine*. November–December 1998.

Stein, Joseph. *Fiddler on the Roof*. Premier Performance September 22, 1964.

The Prince of Egypt. Wells, Simon, Brenda Chapman and Steve Hickner, directors. Dreamworks Animation. DVD, 2006.

The Ten Commandments. DeMille, Cecil B., director. Paramount Pictures, 1956.

Teng, Vienna. "The Atheist Christmas Carol." *Warm Strangers*. CD, 2004.

"The Toy That Saved Christmas." *VeggieTales*. Olsen, Chris and Phil Vischer, directors. World Entertainment. DVD, 1999.

Teresa, Mother. "Brainy Quote." No pages. Online: http://www.brainyquote.com/quotes/quotes/m/mothertere107032.html.

Thurman, Howard. "Mysticism and Social Change." *Eden Theological Seminary Bulletin*. Spring 1938.

Thurman, Howard and Luther E. Smith, *Howard Thurman: Essential Writings*. Indiana: Orbis, 2006.

Tolstoy, Leo. *Master and Man: A Story by Tolstoy*. Rockville: Arc Manor, 2008.

Trungpa, Chogyam. *The Pocket Chogyam Trungpa*. Boston: Shambhala, 2008.

Tugwell, Simon. *Early Dominicans: Selected Writing*. Classics of Western Spirituality. Mahwah, NJ: Paulist, 1982.

Vanier, Jean. *From Brokenness to Community*. Mahwah, NJ: Paulist, 1992.

Vivekananda, Swami. *Christ: The Messenger*. Vedanta Center, 1900.

Weil, Simone and Sian Miles, ed. *Simone Weil: An Anthology*. New York: Grove, 1986.

Welwood, John. *Challenge of the Heart: Love, Sex and Intimacy in Changing Times*. Boston: Shambhala, 1985.

Wilber, Ken. *One Taste*. Boston: Shambhala, 2000.

———. *The Simple Feeling of Being*. Boston: Shambhala, 2004.

Wilber, Ken, et al., *Integral Life Practice*. Boston: Shambhala, 2008.

Wilber, Ken and Treya Wilber. *Grace and Grit: Spirituality and Healing in the Life and Death of Treya Wilber*. Boston: Shambhala, 2001.

Winnicott, Donald Woods. *Home is Where We Start From: Essays by a Psychoanalyst.* New York: W.W. Norton, 1990.

Yaconelli, Mark. *Wonder, Fear and Longing: A Book of Prayers.* Grand Rapids, MI: Zondervan, 2009.

Zielinski, Barbara. "Mysticism in community." *Catapult Magazine.* Vol. 5, Num 16 (September 8, 2006). No pages. Online: https://www.catapultmagazine.com/lets-get-together-4/article/mysticism-in-community.

Zinn, Howard. *A People's History of the United States.* New York: Seven Stories, 2004.

Index

Absurdity, 51, 176–78
Abuse, 54, 57, 63–64, 67, 81, 87, 102, 109, 110, 118
Alderman, Tracy, 50–51
Anger, 22, 50, 57, 63, 73–75, 77, 78–83, 84, 86, 87, 89, 103, 104, 108
Apartheid, *See* South Africa
Assertiveness, 88–89
Assumptions, 104–8, 114, 116, 127, 148, 185, 188
Avalokiteshvara, *See* Tara

Bard, Carl 114
Basu, Kajal, 51
Beguines, 149, 151
Bhikkhu, Bodhi, 64
Bhikkhu, Phra Santikaro, 8
Big Mind, 53
Bistami, Bayezid, 143
Bodhisattva, 28, 69
Body and Soul, 27
Bonhoeffer, Dietrich, 59
Boswell, James, 41
Brahma, 14, 15
Buber, Martin 131, 154–56, 162
Buddha, 5–8, 54, 38, 64, 69, 139
Buddhism, 5–8, 110, 157

Capacity for Belief, xxii
Capacity for Concern, 63, 65, 68, 70
Capps, Donald, 153
Carnegie, Dale, 85
Chodron, Pema, 66
Cognitive Pillar, 20–21, 186

Community, 29, 31, 48–49, 76, 77, 84, 87, 131–35, 152–59, 165, 180, 185
Compassion, 5, 6, 8, 19, 39, 58, 61, 63–65, 91, 157, 164
Compassion, Idiot, 39, 65–71
Compassion, Yin and Yang, 69–71
Compassionate Detachment, 110
Comradeship, 121
Contemplation, 8, 11, 137
Coolidge, Calvin, 1

Dabrowski, Casmir, 173
Dalai Lama, 61, 64, 69, 167
Dana, 5
Davis, Ellen, 74–75, 85, 94, 97
Davis, Ruth, 50
Davis, Stuart, 62
Day, Dorothy, 163
Deida, David, 22, 126
De-identification, 127–28
Discipleship, xii, 59

Ecclesiastes, xiii
Eckhart, Meister, 9–13, 35, 37, 38, 46, 71, 142, 144, 146, 178
Einstein, Albert, 99
Elmer, Duane, 67
Emerson, Ralph Waldo, 154
Enlightenment, xii, 18–20, 38–39, 48, 109, 137, 144, 145
Ephesians, 19–20
Eschatology, 174
Ethical Pillar, 37–44
Exercises, 22, 28, 120–21, 126
Exodus, 3, 54

Extended Grace Liturgy, 36, 171, 183–85

Faith, 170–73, 185
Family Relationships, 125–28
Father Thomas Keating, *See* Keating, Father Thomas
Faulkner, William, 77
Fear, xi, xii, xxiii, 22, 51, 57, 74, 78, 83–86, 88, 152, 177, 179, 180
Featherstone, Rudy 36
Fiddler on the Roof, 129
Forgiveness, 44, 109–11, 166
Four Agreements, The, 99–115
Fox, Matthew, 64
Friendship, 121–24, 127, 134
Fromm, Erick, 160

Generosity, 7
Genesis, 27
Genpo Roshi, 53
Gerasene, Man from, 23
Gibran, Kahlil, 58
Glucklich, Ariel, 48–49
Golden Rule, 107
Gospel of John, xx, xxii, xxiii, 31, 33, 34, 153, 155, 177, 181
Gospel of Luke, 12, 30, 99–115
Gospel of Mark, 23
Gospel of Mary, 34
Gospel of Matthew, 2, 32, 39, 40, 42
Graham, Beverly, 165
Guilt, 61–63, 65–68, 82, 102, 111, 115

Hafiz, 16–17
Hamman, Jaco, 75, 132
Hart, David Bentley, 97
Hebrews, 20
Heifer Project, 6
Heine, Heinrich, 111
Hinduism, 14–16, 47–48, 138
Hope, 2, 5, 12, 29, 162, 173–76
Huxley, Aldous, 139, 141

Incarnation, 25, 154, 171, 184
Integral Institute, 21, 22, 25, 40, 155
Integral Practice, 20, 28, 37, 43, 186–87
Interfaith, 172

Intimacy, 31, 82, 116–18, 119, 122, 125, 128
Isadore, Rabbi, 158–59
Isaiah, xiii, 169

James, William, 139
Jesus, 8–16, 19, 23, 25, 26, 29, 30–37, 39, 40–41, 46–59, 62, 64, 65, 83, 99, 102, 152–53, 155, 156, 161, 165, 167, 171, 173, 177, 180, 181
Job, 91–98, 99, 100
John the Baptist, 168, 177
Joseph, 12, 13
Judaism, 1–4, 61, 91, 133, 138

Kahlil Gibran, *See* Gibran, Kahlil
Karuna, 6
Keating, Father Thomas, 32, 144
King, Martin Luther Jr., 76–77, 78
Koen of the Dry Well, 38

Ladinsky, Daniel 17
Lament, 61, 72–78, 86–89, 114, 164
Lanzetta, Beverly, xix, 59, 177–78
Law, Eric, 188–89
Lawrence, D.H., 147–48
Leong, Kenneth, 8
Lerner, Harriet, 117
Lerner, Rabbi Michael, 61
Lies, 99–101
Life Positive, 51
Loder, Ted, 135
Loin-pres, 148, 149
Love, xx, xxi, 10, 13, 22, 40, 55, 58, 61, 63, 65, 69, 82, 103–4, 113, 115, 130–31, 138, 146–50, 167–70, 181
Luther, Martin, 164–65

Management by Strengths (MBS), 120
Mandela, Nelson, 91
Margareta Contracta, 49
Mary Clarke, see Mother Antonia
Mary of Magdala, 33–34, 35, 37
Mary, Mother of Jesus, 9, 11, 12, 13, 57
Masks, 24–25, 117
May, Gerald, 84, 85, 89, 150, 152
McConnell, Carmel, 120

index

Mechthild von Hackeborn, 49
Mechthild von Magdeburg, 55
Meditation, 11, 32, 57
Meister Eckhart, *See* Eckhart, Meister
Merton, Thomas 18, 43, 65, 98, 115, 139, 144, 152, 155, 157, 162, 166
Messiah, 3, 4
Metta, 5
Micah, 156
Mindfulness, 43, 150, 186
Miracle of Turning Water Into Wine, 177
Mistakes, 9, 12, 44, 89, 102, 109, 111
Monkey and the Fish, 67–68
Moses, 1–4, 54
Mother Antonia, 55
Mother Teresa, 41
Mystic, xix, 10, 11, 19, 32, 84–85, 136–39, 171, 174–75
Mysticism, Activism 156–66
Mysticism, Community, 152–56
Mysticism, Erotic, 146–50
Mysticism, Nature, 145–46
Mysticism, Suffering and Joy, 48–50, 150–52

Nisargadatta Maharaj, 48
Nouwen, Henry 159, 161

O'Connor, Joey, 90
Obama, Barack, 75, 77, 78
Oldenburg, Ray, 133
Operation Lunch Sack, 165

Pain, 97
Pain, Emotional, 51–56
Pain, Physical, 46–51
Pain, Spiritual, 51, 56–59, 83
Parable of Lazarus and the Rich Man, 99–115
Parable of Sewing Seeds, 41–44
Pascal, Blaise, 54
Paul, Margaret, 53
Paul, Saint, 19–20, 27, 28, 138
Philippians, 28
Physical Pillar, 20, 26–30, 186
Play, 28, 132, 139, 178
Porete, Marguerite, 149

Positive Disintegration, 173
Poverty Statistics, 62
Praise, 74–76, 85, 86, 126
Prayer, 32, 57, 74, 85, 88
Prayer, Apophatic and Cataphatic, 140, 142
Prayer, Centering, 32–33
Prayer, Contemplative, 32–33
Psalms, 72–89
Psychodynamic Pillar, 20, 21–26, 186
Putnam, Robert, 133–34

Quakers, 154, 165

Rabi'a, 138
Ramakrishna, 14, 15, 16
Rebirth, xii, 19, 29
Repentance, 61–62, 164
Resurrection, 15, 30, 34, 37, 47, 54, 109
Richo, David, 79, 81, 85, 88
Rilke, Rainer Maria, 44, 152
Rinpoche, Chogyam Trungpa, 39, 65
Romans, 9
Rosh Hashanah, 61
Ruiz, Don Miguel, 99–115, 117
Rumi, 143, 146, 151

Salvation, xii, 37, 48, 49, 133, 156
Satan, 92–93
Schneider, Reinhold, 59
Seisetsu, 8
Self-Harm, 50–51
Self-Acceptance, 113, 117, 188
Shadow, 23–24, 120, 125, 148, 166, 171, 174, 184
Shiva, 14, 15
Siblings, 125–28
Significant Other, 128–31
Silence, 32, 43, 94, 97, 143, 154, 189
Soelle, Dorothee, 48, 56, 58, 84, 136–66
Soloveitchik, Rabbi Joseph, 153–54
Song of Songs, 146
South Africa, 158, 163
Spiritual Pillar, 20, 30–37, 186
St. Francis of Assisi, 160
St. John of the Cross, 54, 58, 137

index

Suffering, 29, 31, 38–39, 40, 46–59, 61, 62, 70, 75, 78, 91, 102, 168
Sufi, 138, 139, 143

Tara, 69, 70
Teng, Vienna, 175
Theology of Glory, xxiii, 30, 162
Theory of Everything, 19
Thich Nat Hanh, 150–51
Thurman, Howard, 13, 161
Tolstoy, Leo, 161
Touch, 30, 33, 65
Transcendence, 20, 51, 139, 142
Transformation, xix, xxi, 4, 30, 31, 59, 82, 142, 174–75
Translation, 30, 42, 142
Trenshaw, Cynthia, 55
Tugwell, Simon, 156
Tutu, Arch Bishop Desmond, 163

Upanishads, 138

Vanier, Jean, 154
Vidyuddeva, 40
Virgin, 9–12, 171, 173
Vishnu, 14, 15
Vivekananda, Swami, 15, 16
Vulnerable, 29, 53–54, 73, 76

Weil, Simone, 51, 58–60, 159
Welwood, John, 82
Wilber, Ken, 10, 18, 20, 40, 118, 136, 138, 139, 142,155
Winnicott, D.W., xxii
Women, 33, 78, 143, 149
Work Relationships, 119–21
Worry, 83–86, 88, 139

Zen, 8, 39, 136
Zinn, Howard, 164